Think No EVIL

McDougal & Associates

Servants of Christ and Stewards of the
Mysteries of God

Think No EVIL

A Guide to Faith for Homeschoolers

by

Taun Mizell

You may contact Taun Mizell through the publisher at: info@thepublishedword.com

Published by:

McDougal & Associates
18896 Greenwell Springs Road
Greenwell Springs, LA 70739

www.thepublishedword.com

McDougal & Associates is an organization dedicated to spreading the Gospel of the Lord Jesus Christ to as many people as possible in the shortest time possible.

ISBN: 978-1-940461-84-7

Printed on demand in the U.S., the U.K. and Australia
For Worldwide Distribution

DEDICATION

This book is dedicated to Dr. Fred Malone, a man gifted by God with the heart of a shepherd and the clear understanding of the Word of God, a teacher of Christ the Son in all His fullness.

ACKNOWLEDGMENTS

I want to acknowledge the many good teachers I have been privileged to study under in the places we have lived. I am also grateful to the many authors I have read who tackled the darkness in their time and reminded the readers that Jesus Christ is our sure hope and peace in the midst of trials. These were men singularly gifted by God to speak to those who despised the Lord and His Word. Today there are men who are called by God to speak clearly and warn believers not to be deceived by the cunning craft of those who call themselves "Christians" but are really wolves hiding under sheep's skin.

CONTENTS

AUTHOR'S PREFACE

In the beginning, God created the universe and put man upon the earth. We have our being because He holds our breath, our very lives, in His hands. It is clear from all that is contained within our world that there is a complex and interrelated design present. And where design exists, so, too, does purpose. We are designed to communicate, to love, to create beauty and to worship, to understand the past and the future and to know our God. [1]

In the beginning, man lived in harmony and peace with God. However, man chose to disregard the Word of God and spurned the love of God; therefore, God's consequences rolled down into the history of our world. We were severed from the only source of love, the Fountain of Life. Sin, instantly embedded within our soul and bonded permanently to our being. [2] Therefore, everything we think and do flows out of a mind that God calls "corrupt." Corruption cannot bring life, but only death. All men are lost, wandering in a land of spiritual darkness, eyes fixed upon small degrees of change within shadows as a substitute for light.

The history of the earth, which we have in glimpses, shows clearly that man is bent toward self-destruction. The thousands of decisions made every day by sin-bound men who are separated from the God who created them cannot result in anything but chaos, evil and desolation!

The Jewish-Christian Scriptures are the only source that speaks clearly and realistically about mankind. The Word of God strips away the mists of culture and tradition in order to reveal the true condition of all men before a holy God.

God allowed our rebellion and did not shield us from the consequences, but out of His infinite mercy came the promise of redemption; the breach would be healed. [3] His children would be set free, [4] our hearts would be soft again, and we would see His glory in fullness of joy.

---

1. Genesis 1:27-4:15, ASV
2. Genesis 3:1-24, ASV and Romans 1-3, ASV
3. John 2:23-3:19 and Romans 5-6, ASV
4. 2 Corinthians 5:14 -21, NASB

INTRODUCTION

This material was created to help the reader understand how the Gospel of Jesus Christ gives mankind insight into our core, by revealing our true character, desires and motivations. For many years I taught Sunday school, as well as Vacation Bible School, and was surprised to find that most of our children have no real understanding of the Bible, the character of God or the qualities of evil found within each of us before we come to know Christ as Savior. Many students graduate without first understanding the necessity of the sacrifice of our Lord Jesus within His Father's comprehensive plan of salvation. Their thinking is vague, and it is clear that many students have no moral or philosophical anchor rooted in the eternal Lord. It is for this reason that many of our church-going students enter college thinking they have faith and leave having none.

The system of education we have set up teaches us that "self-esteem" is of great value. The end result is that most of us have a good opinion of ourselves based upon a subjective internal evaluation that uses how we feel about ourselves as the standard of judgment. We also think in terms of how we are impacted by things rather than thinking objectively or giving consideration to the absolutes of right and wrong. "Good" has now been stretched to include things that previous generations called "evil." The Ten Commandments have been ignored for so long that they have ceased to be the standard which informs us of what constitutes good or evil in both behavior and thinking. We are naive in many ways and do not recognize that this mindset has built for us a useless foundation that serves no one. No one can have and no one builds a good character unless he believes what God has said constitutes both good and evil.

Jesus Christ is our reason for studying the words spoken in the Scriptures and why we practice memorization, for the Scriptures constitute a living tool. The Scriptures are the basic protein of truth needed for spiritual growth. The scriptures found within the lessons of this book and those found within the footnotes form the backbone of all the lessons. The Bible informs our minds of Christ and, through it, our Father spreads His blueprint of truth out before us, giving us knowledge and direction. This living Word provides protection during spiritual battles with the force of darkness and gives us insight into the heart of God. The Spirit, using the Holy Word, informs us of the eternal truths of our loving God, comforts us through difficulties, warns us of evil, rebuking us and correcting us when it is needed. The Word of God enlightens our minds, and through the work of the Holy Spirit, gives us greater love for and understanding of our loving and merciful Savior. The engrafting of this Word of truth into our minds allows the indwelling Spirit to apply the Scriptures to ourselves and to situations as we move through life, giving us both the faith and the wisdom to follow Jesus Christ. Jesus teaches us what constitutes both good and evil in thought, word or deed, so that we can love each other.

There are five sections in the text which consider our spiritual blindness and that of Israel in the Old Testament. Notes to the teacher regarding these can be found at the end of the book.

PART I

THE NATURAL MAN

CHAPTER 1

MAN'S THINKING

The Scriptures reveal to us that out of our heart, or mind, comes real evil with long-term results which impact families and nations. Mankind's mental assessment of being basically good is subjective and woefully inaccurate. Our self-perception is biased, and without wisdom from God, we fail to see the scope of the evil that indwells us.

And God saw that the wickedness of man was great in the earth, and every <u>imagination</u> [1] of the thoughts of his heart was only evil continually.   Genesis 6:5, ASV

I will not again curse the ground any more for man's sake; for the thoughts of man's <u>heart</u> [2] is evil from his youth nor will I smite any more everything living as I have done.   Genesis 8:21

The thoughts of the wicked are an <u>abomination</u> [3] to the Lord, but the words of the pure are pleasant words.   Proverbs 15:26

The Lord said, I have spread out my hands all day long unto a rebellious people, which walk in a way that is not good, after their own thoughts ... .   Isaiah 65:2

And the Spirit of the Lord said unto me, Speak, Thus says the Lord ... , for I know the things that come into your mind, every one of them.   Ezekiel 11:5

Jesus was in Jerusalem for the Passover and many believed in his name when they saw the miracles he performed. But Jesus did not entrust himself unto them, because he knew all men, and did not need anyone to testify of man: for he knew what was in man.   John 2:23-25

... Do you not understand that whatever enters a man from the outside cannot defile him, because it does not enter his heart, but his stomach, and is eliminated ... . What comes out of man, that defiles him, for from within out of the heart of men proceed evil thoughts, adulteries, thefts, <u>fornications</u>, [4] murders, covetousness, wickedness, deceit, <u>lasciviousness</u>, [5] an evil eye, blasphemy, pride, foolishness and this defiles the man.   Mark 7:18-23, NKJV

---

1. Imagination: a form; figuratively conception (that is, purpose): thing framed, mind, work, imaginations.

2. The word *heart* when used in Scriptures, most often means (the center) the mind/will.

3. An abomination: something (morally) disgusting, that is (as noun) an abhorrence; especially idolatry or (concretely) an idol.

4. Fornications: harlotry, to act as a harlot, that is, to indulge in unlawful lust of any kind (including adultery and incest).

5. Lasciviousness: the lack of legal, moral or sexual restraint, sensuality, filthy, wantonness (the opposite of self-control) (Strongs). Licentious, libertine (AHD).

QUESTIONS ON THE FACT THAT THE LORD IS AWARE OF ALL OUR THOUGHTS
(ALWAYS WRITE YOUR ANSWERS IN YOUR NOTEBOOK.)

1. **When do we begin to think evil thoughts? Why couldn't Jesus trust men?**
2. **How do we walk and why do we walk in this way?**
3. **What defiles men and where do evil deeds originate?**
4. **How does this information impact your understanding?**

Our Lord knows our thoughts and the intentions of our hearts. Being self-absorbed, we do not naturally think of the Lord. [6] The Lord said in His law that man's obligation was to love, worship and serve Him alone. [7] It is impossible for us to love, worship and serve God if we do not think of Him at all and this is one proof of our sin. So what is sin? God did not leave the definition of sin in the hands of men but clearly illustrated sin by laws made against sinful thoughts and acts, so that all men are without excuse. God's moral laws are summed up in the Ten Commandments, those wonderfully concise moral laws given by God to Moses for his people. [8] The Commandments were given to help all men understand the nature of sin, their rebellion and their obligations to God. [9] 1 John 3:4-6 states that, *"sin is the transgression of the Law"* and *"whoever sins has not seen God nor known him."* The Lord has defined sin as the breaking of His law, and we all break His law by word, thought and actions, which flow out of our determined will, and because of this sin we cannot know God. This sin is an innate part of everyone's nature; there was never a time from our birth that we were without this innate selfishness. God has said, *"The soul that sins shall die"* (Ezekiel 18:4 and 20, NKJV). According to the Law of God there is no remission or forgiveness of sins without the shedding of blood. [10] Every sin deserves a sentence of death for *"the wages of sin is death"* (Romans 6:23, NKJV), [11] and every sin requires atonement in blood.

We decide things all the time, using our mind, and our sin nature has compromised our ability to think clearly. We do not know ourselves; therefore we cannot honestly evaluate self because we are deceived by our own sinfulness. We believe we are right in choosing our own way, but the Lord warns us that our way, which feels so right, is, in fact, so wrong that it leads to death. The Lord has promised us that if we seek Him with all our heart/mind and soul He will give us the ability to love Him and others as He intended.

---

6. Psalm 10:4: *"The wicked, through the pride of his countenance, will not seek after God: God is not in all his thoughts."*
7. Exodus 20 contains the Ten Commandments. The first four are our obligation to God, and the other six are sin defining.
8. God also gave the ceremonial laws with detailed instructions guiding temple worship.
9. Exodus 12
10. Hebrews 9:22: *"Almost all things are by the law purged with blood; and without shedding of blood is not remission."* Remission, freedom; (figuratively) pardon: deliverance, forgiveness, liberty, remission (see Hebrews 9:11-28).
11. Romans 6:23: *"For the wages of sin is death; but the gift of God is eternal life through Jesus Christ our Lord."*

MEMORIZE THE PROVERBS VERSES
(WORK ON THEM IN CLASS.)

There is a way that seemeth right unto a man, but the end therefore is the way of death.

Proverbs 16:25

All the ways of a man are clean in his own eyes; but the LORD weights the spirits.

Proverbs 16:2

In those days, there was no king in Israel; every man did that which was right in his own eyes.

Judges 21:25

For as a man thinks in his heart, so is he ... .

Proverbs 23:7

QUESTIONS ON HOW THE NATURAL MAN THINKS

1. **What does the natural man believe about himself?**
2. **What standard does the natural man use in determining what is right or wrong?**
3. **Explain how Proverbs 23:7 relates to John 2:23-25 and Mark 7:14-23.**
4. **What provision has God made for us in Deuteronomy 4:29, 1 Kings 8:56-58 and Psalm 10:17?**

It is important to remember that speech and actions flow out of our minds. We take for ourselves the prime role in the determination of all our beliefs and actions. There is nothing that touches us that we do not store away, reconfigure, devalue or disregard in the process of developing the content of our mind and the patterns of thinking that guide us throughout our lives. But God's thoughts are not like our thoughts, and His ways are not like our ways. The Lord has promised us that if we seek Him with all our heart, we will find Him, and that He inclines our hearts unto Him, to walk in all His ways. *"But from there you must <u>seek</u> [12] the LORD your God, and you will find Him if you search for Him with all your heart and all your soul"* (Deuteronomy 4:19, NASB). [13] *"I will put My Spirit within you and will cause you to walk in My statutes ..."* (Ezekiel 36:27) **[To Memorize, both].**

---

12. Seek: to tread or frequent; usually to follow, that is pursuit or search; by implication, to seek or ask; specifically to worship.
13. See also 1 Kings 8:56-58 and Psalm 10:17

CHAPTER 2

MAN AS A FREE AGENT

We assume that we are free agents, able to determine our own path. We, as natural men, routinely make internal, mental choices, trusting ourselves. We are essentially a law unto ourselves. In the Scriptures, the phrase, *"natural man"* means the unchanged, unconverted, carnal, sin-bound man, ruled by his own flesh, fulfilling the desires of his own heart and mind.

Jesus is very plainspoken. He said, *"I say to you whoever commits sin is the servant of sin"* (John 8:12-44). Man's natural transgression of God's law is the evidence that the bondage to sin exists, and that men are under the control of the sin nature. In our natural state, we are the servants of sin, knowing how to sin, but we don't know God.

Paul, speaking to believers, described their true spiritual condition before they were converted by God:

And He has made you alive, who were dead in trespasses and sins; in which you once walked according to the course of this world, according to the prince of the power of the air, the spirit that now works in the children of disobedience; among whom we also had our way of life in times past, in the lusts of our flesh, fulfilling the desires of the flesh and of the <u>thoughts</u>; [14] *and were by nature the children of wrath, even as others.*

Ephesians 2:1-3, NKJV [To Memorize]

For who among men knows the things of a man except the spirit of man within him? So also no one knows the things of God except the Spirit of God ... But a natural man does not accept the things of the Spirit of God, for they are foolishness to him; and he cannot understand them, because they are spiritually appraised.

1 Corinthians 2:11 and 14, NASB [15] [To Memorize]

In Romans, Paul discussed the lack of merit of both Jew and Gentile:

For when ye were the servants of sin, ye were free from righteousness.

Romans 6:20

There is none righteous, no not one: there is none that understands, there is none that seeks after God. All have gone out of the way ... . None do good, no not one ... . No flesh shall be justified in God's sight: for by the law is the knowledge of sin.

Romans 3:10-20, MKJV

---

14. Man spends his life fulfilling the desires of the body and of the thoughts of the mind.
15. The KJV of 1 Corinthians 2:14 says, *"Neither can he know them, because they are spiritually discerned."*

King David tells us, in Psalms, that man does not <u>seek</u> [16] God: *"The wicked, through the pride of his countenance, will not seek after God: God is not in all his thoughts"* (Psalm 10:4 JV). [17]

The disciple James stated, *"For whosoever shall keep the whole law, and yet offend in one point, he is guilty of all. For He that has said, Do not commit adultery, also said, Do not kill. Now if you commit no adultery, yet if you kill, you are become a transgressor of the law"* (James 2:10-11).

QUESTIONS ON THE NATURAL MAN FROM EPHESIANS 2:1-3, ROMANS 3:10-20, 1 CORINTHIANS 2:14, PSALM 10:4 AND JAMES 2:10-11
(READ THE SELECTIONS IN CONTEXT IN YOUR BIBLE AND THEN WRITE YOUR ANSWERS TO THE FOLLOWING QUESTIONS FOR EACH SELECTION IN YOU NOTEBOOK.)

1. Write down what we learn about men, sin and the Law from each selection.
2. If God is not in our thoughts, what are we?

Man's ability to love has also been compromised by sin. Jesus said, *"Thou shalt love the Lord thy God with all thy heart, and with all thy soul, and with all thy mind. This is the primary and great Command and the second Command is to love your neighbor as yourself"* (Matthew 22:36-40). Do we do this? In our natural state, we do not have the capacity to love God or man as God has intended. The Bible gives us the basic principle that man is born with sin bonded to his nature, having a sin nature that naturally transgresses the law of God. As a natural man, we are not under God's guidance, nor do we follow God's laws, but we do follow our own perceptions and the various belief systems invented by man under the influence of Satan. Man's firm belief that personal autonomy is real is just an illusion.

---

16. To seek God: properly to tread or frequent; usually to follow, that is pursuit or search; by implication to seek or ask; specifically to worship.

17. See also Romans 1:15-32, 2:1-13 and 3:20-31. This is said of the natural man, whether Jew or Gentile.

CHAPTER 3

GOD'S ASSESSMENT OF MAN'S THINKING

Our God has abundant mercy as part of His nature, and He understood the corruption that would result from the selfishness of Adam (and our selfishness) even before the world was made. Our Lord was not surprised because He knew the course fallen man would take before He created him. The Lord purposed abundant mercy out of His storehouse of grace and sent Jesus Christ to redeem men. His plan was to make a new kingdom made up of men who would each yield their heart, mind and will to Christ Jesus, fulfilling the good purposes of the Father.

[MEMORIZE THREE OF THE FOLLOWING VERSES]

The _heart_[18] is deceitful above all things, and exceedingly corrupt: who can know it? Jeremiah 17:9, ASV

Woe unto them that are wise in their own eyes, and prudent in their own sight!　Isaiah 5:21

You did not listen but walked in the counsels and the thoughts of your evil heart. Jeremiah 7:24, ASV

O, Lord, I know that the way of man is not in himself; it is not in man who walks to direct his steps.
Jeremiah 10:23, ASV

He that planted the ear, shall he not hear? He that formed the eye, shall he not see? He that chastises the heathen, shall he not correct? He that teaches man knowledge, shall he not know? The Lord knows the thoughts of man are _vanity_. [19]
Psalm 94:9-11

The sacrifice of the wicked is an _abomination_ [20] [hateful] to God; how much more when he brings it with a wicked mind?
Proverbs 21:27

QUESTIONS ON GOD'S ASSESSMENT OF MAN'S THINKING
(WRITE DOWN WHAT YOU LEARN FROM EACH SELECTION IN YOUR NOTEBOOK.)

1.　Based on the above scriptures, what is God's assessment of mankind?
2.　Compare this to Romans 1:1-2:16 and write down what you learn.

---

18. The heart: also used (figuratively) very widely for the feelings, the will and the intellect. (Strongs)
19. Vanity: empty, useless, no satisfaction.
20. Abomination: something morally disgusting, that is an abhorrence.

3. Look up Proverbs 1:30-31, Jeremiah 6:19, 17:10, 25:14 and 32:19.

The Lord has a set hatred of evil as part of His character and will not compromise with sin at all. In our natural state of sinfulness, we allow self too much slack, constantly making compromises. Even as our conscience protests, we create even more corruption within ourselves. *"And God looked upon the earth, and behold, it was corrupt; for all flesh had corrupted his way upon the earth"* (Genesis 6:12). *"As I live, saith the LORD God, I have no pleasure in the death of the wicked; but that the wicked turn from his way and live: ... . Turn you from your evil ways; for why will you die?"* (Ezekiel 33:11). The Lord does not enjoy destroying the wicked, but His law requires justice so that every moral law broken by word, thought or deed receives a just sentence of death. Jesus said, *"But I say unto you, that every idle word that men shall speak, they shall give account in the Day of Judgment. For by your words you shall be justified, and by your words you shall be condemned"* (Matthew 12:36-37). [To Memorize]

Paul wrote, *"For we must all appear before the judgment seat of Christ; that every one may receive the things done in his body, according to that he has done, whether it be good or bad"* (2 Corinthians 5:10) [To Memorize]

The Lord has told us that all men will be held accountable for their deeds and the fruit of those deeds, as well as the word he speaks. Read the following five references in context and the selections quoted and briefly discuss them, writing down what each reveals about accountability.

1. What does *"eat the fruit of their own way"* mean? (Proverbs 1:30-31 and 33)
2. What does *"the fruit of your own thoughts"* mean? (Jeremiah 6:19)
3. What does these verses mean? (Jeremiah 17:9-10)
4. What is taking place in verses 1 through 5? (Jeremiah 25:1-5)
5. Who was being repaid for the evil done against Israel? (Jeremiah 25:14)
6. To what degree does God hold men accountable? (Jeremiah 32:18-19)

Out of His goodness, the Lord set His love upon sinful, rebellious men, men without a single redeeming quality. He chose to send His Son to lay down His life to save men, not to leave us in spiritual darkness. *"For God so loved the world, that he gave his only begotten Son, that whosoever believes in him should not perish, but have everlasting life. For God sent not his Son into the world to condemn the world: but that the world through him might be saved"* (John 3:16-17). *"Verily, verily, I say unto you, He that hears my word, and believes on Him that sent me, has everlasting life, and shall not come into condemnation; but is passed from death unto life"* (John 5:24). [To Memorize]

The grace of God is greater than our sin natures and will, over our lifetime, undo the evil done in our heart/mind.

CHAPTER 4

THE LAW

God called Abraham to come out of the land of Ur, which was ruled by the Chaldeans. [21] Abraham followed the Lord's instructions and went into the land of the Canaanites. The Lord made specific promises to Abraham concerning the future of his family. Abraham had a son named Isaac, whom God appointed as the official heir to the Abrahamic promises. The second son of Isaac, named Jacob, was chosen by God to be the legal heir of the Abrahamic promises and blessings. Jacob had 12 sons who would be the heads of the 12 tribes which inherited the promises and blessing given to their father Abraham. Gods' chosen people are the descendants of Abraham. These people, chosen by God, are the Jews, and Hebrew, their native language, is still spoken today.

The Jewish people lived in Egypt for 430 years, first as herdsmen, and then, as slaves. God told Moses that He would keep His promise to Abraham and redeem them from the Egyptians and give them a land of their own, *"I did swear to give it to Abraham, to Isaac, and to Jacob; and I will give it to you for a heritage ..."* (Exodus 6:8). [22] Soon after the people were led out of Egypt, in the third month, they were near the entrance into the Promised Land. During that month, God told Moses to send one man from each of the 12 tribes of Israel to evaluate the land. Ten men returned from searching the land, and because they were afraid of the people of the land, they refused to do as God commanded. The other two men, Caleb and Joshua, advised Moses that the Land was bountiful and that they were ready to follow God into the Land. Upon hearing the reports, the people also turned against Moses, refusing to do as God commanded. God's punishment for their refusal to obey and enter into the Promised Land was one year in the desert wilderness for each of the 40 days spent as scouts. [23] They spent 40 years wandering in a harsh land, until the day the Lord called them to go into the Promised Land. He called them together before Mt Sinai and gave the people laws to live by and many instructions to follow. In its totality, this was called the Sinai Covenant.

God's moral law is presented in the Ten Commandments, also called the Decalogue, [24] and is a part of the Sinai Covenant. God told Moses to write down the Ten Commandments, as well as many of the civil statutes to govern the nation and many ceremonial laws for tabernacle worship. [25] These three parts — the older Moral Law (Decalogue), the Civil Law, and the Ceremonial Law (which directed the worship of the living God), formed the Sinai Covenant and, in summation, are also called "The Law."

---

21. See Genesis 11:27-12:8, 13:14-18, chapters 15-17 and 21:1-8
22. See also Exodus 6:6, Deuteronomy 9:4-5 and 2 Samuel 7:23 for the reason for driving out the nations.
23. See Numbers 13 and Deuteronomy 1
24. Deuteronomy 5:8-21, Ver? *"You shall have no others gods before Me. You shall not make any idol nor shall you worship or serve them. You shall not take the name of the Lord in vain. Keep the Sabbath day for it is holy. Honor your father and your mother. You shall not murder, you shall not commit adultery. You shall not steal, you shall not lie. You shall not covet a neighbors wife or anything that belongs to your neighbor."* These are also seen in Exodus 20.
25. See Deuteronomy 9, 10:1-5 and Exodus 34:1

The Jewish people were to keep the Sinai Covenant fully to the last detail because this was the will of God. The keeping of these commandments was the condition God made for them receiving blessings. The Sinai Covenant, or Law, covered all areas of the life of the Jewish people. The civil laws provided boundaries to keep them from oppressing one another and to keep them from making alliances of any kind with the surrounding ungodly peoples. The religious laws were to keep the difference between the Holy and the profane very sharp. [26] God used the Ten Commandments, the moral law, to teach the people their sin before Him. He used the various commands and judgments to protect and preserve His people, which made them distinctly a people under God.

The people began to focus upon outward compliance, mistakenly believing that the laws, statues and sacrifices were a system of performance-based salvation. But all the laws were external and could not remake the internal man bound by the sin nature. The people overlooked the fact that salvation is given by God alone and cannot be earned. This was a salvation which changed the heart\mind of men, to seek the Lord, to love Him with all their being and to submit to Him in obedience, as did their father Abraham. There was no performance-based salvation then, nor is there today. These laws were to teach the people what constitutes sin and guide the people to honor the Lord with their lives and love one another, acting as a light to all the surrounding peoples until Messiah should come.

Hear, O Israel: The Lord our God is one Lord: and you shall love the Lord your God with all your heart, and with all thy soul, and with all thy might. And these words, which I command you this day shall be in your heart: and you shall carefully teach them unto your sons, and shall talk of them when you sit in your house, and when you walk by the way, and when you lie down, and when you rise up. Deuteronomy 6:4-7, MKJV [To Memorize]

QUESTIONS ON THE LAW FROM EXODUS 20, DEUTERONOMY 4:1-40 AND CHAPTERS 5, 6 AND 7
[LIST AS MANY OF THE TEN COMMANDMENTS AS YOU CAN FROM MEMORY. THEN LOOK THEM UP AND WRITE THEM DOWN TO HELP YOU REMEMBER THEM BETTER. READ THE PASSAGES IN CONTEXT AND THEN WRITE IN YOUR NOTEBOOK THE ANSWERS TO THE FOLLOWING QUESTIONS:]

1. Where did the Law come from?
2. Deuteronomy 4:25-29 is a promise given to the people. What are its conditions?
3. What was the condition agreed to by the people (see Deuteronomy 5:27)?
4. What was the result of their words?
5. What was God's desire for His people?
6. What did God say was the purpose for the statutes, judgments and commandments?

---

26. Ezekiel 44:23 *"Moreover, they shall teach My people the difference between the holy and the profane, and cause them to discern between the unclean and the clean."*

The Law is spiritual and good, but it has no ability to change the internal mindset of anyone under bondage to sin. [27] The Law is the truth that exposes the sin nature and drives men to his knees before God, for it cannot be kept by anyone ruled by self. This was not its purpose. One reason for the moral Law was to give us the knowledge of what constitutes sin.[28] The moral Law focused attention on the sinfulness of all sin, and sin is alive within us, but comes out of our mind's\heart's dark closet when it is identified and credited to our account. All men sin, whether they live under God's law or they live under their own law. All are justly condemned and guilty before God. [29] All men die because of this inheritance of sin, brought upon mankind by Adam's willful rebellion. The Ten Commandments also give us some knowledge of God, as well as our obligations to Him. We gain insight by contrasting the character of godly love, that values others above self, with the negative commandments. If we love, we will not lie, take advantage of one another, steal or commit adultery or any of the other things men do against their fellowman. All men everywhere are called to follow this moral Law, and it will be the standard that God uses in judgments issued against men because it is eternal in nature, and its teachings are one reflection of the character of the living God. [30]

To some degree, the moral law of God has also been written on the hearts of men since the beginning of creation. All Gentile or non-Jewish cultures also have a system of laws, and some of their beliefs reveal the stamp of God's moral law. Romans 2:14-15 states: *"For when the Gentiles, who do not have the law, by nature do the things in the law, these, although not having the law, are a law unto themselves: who show the work of the law <u>written in their hearts, their conscience also bearing witness</u>, and between themselves their thoughts accusing or else excusing one another"* (NKJV).

This God-given compass found within the heart of men is twisted because of our sin nature. It is also influenced by the moral and cultural mores of our group. But we all have, to some degree, an internal awareness that responds to being wronged. We may steal from others but resent anyone taking our things. We may lie but hate anyone who deceives us. Out of His abundant grace, the Lord gave us the Law that we might identify and put to death our sins against each other and against Him. This witness, that even natural man has some remnant awareness of this law left within, is universal. We are also given a conscience to help govern our sin-harnessed mind, will and emotions, [31] and it serves as a restraining influence upon our evil. But there is a process by which repetition of sin can cause man to become seared [32] in his own conscience, rendering it defiled. [33] Eventually the conscience ceases to convict of sin, as our hearts\minds\will\emotions become sin-hardened and terminally self-absorbed. We are all spiritually blind under the

---

27. See Romans 7:14

28. Romans 3:20 *"Therefore by the deeds of the law there shall no flesh be justified in his sight: for by the law is the knowledge of sin."*

29. See Romans 2:12

30. See Acts 17:30-31

31. John 8:9 *"When they which heard (it), being convicted (by their own) conscience, went out one by one, beginning at the oldest, (even) unto the last: and Jesus was left alone, and the woman standing in the midst."* See also Acts 24:16, Romans 9:1 and 13:5.

32. 1 Timothy 4:2 *"Speaking lies in hypocrisy; having their conscience seared with a hot iron."*

33. 1 Corinthians 8:7 *"Howbeit there is not in every man that knowledge: for some with conscience of the idol unto this hour eat it as a thing offered unto an idol; their conscience being weak is defiled."* Titus 1:15 *"Unto the pure all things (are) pure: but unto them which are defiled and unbelieving (is) nothing pure; but even their mind and conscience is defiled."*

influence of sin, until the day comes that the Spirit opens our heart\mind to hear and believe the truth of the Word of God.

But the Law condemns sinners, and God was *"not willing that any should perish but for all to come to repentance,"* (2 Peter 3:9). Therefore He extended yet more mercy through His Son unto men. *"But where sin abounded grace did much more abound: so that as sin has reigned to death, even so grace might reign through righteousness unto eternal life by Jesus Christ our Lord"* (Romans 5:20-21, MKJV). Out of His abundant love and grace, God sent Jesus to live a perfect, sin-free life that fulfilled all the conditions promised in the Sinai Covenant for our blessing. Then Jesus laid down His life for us, taking the penalty we deserved for our sin. The Lord's purpose was to overrule our sin nature through the power of the indwelling Spirit of His Son Jesus, so that we might truly love Him and love one another. God has ordained that sinful man can only be saved by His grace (loving compassion and abundant mercy), not by keeping the Law. Grace is available only because of the sacrifice of the innocent and pure Jesus, the long-awaited Messiah. This grace works through our God-given faith being placed in Jesus Christ, as the <u>propitiation</u> [34] for all our sin. [35] God's grace is a gift which causes us to yield our hearts and lives to follow Jesus. *"Through Him we also have access by faith into this grace in which we stand ..."* (Romans 5:2, MKJV).

Grace, extended through the power of the indwelling Spirit of Christ, produces within us the ability to love our Lord and also to love other people. This grace from our Lord gives us motivation and power for our efforts to honor Him by our less-than-perfect efforts to keep His law. Our love for God comes from hearts and minds suffused with Christ's love, which surpasses knowledge, [36] a love that constrains us. [37]

QUESTIONS ON ROMANS 2:12, 5:1-2, 15, 17-21, 2 PETER 3:9 AND HEBREWS 8 & 9
(READ THE CONTEXT OF THESE REFERENCES AND THEN ANSWER THE FOLLOWING QUESTIONS, PUTTING YOUR ANSWERS IN YOUR NOTEBOOK.)

1. What do we learn about Jesus Christ in these references?
2. What has the Lord given to man that restrains his natural evil?
3. What is the meaning of Hebrews 9:22?

---

34. *Propitiation*, that is, (concretely) an atoning victim, a word relating to the expiration of air from the lungs, also the lid of the Ark in the Temple, mercy seat, propitiation.

35. Romans 3:21-28 *"Being justified freely by his grace through the redemption that is in Christ Jesus: Whom God has set forth (to be) a propitiation through faith in his blood, to declare His rightness for the remission of sins that are past, through the forebearance of God; to declare, (I say), at this time His righteousness: that He might be just, and the justifier of him which believes in Jesus."* See also 1 John 2:2-5 and 4:7-13.

36. See Ephesians 3:14-19

37. See 2 Corinthians 5:14

CHAPTER 5

SPIRITUAL DARKNESS

Spiritual darkness is our natural state, and I have used Romans 8:6-8 and 13, 1 Corinthians 2:12-14 and Ephesians 2:1-3 and 4:17-19 to illustrate that spiritual darkness. Paul wrote all three of these books, and the terms he used to describe the unconverted man are, practically speaking, interchangeable. He used the term *the carnal mind* when referring to the natural man with his sin nature. [38] The King James Version of the Bible uses the word *flesh* to describe the carnal mind.

QUESTIONS ON ROMANS 8:6-8, 13 (MKJV)
WRITE THE ANSWERS TO THE FOLLOWING QUESTIONS IN YOUR NOTEBOOK.
READ THE FOOTNOTES AS YOU ENCOUNTER THEM.

For to be carnally minded is death … . Because the carnal mind is <u>enmity</u> [39]against God: for it is not subject to the law of God, neither indeed can it be … . So then they that are in the flesh, cannot please God. … For if you live according to the flesh, you will die.
Romans 8:6-8 and 13, MKJV

1. **What are the characteristics of the carnal man?**
2. **Why is the carnal mind said to be death?**
3. **What are the consequences of the carnal mind following the carnal nature?**

Our Lord has identified clearly for us the true nature of men, identifying the mind as the center from which our evil flows. As "natural men," we are unaware that we exist in spiritual darkness. 1 Corinthians 2:12-14 uses this term *natural man,* meaning the carnal mind and flesh, unconverted, harnessed by sin in the mind, emotions and will.

QUESTIONS ON 1 CORINTHIANS 2:12-14 (MKJV)

For the natural man does not receive the things of the Spirit of God for they are foolishness to him: neither can he know them, because they are spiritually discerned.   1 Corinthians 2:14, MKJV

---

38. *Carnal,* pertaining to the flesh (the carnal mind, carnal nature, or flesh is the same as the natural man). See Romans 8:6-8.
39. Enmity, hostility; by implication, a reason for opposition: enmity, hatred.

1. What do men know about the things of God?
2. Why do men need to understand the things of God?
3. What does the carnal man think about the things of God?

We are spiritually dead. Therefore we live to fulfill the desires of our heart\mind. Without the Lord's intervention, no man would know or care about the things of God. The Holy Spirit must give us faith, with its spiritual discernment, to seek the Lord and His ways. Then we must have spiritual re-birth to love our holy Father and follow His ways.

QUESTIONS ON EPHESIANS 2:1-3

And you hath he quickened, who were dead in trespasses and sins; wherein you once walked according to the course of this work, according to the <u>prince of the power of the air</u>, [40] the spirit that now works in the children of disobedience: among whom we all also had our conservation [way of life] in times past in the lust of our flesh, fulfilling the desires of the flesh and of the mind; as you were by nature children of wrath, even as others.

Ephesians 2:1-3

1. What was our former condition?
2. What does the phrase *"you walked according to the course of this world"* mean?
3. What was our nature?
4. What spirit did we have and what was our destiny?

As natural men, we are all walking along in the world's cultures, under the influence of Satan, dead in our trespasses and sins, with our minds giving value to and assent for whatever the world surrounding us values. Busy pursuing the desires of our bodies and minds, we suppress conscious awareness of the Lord that made us, for He holds no value for us.

QUESTIONS ON EPHESIANS 4:17-19 (ASV-1901)

This I say therefore, and testify in the Lord that you no longer walk as the Gentiles also walk, in the vanity [41] of their mind, having the understanding darkened, being alienated from the life of God through the ignorance that is in them, because of the blindness of their heart; who being past feeling have given themselves over unto <u>lasciviousness</u>, [42] to work all <u>uncleanness</u> [43] along with greediness.

Ephesians 4:17-19, ASV1901

---

40. *Prince of the power of the air*, that is the ruler who has mastery, who is actively working, effectual upon the children of unbelief, in other words, Satan.
41. *Vanity*, inutility (futility);(useless, empty, pointless, of no value) figuratively, transientness; moral depravity.
42. *Lasciviousness*, legal, moral and sexual immorality, sensuality, lust, licentiousness, filthy, wantonness.
43. *Uncleanness*, impurity (the quality), in this case, morally impure.

1. **What prevents us from knowing God?**
2. **What does it mean to be *"alienated from the life of God"*? How? Why?**

Ephesians tells us that because we are spiritually dead we have no capacity to love God. We are separated from the living God and cannot know Him. Rebellion against authority and any restraints is part of our sin nature, even from a very young age. We are like the people in "The Lord of the Ring" trilogy, for it is as if we are all born bonded to the Ring of Mordor. The ring gives the dark lord immediate access to the mind. We are all twisted by sin to some degree, as was Boromir, the "Syth," or Gollum\Smeagol. They were continually influenced by the pull of darkness from within and without. Our sin nature pulls us toward evil, like the Ring of Mordor. The commandments that God has given to men illustrate the sin nature's inclinations, so that we might identify our sin and our true nature. [44]

However, the Lord was kind to men, fulfilling the conditions for blessing given at Mt. Sinai for us through Jesus. Jesus never pursued evil. His thought and His speech was pure. His death and all of His works benefited men. Because of this, believers can be reconciled to God and grafted into His family. Jesus comes to live within us through His indwelling Spirit, [45] so that we might be the recipients of His love and righteousness. Our Lord Jesus changes our hearts\minds, giving us, through Himself, the power and motivation to love both God and our fellowmen, thereby fulfilling God's commandment, *"And you shall love the Lord with all Your heart, soul, mind and with all your strength, ... and you shall love your neighbor as yourself"* (Mark 12:30-31). Jesus told Nicodemus, a ruler of the Jews, that he had to be born again to see the kingdom of God." [46] We, as natural men, must have this spiritual re-birth to change our heart\mind, so that we can think and live a new way through love. [47]

---

44. Romans 3:20 *"Therefore by the deeds of the law there shall no flesh be justified ... : for by the law (is) the knowledge of sin."*
45. See John 14:1-31
46. See John 3:1-8
47. Love that is motivated and powered by the living God through His precious Son Jesus.

CHAPTER 6

THE FLESH AND THE SPIRIT

The changed, or converted, man is operating from a new spiritually awakened mind, indwelt by the Holy Spirit. [48] This spiritual awareness is a function of the "new birth." The indwelling of the Spirit of God was the fulfillment of a promise made to Israel by God through the prophet Ezekiel. [49]

A new heart will I give you and a new spirit will I put within you: and I will take away the stony heart our of your flesh, and I will give you a heart of flesh. And I will put my spirit within you, and cause you to walk in my statutes, and you shall keep my judgments, and do them! Ezekiel 36:26-27 [50]   **[To Memorize]**

Let us again use Romans 8:1-14, Ephesians 2:1-6 and 1 Corinthians 2:11-14. Read the additional information given in the added verses and see the contrast between the spiritual deadness of natural man and the converted man who is filled with the Spirit of God.

QUESTIONS ON ROMANS 8:1-14
(NOTE THE CONTRAST BETWEEN THE FLESH [NATURAL\CARNAL MIND] AND THE SPIRIT [UNDERLINED].)

For to be carnally minded is death; <u>but to be spiritually minded is life and peace</u>. Because the carnal mind is enmity against God; for it is not subject to the law of God, neither indeed can be. So then they that are in the flesh cannot please God. <u>But you are not in the flesh, but in the Spirit, if indeed ... that the Spirit of God dwell in you</u>. Now if any man has not the Spirit of Christ, he is none of his. <u>But if the Spirit of him that raised up Jesus from the dead dwell in you, He that raised up Christ from the dead shall also quicken your mortal bodies by his Spirit that dwells in you</u>. For if you live after the flesh, you shall die; <u>but if you through the Spirit do mortify[51] the deeds of the body, you shall live. For as many as led by the Spirit of God, they are the sons of God</u>.   Romans 8:6-9, 11, and 13-14 **[To Memorize]**

Who is the Spirit-filled man?
3. **How is it possible for him to be in the Spirit?**
4. **What was his life like prior to the indwelling of the Spirit?**
5. **How does he live now? What is the focus of his life now?**
6. **What understanding does Jeremiah 17:9 give us about our righteousness?**

---
48. See John 3:14-21, 36 and John 14:1-15:18
49. See Ezekiel 36:26-27 (NASB)
50. See what our Lord Jesus said in John 14:15-27.
51. Mortify: to kill, (cause to be) put to death, to deaden ie (fig) to subdue (see Romans 3:18 and Colossians 3:5)

7. Whose righteousness is mentioned in verse 10?
8. If you are spiritually minded, what two graces are extended to you?
9. Write a description of the natural man and the Spirit-filled man.
10. What does Ezekiel say the Spirit will do?

When we are born again, we are redeemed from under the wrath of God and reconciled to God. Jesus procured for us this peace with His heavenly Father. Jesus comes to indwell us, imparting new life unto us by His Spirit. The Spirit of Christ gives us the desire to know God and to please Him. He brings us to the point of genuine sorrow over our hardness of heart and our willful disobedience, which leads us to repentance. [52] His work in our heart sets us free from bondage to sin. We are freed from guilt, for we were once saturated with evil, but now have been forgiven for each sin. We are grateful and thankful for such mercy given us by our Lord and Savior. This leads us to put to death the deeds which spring from our "flesh." We are given the ability through His Spirit to begin to know and love the Lord as He has commanded. *"And you shall love the Lord with all our heart, soul, mind, and with all your strength"*(Deuteronomy 6:5, NKJV).

QUESTIONS ON JOHN 14:1-27
(READ THE WHOLE CHAPTER AND THEN PUT THE ANSWERS TO THE FOLLOWING QUESTIONS IN YOUR NOTEBOOK.)

Jesus said unto him, I am the way, the truth, and the life: no one comes unto the Father except through me.
John 14:6, NKJV [To Memorize]

Peace I leave with you, my peace I give unto you: not as the world gives, I do give to you, Let not your heart be troubled, neither let it be afraid.
John 14:27, NKJV [To Memorize]

1. If you love the Lord Jesus, what will you do in your life?
2. Who is the Comforter and where does He live?
3. What is one of the jobs of the Holy Ghost?
4. Why is He called the Spirit of truth?
5. What is the connection between believers and the Father?
6. What proof is there that you love both the Son and the Father?
7. What do you know about yourself if you do not value the Word of the Father?

One job of the indwelling Spirit of Jesus is to cause us to walk in the ways of God, by teaching us through His Word how to love others. This godly love will not break the commands of the Father easily because our heart\mind has been changed. If we have been "born again" by the Spirit of Christ, we are learning to love Jesus and will now have a Spirit-given bias to obey His truth.

---

52. 2 Corinthians 7:10 *"For the sorrow that is according to the will of God produces a repentance without regret, leading to salvation, but the sorrow of the world produces death"* (NASB). Luke 5:32 *"Jesus said, 'I have not come to call the righteous but sinners to repentance."* Also see 2 Timothy 2:24-26.

QUESTIONS ON 1 CORINTHIANS 2:11-14 (MKJV)

For who among men knows the thoughts of a man except the spirit of the man which is in him? Even so the thoughts of God no one knows except the Spirit of God. Now we have received, not the spirit of the world, but the Spirit who is from God, so that we may know the things freely given to us by God, which things we also speak, not in words taught by human wisdom, but in those taught by the Spirit, combining spiritual thoughts with spiritual words. But a natural man does not accept the things of the Spirit of God, for they are foolishness to him; and he cannot understand them, because they are spiritually appraised.

1 Corinthians 2:11-14, NASB **[Memorize the Last Verse]**

1. **How does a man know or assess other men?**
2. **How does he think about God?**
3. **Why is it that the natural man can never know the things of God?**
4. **What is one of the purposes of the Spirit?**
5. **How does the Spirit teach us the things of God?**

We must have the Spirit of God to understand the things of God. True wisdom comes from the living Word of God, not from the thoughts (dead philosophies) of men through the ages. In our past, we believed the various philosophies and perceptions of men, which were (and still are) under the influence of Satan, the ruler of the world systems since the Fall. In our natural state, we fulfilled the lust of our bodies and our minds. We were in bondage through sin, under the influence of evil.

QUESTIONS ON EPHESIANS 2:1-10 (MKJV)

And He has made you alive, who were once dead in trespasses and sins, in which you once walked according to the course of this world, according to the prince of the power of the air, the spirit that now works in the children of disobedience; among whom we also had our way of life in times past, in the lusts of our flesh, fulfilling the desires of the flesh and of the thoughts, and were by nature the children of wrath, even as others. But God, who is rich in mercy, for His great love wherewith He loved us, even when we were dead in sins, has made us alive together with Christ (by grace you are saved), and has raised us up together and made us sit together in the heavenly (places) in Christ Jesus, so that in the ages to come He might show the exceeding riches of His grace in His kindness toward us through Christ Jesus. For by grace you are saved through faith, and that not of yourselves. It is the gift of God, not of works, lest anyone should boast. For we are His workmanship, created in Christ Jesus to good works, which God, has before ordained that we should walk in them.

Ephesians 2:1-10, MKJV **[To Memorize, last 4 verses]**

1. What does it mean to "walk according to the course of the world"?
2. Why did God step into the world of men? And what great kindness did He do?
3. What did we think about and do when we were children under wrath?
4. How do we obtain faith?
5. What are we supposed to do differently when we have faith? Why?

THE WAR OF THE FLESH AGAINST THE SPIRIT

There will always be war between our flesh and the indwelling Spirit of Christ because we have a remnant of sin that remains. The Lord left this imprint of sin within us because we need to struggle against the flesh, which is very demanding. We grow spiritual muscles as we overcome the carnal desires of the flesh and the mind[53] by the Spirit's work within us. He gives us understanding of the Scriptures and the gift of belief so that we can grow in grace and the knowledge of the Lord. We begin to have a better appreciation of the importance of God's will and the explicit words written to expose all our slavery to self-interests.

In Genesis, we follow Abraham's life and the life of his son Isaac. Isaac had twin boys. Esau was the older son and was, therefore, entitled to all the blessings, plus a double portion of Isaac's wealth, including all flocks of sheep and goats. The younger son was named Jacob, and he was his mother's favorite. Jacob tricked Esau twice to get both the birthright and the blessings.[54] This meant that Jacob became the future, the one through whom and for whom God worked to bring His plan of salvation for the people of His future Kingdom. Jacob had to flee from his brother in order to live.

Years later, there came a great famine, and Jacob's large family faced starvation. Jacob was an old man by then. Ten of his sons were herders, but Benjamin, the youngest, was still at home with Jacob. Joseph, the eleventh son, was thought to be dead. But Joseph was still alive in the land of Egypt and was a powerful man, second only to Pharaoh. Jacob sent his sons to buy gain in Egypt. Sometime later, Joseph invited the entire clan to come live in Goshen.[55] This clan became the twelve tribes of Israel, and their haven for rest stretched into 400 years of occupation. By this time, the people of Israel (Jacob) had become harshly treated slaves to another Pharaoh.

When the evil of the people in the old land reached saturation level, God had promised Abraham he would bring His descendants out of Egypt. Now was the time, and God raised up Moses to do His will and bring His people out.

Our Lord has very long-range plans for individuals and nations, to accomplish His certain will. This internal war that all Christians experience will be won, as the Lord brings us into His Kingdom. None can bring himself into compliance, nor will the Lord's plans be circumvented. This does not mean that our choices do not matter, because the Spirit leads us where God has called us to walk, with the particular difficulties we encounter along the way. Whatever choices we make, God is there, and He never leaves us. We are His workmanship created in Christ Jesus.

53. See Ephesians 2:3 and Romans 12:2
54. Genesis chapters 29-33 and 35-36. This is a good read.
55. Sixty-six people came into Egypt, all of Jacob's descendants (Genesis 46). Jacob was now called Israel by the Lord.

PART II

THE SPIRIT-FILLED MAN

CHAPTER 7

CONVERSION

Remember from earlier lessons that the natural man cannot understand the things of God, for they are spiritually discerned. Our mind is the center from which everything is considered, adopted and applied. The content of our minds is a product of our life learning, and our sin nature has led us to devalue, ignore, suppress [56] or deny the entrance of anything pertaining to the Lord. Therefore to understand the things of God, we must have a new nature imparted to us. Our minds are transformed through the Spirit by the truths of Christ Jesus, to think and function in the new way of godly love. This is why we study God's Word.

QUESTIONS ON EPHESIANS 4:17-24
(READ THE REFERENCES AND THEN ANSWER THE FOLLOWING QUESTIONS, WRITING THE ANSWERS IN YOUR NOTEBOOK.)

This I say therefore, and testify in the Lord, that you henceforth not walk as other Gentiles [nations] walk, in the vanity [futility] of their mind, having the understanding darkened, being alienated from the life of God through the ignorance that is in them, because of the blindness [57] of their heart: who being past feeling have given themselves over unto <u>lasciviousness,</u> [58] to work all uncleanness [sexual/moral impurity] with greediness. <u>But you have not so learned Christ, if indeed you have heard Him and were taught by Him, as the truth is in Jesus. For you ought to put off</u> [59] <u>the old man [self, according to our old way of thinking \ living before) who is corrupt</u> [60] <u>according to the deceitful lusts,</u> [61] <u>and be renewed</u> [62] <u>in the spirit of your mind. And you should put on</u> [63] <u>the new man, who according to God was created in righteousness and true holiness.</u> Ephesians 4:17-24

---

56. Romans 1:18-20 *"For the wrath of God is revealed from Heaven against all ungodliness and unrighteousness of men, who suppress the truth in unrighteousness, because that which may be known of God is manifest in them; for God has showed (it) unto them. For the invisible things of Him from the creation of the world are clearly seen, being understood by the things that are made, (even) His eternal power and Godhead; so that they are without excuse :... ."*
57. Stupidity or callousness, blindness, hardness.
58. *Lasciviousness,* lacking legal or moral or sexual restraints, wantonness (the opposite of self-control or personal restraint).
59. *Put off,* to put away (literally of figuratively): cast off, lay aside, and lay down.
60. *Corrupt,* to pine or waste: properly to shrivel or wither, that is to spoil (by any process) or to ruin (especially figuratively by moral influences, to deprave):- self corrupt, defile, destroy.
61. *Lusts,* a longing (especially for what is forbidden): concupiscence, desire, to lust after (desires of the mind and body).
62. Renew, to renovate, that is reform.
63. *Put on,* (in the sense of sinking into a garment); to invest with clothing.

1. What does it mean to *"walk in the vanity of their mind"*? Who is the *"old man"*?
2. How does he live and why does he live this way? How do lusts deceive him?
3. What is the focus of his life and what is his relationship with God?
4. What does it mean to be *"renewed in the spirit of your mind"*?

QUESTIONS ON JOHN 3:1-21 AND NUMBERS 21:1-9
(THE SECOND PART OF THIS CHAPTER IS ON THE NEW BIRTH. REMEMBER, WE ARE COMPARING THE BELIEVER WITH THE UNBELIEVING NATURAL MAN, TO UNDERSTAND THE VAST DIFFERENCE IN THINKING BETWEEN THE TWO.)

Now He which established us with you in Christ, and has anointed us, is God; who has also sealed us, and given the earnest (down payment or guarantee) of the Spirit in our hearts. 2 Corinthians 1:21-22

In whom you also (trusted), after you heard the word of truth, the gospel of your salvation: in whom also after you believed, you were sealed with the holy Spirit of promise, which is the earnest (down payment) of our inheritance until the redemption of the purchased possession, unto the praise of His glory. Ephesians 1:13-14 **[To Memorize]**

Those who trust and obey Christ do so because His work of redemption has been applied to their souls, and this is called being "born again." This gift of salvation makes it possible for us to love the Lord. Hebrews 9:14 says that Christ has also *"purged our conscience from dead works to serve the living God,"* for our conscience had been degraded and twisted by sin. We are also sealed for God by the entrance of the indwelling Holy Spirit. His <u>seal</u> is permanent and irrevocable. [64] We cannot lose our salvation because we did nothing to merit it; it was a gift from the Father through His most precious Son.

1. What is the meaning of the three things Jesus said about being <u>born</u> [65] again?
2. What does the wind have to do with regeneration by the Spirit?
3. Jesus mentioned Moses and the serpent. Why?
4. Who is the *"Son of Man"*? What power does this *"Son of Man"* have?
5. What is the meaning of the phrase *"<u>believes on him</u>"* [66] and how is this similar to the example that Jesus gave?
6. What is the condition placed upon those desiring everlasting life? Why do people hate the light?

---

64. *Sealed*, to stamp (with a signet or private mark) for security or preservation (literally or figuratively); by implication to keep secret, to attest: seal up, stop. Having a uniting or joining (a copulative) and sometimes a cumulative force.
65. Born, to procreate (properly by father but by extension the mother); figuratively to regenerate: beget, be born, bring forth, conceive, be delivered of, make, spring.
66. *Believes on him*, to have faith (in, upon, or with respect to, a person or thing), that is, credit; by implication to entrust (especially one's spiritual well being to Christ): believe, commit to (trust), put in trust with.

In depending upon Jesus alone, we, too, can overcome the world. We have new life under the guidance and power of the Spirit of Christ Jesus. We are freed from the domination of sin and self, to love God and serve man. In focusing our hearts upon Christ, we remember what Jesus has accomplished on our behalf and the great love He has for us. In trusting Him, our mind calms, our heart melts and our will is renewed to joyfully follow Him. In Jesus, we can live with internal peace, even in the midst of the seas of stress surrounding us. The Spirit keeps our mind focused upon Jesus, and His gift of faith [67] will keep us holding to His promises and truth.

These things I have spoken to you, so that in Me you may have peace. In the world you have <u>tribulation</u>: [68] *but take courage; I have overcome the world.*   John 16:33, NASB **[To Memorize]**

As we began to practice obedience in faith\trust, we become more aware of the depth of our sin. We realize that remaining sin grips like ligaments attached to bones, and it takes the power of Christ to eradicate the old patterns of sin and sinful responses. We must continually run to our Father for protection and power in order to stand in this battle between our flesh and our mind. It is a conflict to be enjoined every day for the rest of our lives. Giving up is not an option, for God has ordained that we must struggle to gain spiritual muscles and spiritual understanding. All of the creatures born from the shell struggle to gain strength to exit the shell, and we must gain strength to understand and yield self to the Spirit, as He applies the gifts of salvation, repentance, faith, justification, sanctification and love for God and man. God has also reconciled His children to Himself and has communication with them through prayer. None of these things come naturally to our self-centered hearts, but, rather, come through the Spirit of Jesus Christ, as He does His work in our heart\mind.

We walk each day by faith, trusting our Lord Jesus, as He works in us, putting into practice His truth. Faith does not make the Law void. Faith actually establishes the Law in our heart\mind because love for God and man is the substance of the Law.

---

67. Ephesians 2:8 *"For by grace are you saved through faith; and that not of yourselves: (it is) the gift of God ... ."*
68. *Tribulation*, pressure (literally or figuratively): afflicted, anguish, burdened, persecution, tribulation, trouble.

THE LAW OF THE SPIRIT IN CHRIST

In the first sentence in Romans 8:1, Paul said something amazing, *"There is therefore now no condemnation to them which are in Christ Jesus, who walk not after the flesh, but after the Spirit."* The presence of Christ Jesus within us produces an intention that is set to follow the Spirit, not the flesh (self), for He has given to us a bias toward hearing and keeping His truth. *"This I say then, Walk in the Spirit, and you shall not fulfill the lust of the flesh"* (Galatians 5:16). To *"walk in the Spirit"* is to walk under the guidance of the Spirit as He uses the Word of God to change how we think and what we think. This new principle working within believers is called *"the law of the Spirit of life in Christ Jesus."*

There is therefore now no condemnation to them which are in Christ Jesus, who walk not after the flesh, but after the Spirit. For the law of the Spirit of life in Christ Jesus has made me free from the law of sin and death that the righteousness of the law might be fulfilled in us, who walk not after the flesh, but after the Spirit. For they that are after the flesh do mind the things of the flesh; but they that are after the Spirit the things of the Spirit. Romans 8:1-5 **[To Memorize]**

QUESTIONS ON ROMANS 8:1-16

1. **What is the great weakness of the Law (v3)?**
2. **Why is the Law called *"the law of sin and death"*?**
3. **Why is the carnal mind\flesh alien to God?**
4. **What does it mean *"to be spiritually minded"*? What is the benefit of it for us?**
5. **Why is there no condemnation for those who are in Christ Jesus?**
6. **What is the strength of the new law of the Spirit of life in Christ?**
7. **What is the condition of this promise?**
8. **What are the two conditions of operation of this new law?**
9. **Who are the sons of God?**

Those who do not have the Spirit dwelling within do not belong to God. Remember that the unbeliever has a mindset that focuses upon the concerns of the sin nature (flesh). He is busy fulfilling the desires of his heart\mind and body. The things of God are alien to his nature, and He cannot keep the moral law, the Ten Commandments. Those who have the Spirit dwelling within belong to God. He has sealed us and marked us as His. His Son indwells us through His Spirit, and God has adopted us into His family. Believers are learning to walk in love, remembering the true Word of God each day and being led by the Spirit of God. The rightness of the Law is acknowledged by believers. Why? We see that His truth revealed in the Law is absolutely necessary for this new life of love toward God and men. Studying the Scriptures to learn who God is, His evaluation of human beings and His desire for all the nations, as well as each of us individually, are just some of the things we need to understand. Under the Sinai Covenant, the people had promised to keep God's laws and judgments but failed miserably. God promised, in Isaiah 9:6-7, to send a child who would fill all of these names: Wonderful, Counselor, Mighty God, Eternal Father and Prince of Peace. A Son was to be given and the government would be upon His shoulders. His rule would never end nor the peace it was to bring. He would sit upon the throne of David, and His Kingdom would uphold righteousness and justice forever. Jesus Christ fulfilled the covenant at Sinai, as well as all the other covenants that God instituted.

The New Testament brings to us the beauty of Jesus Christ, as the promised Son of God. His holy life, coming from a pure mind and body, was necessary to fulfill the plan of His Father. Jesus kept the Law of God perfectly, as was His nature. The Father could justify us by the Son's sacrifice for our sin natures, and His Son's perfect obedience could be put to our account. Our knowledge of the Father's and Son's love for us is becoming the motive for our walk.

God has prescribed means[69] that He designed to produce holiness within each one of His children. Salvation is worked within each person by the Holy Spirit, as we read the Scriptures to inform the mind and open our understanding to the things of God. We are given faith in Christ as our Redeemer, and this is a gift from God, not about anything that we do. We are to join ourselves to Christians in the area in which we live. Find one church where the pastor is preaching and living the whole counsel of God, and become a real part of that fellowship of believers.

We grow spiritually as we cultivate obedience to the Lord Jesus, and our love for the Lord Jesus increases. When we have demonstrated to those around us and in the church body, that the changes in our thinking and living are real, then we are ready to be baptized, to show publicly that we have been buried with Christ and resurrected to new life in Him.

God calls believers to be active, not passive members of the Body of Christ. This is absolute necessary because we need to know each other fairly well in order to love, encourage, aid and even rebuke one another when necessary. It all takes time and fellowship. We are told this in the New Testament, and the admonition we are given is not to forsake the gathering together to meet to worship the Lord as some did.[70]

The Lord's Supper is the call to the church for the members to worship God and remember Christ who loves us and gave Himself as our substitute, bringing forgiveness for the unpayable debt due as a result of our sin. We are called to look at the Lord Jesus again and take account of the sacrifices He made on our behalf. His Cross is His visible declaration of His remarkable love for believers, when we were yet His enemies. Seriously contend with your mind and heart, out of which our

---

69. *Means:* Signifying a way to an end (*American Heritage Dictionary*). But our God has chosen certain means to be implemented that cause us to grow in faith, grace, knowledge and greater understanding as well as battling sin.

70. See Hebrews 10:19-26

deeds come and the thoughts that are apart from God and yield yourself to the Spirit's conviction of sin.[71] For we are judged by God when we have regard for particular sins. Whenever sins are working within, we must pass judgment against them with serious intent to lay them down today and walk away. The power, motivation and understanding for the destruction of our wrong deeds, our wrong motives and wrong thinking are provided through the indwelling Spirit of Christ. As we read the Holy Word, the Spirit begins His work, opening our understanding.[72] Therefore, we have no valid excuse to hold to sin. We will be disciplined by the Lord so that we will not be condemned along with the world. Even when you walk away from sin, you must be seeking to repair the damage to others. There is always damage to others when love is forgotten and selfish desires rule us.

Habitual prayer along with verse memory and serious study leads to a growing understanding of biblical doctrines. These practices form another part of the method God has chosen to guide and comfort us. He has sent the Spirit to indwell us, to seal us for Himself and promote this communication. The Spirit actively opens our mind and heart to give us understanding of the Scriptures so that we see the whole truth and respond to the Lord with humility and grace through His Spirit.[73] We cannot stand alone. We are His body singly and co-operatively, and we cannot love one another without entering into consistent prayer for each other, our families, our government and other Christians all over the world. We all have blind spots, and we need to ask the Lord to give us all insight so that we do not become hypocrites.

Christ's gathering of believers together in local communities is real but invisible to men. But men do judge the visible church for the church is watched and evaluated by the conduct and speech of the members. Satan desires to destroy our faith, unity and our witness before our community. This church is of God's making, and He designed how it is to function in this world.

---

71. See 1 Corinthians 11:31-32
72. See Hebrews 4:12-16
73. See Hebrews 3

CHAPTER 9

THE SPIRIT OF CHRIST DWELLING WITHIN US

A war exists within us because of the pull of old sinful habits of thinking and behavior, which stands against the Spirit of Christ that indwells us. We were carnal in nature, spiritually dead under the yoke of sin and without merit before God. We could not let go of our natural propensity for sin, but God is faithful and has made for us a way of escape.

QUESTIONS ON ROMANS 8:26-39

1. Who intercedes on our behalf?
2. Those who love God and are called according to His purpose can know what?
3. What amazing information are we given in these verses?
4. What do we know about the love of God? And where is this love?

Paul thought that he kept the moral law, until the Holy Spirit convicted him of covetousness.[74] He was carnal [75] in nature, spiritually dead under the yoke of covetousness and without merit before God. When salvation came to Paul, the Holy Spirit opened his mind to understand that the moral law was not a standard for gathering merit, but rather a standard for death, applied because of the evil in his (and our) failure to keep the Law. As the illumination of the indwelling Spirit progressed, Paul recognized his many sins and found himself trapped in an internal war between his mind (that loved the Lord and His laws) and his flesh (that still had remaining sin). He cried out, *"O wretched man that I am! Who shall deliver me from the body of this death?"* (Romans 7:24). When the Holy Spirit gave Paul insight into the work of Christ Jesus, he almost shouted, *"(There is) therefore now no condemnation to them which are in Christ Jesus, who walk not after the flesh, but after the Spirit. For the law of the Spirit of life in Christ Jesus has made me free from the [just condemnation] law of sin and death"* (Romans 8:1-2). [76]

QUESTIONS ON 1 CORINTHIANS 2:1-16 AND 3:18-23
(READ THE 1 CORINTHIANS SELECTIONS CAREFULLY, DISCUSS THEM FULLY AND ANSWER THE FOLLOWING QUESTIONS IN YOUR NOTEBOOK.)

---

74. See Romans 7:7-13
75. See Romans 7:14
76. Read through verse 14 to understand it more fully.

But as it is written, eye has not seen, nor ear heard, neither has entered into the heart of man the things which God has prepared for them that love Him. But God has revealed (them) unto us by His Spirit: for the Spirit searches all things, yes, the deep things of God. 1 Corinthians 2:9-11 [To Memorize]

1. In verses 10 through 12, who can receive the things of the Spirit of God?
2. Why is the contrast given between the wisdom of men and the wisdom of God?
3. How do we receive the things of God?
4. Considering verse 14, why can't the natural man receive the things of God?
5. What does this statement mean: *"We have the mind [77] of Christ"*?

QUESTIONS ON EPHESIANS 1:1-2:22
(READ THE PASSAGE AND THEN ANSWER THE FOLLOWING QUESTIONS IN YOUR NOTEBOOK.)

Remember, believers are no longer judged and condemned by the Law because Christ kept the Law perfectly for us and died in our place. This does not negate the Law, for it is spiritual and good, but God had to make a way by which the once sin-bound man could love and honor Him. We can begin living, believing the truth of the Scriptures and yielding to the conviction of the Spirit, so that we will overcome the carnal desires of the heart and mind. How does this change us? Jesus has permanently bonded Himself to us, living within us, changing the intention of our hearts from terminal selfishness to seeking God with all our heart, soul and mind and loving our neighbor.

1. Describe the order in which God brought about the salvation of the saints.
2. What is the time scale and what is the purpose of God's choosing?
3. What are the benefits the saints (believers) receive?
4. Why do believers receive such amazing benefits?
5. What does Paul want us to understand about Christ and the gifts we have received?
6. Exactly what is his prayer for the saints (believers)?
7. In light of this prayer, how should we pray for one another?

The Lord sent His Spirit to teach us, to lead and guide us, through the application of the Scriptures to our lives. He is primarily teaching us the godly ways of real love, so that we can love God and our fellowmen. The Lord Jesus gave us the principles found in all the Scriptures, to renew our minds through the continuous and careful consideration of His Word. This consideration leads to an ever-stronger belief and the adoption of the principles discovered there. This, in turn, leads to the rejection of the principles of the world.

---

77. *Mind*, the intellect, that is, mind (divine or human: in thought, feeling, or will); by implication meaning: mind, understanding.

EPHESIANS 4
(READ THIS CHAPTER IN YOUR BIBLE AND THEN ANSWER THE FOLLOWING QUESTIONS ABOUT SPECIFIC PORTIONS OF IT IN YOUR NOTEBOOK.)

Remember, the "old man" or old self is the same thing as the natural (sin-bound) man, carnal nature or flesh, with its corrupt mind, deceived by lust and dead in trespasses and sins.

QUESTIONS ON EPHESIANS 4:1-7 AND 11-17

1. How are to walk?
2. Why shouldn't we compare ourselves with other Christians?
3. What is to be our constant mental attitude?
4. What is the purpose of the teachers and pastors within the Church?
5. What is the overall plan for each person?
6. Why is all of this preparation important for us?
7. Why is there no room for pride within the Church?
8. How are we to become mature Christians?
9. Why is it important for all Christians to be like Christ?
10. What is the glue that holds the Body of Christ together?

To walk in love as our Lord commands is very difficult for us. We have been taught to lean on self, and our natural inclinations lead to pride in self. But the Lord has radically changed the point of our lives, putting into our hands the compass of His truth to follow, and He is due North. God's love for us is the reason for salvation, and the sacrifice of Jesus is proof of this love. Honoring the Father through the Son is now the point of our lives. We depend upon His truth, and the assurance of His love gives us the strength to endure in peace of mind. We trust the Lord Jesus.

QUESTIONS ON EPHESIANS 4:17-32

As we Gentiles practice sin, we put deeper grooves into our souls, and the deeper the groove made by us, the less we are able to feel emotionally. We go deeper into sin, trying to recapture those feelings we once were able to experience, until we are imprisoned by the desires of flesh\mind. In salvation, the Lord Jesus opens our minds to see the truth of our imprisonment to sin. We rejoice in understanding that the bondage to sin and sinful desires is broken. In Christ, we are free to learn how to love others as He intended, instead of focusing upon those self-seeking desires as the point of our lives.

1. List the six Gentile characteristics found.
2. What are we to do with "the old man" or "the old self"? Why?
3. Why do deceitful lusts corrupt man?
4. What has to be renewed and why is this necessary?
5. Why put on the new Man?
6. How do you accomplish this command (vs 24-32)?

Fidelity to Christ and reliance upon Him for salvation is part of this faith, and so is having such constancy of obedience to the Word of Christ that it illustrates that such a profession of faith is real. We will never be perfect or free from the need to be alert to our own sinful failures and weakness, so as to prevent more sins of omission or commission. It is a joy to use our renewed minds and think upon the things of God, for He is our life and breath. His love for us, demonstrated in the sacrifice of Jesus Christ, is a great comfort and fuels our efforts to love Him. Paul said, *"I am crucified with Christ: nevertheless I live; yet not I, but Christ lives in me: and the life which I now live in the flesh I live by the faith of the Son of God, who loved me, and gave himself for me."* Galatians 2:20 [To Memorize]

CHAPTER 10

OPENED AND RENEWED MINDS

Remember, we were in spiritual darkness and had no capacity to know or choose the things of God. [78] When we are born again, something miraculous happens. Our mind is changed so that we can know and choose the things of God. We now see clearly, and the Scriptures have become clear and of great value to us. Understanding the Word of God is a gift to us who believe, as is our very belief, and as is the Spirit. [79] Without these gifts, we are unable to comprehend our God or His will. Words convey meanings. The words of God were perfectly preserved, and His words are precise to give us the gift of truth, and this truth is absolute in its nature, as it flows from the God whom we worship.

Commit your works unto the Lord, and your thoughts shall be established.   Proverbs 16:3
                                                                                    [To Memorize]

The preparation of the heart in man, and the answer of the tongue are from the Lord.
                                                                    Proverbs 16:1 [To Memorize]

Now Samuel did not yet know the Lord, neither was the word of the Lord yet revealed unto him.
                                                                                    1 Samuel 3:7

And a certain woman named Lydia, a seller of purple, of the city of Thyatira, which worshipped God, heard: whose heart the Lord opened, that she attended unto the things which were spoken of Paul.
                                                                                    Acts 16:14

The Lord Jesus said, "These are the words which I speak unto you while I was with you, that all things must be fulfilled, which were written in the Law of Moses, and in the prophets, and in the psalms, concerning me. Then he opened their understanding, that they might understand the scriptures."
                                                                                    Luke 24:44-45

All things have been handed over to Me by My Father; and no one knows the Son except the Father; nor does anyone know the Father except the Son, and anyone to whom the Son wills to reveal Him.
                                                                                    Matthew 11:27

---

78. See 1 Corinthians 2:14 and Romans 8:5-7
79. See John 14:17, 15:26, Romans 8:11, 15-16 and 26, 1 Corinthians 2:12-14, Galatians 3:14 and Ephesians 1:13

And Jesus said to him, "Blessed are you, Simon Barjona, because flesh and blood did not reveal this to you, but my Father who is in heaven."   Matthew 16:17

QUESTIONS ON OPENED AND RENEWED MINDS

Jesus was speaking to the disciples about the coming of the Holy Spirit: *"When the Helper comes, whom I will send to you from the Father, that is the Spirit of truth who proceeds from the Father, He will testify about me ... ."* John 15:26

1. **What are the implications of Proverbs 16:1?**
2. **What are the implications of Proverbs 16:3?**
3. **How does God open our individual minds to bring us understanding?**
4. **What is His purpose in opening our minds?**
5. **What is revealed in the Scriptures that is so valuable?**
6. **What is the purpose of the "Helper" seen in John 15:26?**

How do we control our thoughts? Our minds are renewed as we study the living Word of God, to change the way we think and what we think. We build block walls of the Scriptures, to guard and inform our minds. We ask our Lord to protect our minds and cause us to walk under the influence and power of His Holy Spirit. We understand that it is the will of the Spirit to follow the guidelines given for godly behavior and practice, doing as the Lord said in His Word. This means keeping our thoughts and will within the moral limits proscribed in His words, as this reflects active love toward God and man. We are to think like Jesus thinks, to value whatever He values, and to respond like Jesus. In the little book of 1st John, we read this, *"He that says, I know him, and does not keep his commandments, is a liar, and the truth is not in him. But whoever keeps His word, truly in this one the love of God perfected. By this we know that we are in Him. He that says he abides in Him ought himself also to walk, even as He walked."* 1 John 2:4 **[To Memorize]**

We follow the moral commandments so that we might practice the unselfish love illustrated through the conduct and words of Jesus. [80] Contrast this godly love with the negative commands. Godly love does not lie, manipulate others or deceive to get its way. Godly love would never betray trust, as in adultery, and does not covet or steal or kill. Godly love honors and obeys parents. [81] Godly love exercises control over the heart\mind so as to promote the pursuit of purity in both. God-led hearts will refrain from tempting others or coveting the things of another. We are admonished to tell the truth in love, as we practice exercising control over our tongues, remembering always that Jesus loved us so much that He gave His life for our sinful hearts\minds, which were hostile to His way and His Word. Jesus lived on this sinful earth without any stain of sin on Him.

---

80. Jesus quoted the Ten Commandments.
81. See Matthew 15:3-6

The Spirit opened my mind\heart to hear the truth of God in my 30th year. We moved back home a few years after this, and my parents asked me to oversee their cattle during the brief periods they were away. My main duty was to feed the cows at precisely 7 AM every morning, as my parents had done every winter morning for thirty years. Instead of seriously considering why this was necessary, I proceeded to feed the cows at whatever time in the morning I made it to the pastures. The cows began to wander off, after waiting an hour or so for the feed to come. At the end of the second week, they were no where to be found, unless you stayed and honked the horn for at least thirty minutes. Honking the horn was the signal that caused the cows to gather from all corners of the pastures. Because of my semi-obedience, it was necessary for my father to get up at least fifty minutes earlier to begin retraining the cows to respond to the time and food link. It took him some stress-filled extra hours to retrain the cows. He always fed the cows before he began his hour-long commute to work.

That was my first lesson in the foolishness of following my self-centered heart. Instead of obeying the will of my heavenly Father to love one another, I just did what pleased my sense of obedience. I never even considered consulting the Lord. As believers, we bring everything we think and do under scriptural truth, in order to reconsider and actively obey our heavenly Father's command to love one another. Obedience is not just a matter of giving mental assent for the truth. It is imminently involved with changing all our attitudes and ways. Godly love is like an iceberg. We understand a little of it at the surface, but it goes down much deeper than we could imagine. Godly love would have me show up at precisely 7 o'clock to feed the cows. Following the old ways of self-determination can never achieve the objectives of Jesus Christ.

QUESTIONS ON ROMANS 12:2
(HOW DO WE MAKE PRACTICAL APPLICATION FOR OURSELVES OF THE THINGS WE HAVE BEEN STUDYING? READ, AS WELL AS MEMORIZE, THE NEXT THREE VERSES AND DISCUSS THEM. WRITE DOWN THE ANSWERS IN YOUR NOTEBOOK.)

I beseech you therefore; brothers by the mercies of God to present your bodies a living sacrifice, holy, pleasing to God, which is your reasonable service. And do not be conformed to this world, but be trans-formed [82] by the renewing of your mind, in order to prove what is that good and pleasing and perfect will of God. [83]   Romans 12:2

1. **What are we asked to do with our bodies? Why?**
2. **Why is it necessary that our minds be transformed?**

---

82. *Transformed*, to transform (literally or figuratively) "metamorphose," transfigure, change
83. See Romans 12:2 and Matthew 22:37

QUESTIONS ON EPHESIANS 4:23-32 AND COLOSSIANS 3:10

In reference to your former manner of life, you lay aside the old man [self], which is being corrupted in accordance with the lust of deceit [deceitful lusts], and that you be renewed in the spirit of your mind, and that you <u>put on</u> [84] the new man [redeemed self], which in the likeness of God has been created in righteousness and true holiness.   Ephesians 4:22-24, Version ?

And have put on the new man [redeemed self], who is being renewed to a true knowledge according to the image of the One that created him.   Colossians 3:10

1. **What are the old ways of thinking and doing?**
2. **Why is it necessary to continually remove the old ways of thinking and doing?**
3. **What are or the three things that we are to do as we remove the old ways?**
4. **As we are being renewed, whom are we to reflect? Why?**

We are in a war with our old nature's way of thinking, which is imprinted upon us by our years of choosing sin and the influence of the forces of darkness. Our old ways of thinking, speaking and behaving are contrary to the heart of God. This is how we remove the old man: remembering that our minds had no regard for the things of God, we yield to the Spirit of God, as He uses the Scriptures to reveal our false perceptions and beliefs. As the Spirit identifies the false ways of thinking, speaking and responding, we lay aside the old perceptions, evaluations and responses. We place in our hearts\mind the truths found in the Scriptures. Our mind is renewed, as it draws upon these truths from the Word, for they are the thoughts of the living God. The Lord's purpose for us is to internalize His truth as our guideline. We accept the new framework of belief and understanding, incorporating God's views and His evaluations into our heart\mind. He not only teaches us the new ways of thinking, but He engages our heart for change in our behavior. We begin putting into place new ways of living to replace our old-man ways, our old habits of living and responding to life. We put on the new man, that is the new principle of love now operating in us, love which flows from the Father through the sacrificial love of Christ into us by His indwelling Spirit.

Like the Lord of Mordor, Satan sends thoughts into our mind, as crude or sensual suggestions, unkind comments or evaluations of others, things that are evil in content and which will cross the moral line if followed. His purpose is to get us attached to the implanted thought, dwell upon it, embellish it and promote it as if it was our own. These thoughts are certainly not from God and not generally a part of our thoughts after we know the Lord. We can identify such thoughts because they are morally offensive, hateful, unkind, deceptive, foster depression and encourage fear, anxiety or hopelessness. Satan whispers thoughts that cast doubt upon the Word of Jesus or by <u>adding to or</u> taking away from the biblical text, which we are forbidden to do. [85] He will also push

---

84. Put on, (in the sense of sinking into a garment), to invest with clothing (literally or figuratively): array, clothe (with), endue, have (put) on.

85. Revelation 22:18-19 *"I testify to everyone who hears the words of the prophecy of this book: if anyone adds to them, God will add to him the plagues which*

us to focus our attention on something "good" and not on the Lord Jesus. Our pleasures can be a stronghold for Satan to exploit. We all have weaknesses, and Satan will exploit them, if we are not alert. Remember this verse: *"You are from God, little children, and have overcome them; because greater is He who is in you than he who is in the world"* (1 John 4:4, NASB). Remember, take the thought immediately to the Lord, asking Him to remove it, and the Spirit will remove it. Although this battle is often continual, we learn to stop the mental assaults. Learning scriptures which function as a shield or sword is a great help in this particular type of assault. Satan will even twist Bible verses to work against our faith and God's truth.

Submit therefore to God, Resist the devil and he will flee from you.   James 4:7, NASB **[To Memorize]**

Be of sober spirit, be on the alert, your adversary, the devil, prowls around like a roaring lion, seeking someone to devour. But resist him, firm in your faith, knowing the same experiences of suffering are being accomplished by your brethren who are in the world.   1 Peter 5:8-9, NASB **[To Memorize]**

We have been given the ability through Jesus Christ to love God and our neighbor, to learn the truth and practice control of what we think, so that we began to think in the way that Jesus thought. *"For the weapons of our warfare are not carnal, but mighty through God to the pulling down of strongholds; casting down imaginations, and every high thing that exalts itself against the knowledge of God, and bring every thought unto the obedience of Christ"* (2 Corinthians 10:5) **[To Memorize]**

Satan will try to take our peace from us, using anxiety, fear, and worry as crowbars. When the temptation comes to be anxious, worried or upset over circumstances, I take all my cares and concerns to the Lord, understanding that He has the power to guard and protect. *"Be anxious for nothing; but in everything by prayer and supplication with thanksgiving let your request be made known to God, and the peace of God which, passes all comprehension, shall guard your hearts and mind through Christ Jesus"* (Philippians 4:5-7, NASB) **[To Memorize]**

To remember again the larger purposes of the Father and the grace of our Lord Jesus in giving Himself for me, I have found this promise of peace to be absolutely true. Through Jesus our hearts\ minds are kept in a state of peace as our focus is in Him.

I have spoken these things to you that you might have peace in Me. In the world you shall have tribu-lation, [86] *but be of good cheer. I have overcome the world.*   John 16:33, [87] **[To Memorize]**

---

are written in this book; and if anyone takes away from the words of the book of this prophecy, God will take away his part from the tree of life and from the holy city, which are written in this book."

86. *Tribulation,* pressure (literally or figuratively): afflicted, affliction, anguish, burdened, persecution, trouble.

87. See also Psalm 24:5

QUESTIONS ON COLOSSIANS 1:9-16 AND 23-27
(HERE PAUL SHARES HIS CONCERNS AND PRAYERS.)

1. What is included in Paul's prayer?
2. Describe what Christ has done and what His unique characteristics are?
3. What are the positions given to Christ Jesus by His Father?
4. What is the mystery hidden from men but given to the saints (the believers)?

CHAPTER 11

NEEDED ARMOUR

Through the internal work of Jesus Christ, we are to exhibit the fruit of His Spirit—love for God, our neighbors and even those who oppose the truth. The Father has brought us into a loving relationship with Himself through Jesus, the Son. We now have within our hearts\minds joy and thankfulness toward the Father. We joyfully acknowledge our Lord Jesus for His bountiful love that gave us freedom and hope. Through Him, we have gained forgiveness of all our trespasses, spiritual rebirth, peace and reconciliation with God, plus rock-solid faith. [88] This faith is a gift, [89] a moral conviction of scriptural truth, the truthfulness of God, and, by extension, the system of scriptural truth itself. [90] Through the Spirit of Christ, we gain the motivation, power and understanding to walk in God's ways.

QUESTIONS ON GALATIANS 5:13-26

1. **What is the fruit of the Spirit?**
2. **Why do we memorize scriptures?**
3. **Why should our profession match our lives?**

I say then, Walk in the Spirit, and you shall not fulfill the lust of the flesh. For the flesh lusted against the Spirit, and the Spirit against the flesh: and these are in opposition to one another, so that you may not do the things that you please. ...
Now the deeds of the flesh are evident which are (these); adultery, fornication, uncleanness, lasciviousness, idolatry, witchcraft, hatred, strife, jealousy, anger, disputes, dissensions, factions, envyings, murders, drunkenness, revellings and such like: of the which I told you before, that they which do such things shall not inherit the kingdom of God. But the fruit of the Spirit is love, joy, peace, patience, gentleness, goodness, faith, meekness, temperance [self control] ... ." Galatians 5:16-17 and 19-23, NASB

The Lord Jesus prompts us to cultivate this fruit by yielding our hearts\minds in obedience to Him, practicing the love that is learned through His Word. All of these fruits of the Spirit are parts of Jesus' character, and His intention is to integrate these virtues into our hearts\minds. This kind of love responds to the conviction of His Spirit, as we hear and study the living Word. Patience

---

88. See Galatians 5:13-24
89. Ephesians 2:8 *"For by grace are you saved through faith; and that not of yourselves: (it is) the gift of God ... ."*
90. Someone wrote this excellent definition in *Strong's Concordance.*

and gentleness flow from Jesus' cultivation of this mindset within us, a mindset that has no time or circumstantial constraints and which overflows from His uprightness into kindness. Practicing self-control encourages the gifts of patience and gentleness. This new life requires not just a surface purge of visible bad patterns, but a continual Spirit-led plowing of our heart\mind. The Lord shines spiritual light upon our deep-rooted wrong patterns of thinking so that wrong can be identified and removed. His gift of self-control is not a superficial papering over of wrong desires, but the removal of the desires. *"Walk in the Spirit, and you shall not fulfill the lust of the flesh"* (Galatians 5:16).

The example of Jesus' life encourages the gifts of humility and meekness. Meekness is another part of Jesus' character. Consider this: He owned the universe but rode upon a donkey as He entered Jerusalem. [91] The Lord Jesus had nowhere to lay His head [92] and could have built palaces within empires, but instead went from place to place seeking the lost. He never once acted out of pride, vanity, self-glory or self-interest. He humbled Himself [93] to carry the cross because He valued us over His own life, and He was the Creator. [94] We cannot make ourselves meek or humble, but it is Jesus Christ's intention to work these fruits into our hearts\mind, to remove pride and all other falseness within our character. At least five times it is mentioned in the Scriptures that we are to humble ourselves or be humble before God.

Look at the prayer that Paul made for the people of God in Colosse. [95] *"That we would be strengthened by God's power unto all patience and longsuffering with joyfulness"* (Colossians 1:11). Active dependence upon Christ develops trust and strengthens faith, even as His power causes us to grow in faith. We grow in heart\mind, to become more loving, joyful and filled with peace. Thankful acknowledgment of the mercies and works of our God, granted to us through the indwelling Spirit, strengthens the bond of love we have with Christ.

Blessed by the God and Father of our Lord Jesus Christ, who blessed us with every spiritual blessing in the heavenlies in Christ; according as He chose us in Him before the foundation of the world, that we should be holy and without blame before Him in love.   Ephesians 1:3-4 **[To Memorize]**

QUESTIONS ON EPHESIANS 5 AND 6
(READ BOTH OF THESE CHAPTERS TO LEARN THE IMPORTANCE OF THE SPIRITUAL PROVISIONS GOD HAS PUT IN PLACE FOR BELIEVERS.)

Therefore take up the full armor of God, so that you will be able to resist in the evil day, and having done everything, to stand firm.   Ephesians 6:13 (NASB)

---

91. See Matthew 21:1-10
92. See Matthew 8:20 and Luke 9:58
93. Philippians 2:8 "And being found in fashion as a man, He humbled himself, and became obedient unto death, even the death of the cross." See also Matthew 18:4, James 4:6 and 10 and 1 Peter 5:5-6
94. See Colossians 1:12-17
95. See Colossians 1:9-11

QUESTIONS ON EPHESIANS 5

1. How are to walk in the light?
2. Why are we to walk in the light?
3. What are the ways of darkness?
4. How do we redeem the time?
5. What can you learn about marriage in verses 21-33?
6. How does this understanding of marriage give us insight into the relationships within the Church?

QUESTIONS ON EPHESIANS 6

1. Why is it important to keep the Ten Commandments?
2. What does it mean to *"nurture them in the chastening and admonition of the Lord"*?
3. What are *"men-pleasers"* and what is *"eye-service"*?
4. Why is the admonition the same whether we are slaves or free?
5. What does it mean that there is *"no respect of persons"* with God?
6. What is the armor of God and how does each part function?
7. Why do we need the armor?
8. How will your thinking change to follow God? What does love have to do with this?

In Ephesians 6:13-18, we are told: *"Put on the whole armour of God, that you may be able to stand against the wiles of the devil"* (Verse 13). This is why we memorize and meditate upon the Word of God. These practices teach us truth and strengthen our faith in God. *"Take the helmet of salvation"* (Verse 17). Without salvation we are open to the cons of Satan found within the philosophies and reasonings of mere men, even ourselves. We need to keep our thinking free of the speculations of men and cleared of myths, suppositions and false assumptions, as well as superstitions that abound within the Church. *"And the sword of the Spirit, which is the word of God"* (same verse). The Spirit of Christ uses the words of the Scriptures to protect and guide us into God's truth. His truth keeps us from believing and absorbing the value system of Satan, found within the philosophies of men and the cultures of the world. *"Praying always [continuously] with all prayer and supplication in the Spirit, and watching [being aware and alert] ... with perseverance and supplication for all saints"* (Verse 18). Prayer for others, as well as ourselves, is also part of the defensive and offensive weaponry given to us by the Lord. *"Watch and pray, that you enter not into temptation: the spirit indeed is willing, but the flesh is weak"* (Matthew 26:41). [96]

---

96. See also Mark 14:38 and Luke 4:1-15

QUESTIONS ON MATTHEW 21:22, LUKE 6:12 AND 22:45, ACTS 1:14, 2:42 AND 6:4, ROMANS 10:1 AND 12:12, EPHESIANS 6:18, PHILIPPIANS 4:6, COLOSSIANS 4:2-3, 1 TIMOTHY 4:4-5 AND JAMES 5:15-16
(LOOK UP THESE VERSES ABOUT PRAYER AND WRITE DOWN WHAT YOU LEARN FROM THEM IN YOUR NOTEBOOK.)

1. What did Paul pray in Ephesians 1?

All believers are justified by faith, being placed in Jesus alone, as the Perfect Sacrifice, appointed by God, who atoned for our sin. [97] *"For if, when we were enemies, we were reconciled to God by the death of His Son, much more, being reconciled, we shall be saved by His life. And not only so, but we also joy in God through our Lord Jesus Christ, by whom we have now received the atonement"* (Romans 5:10-11). He is the only divine Son of Man who always did those things that pleased almighty God. Jesus was speaking to His disciples when He said, *"And He that sent me is with me: the Father has not left me alone; for I do always those things that please Him"* (John 8:29).

The armor of God is spiritual in nature, but very practical, for we are changed as we practice, in dependence upon the Lord, doing those things He has instructed us. This means that our thinking is changed by studying and memorizing the Word of God. The Scriptures inform our mind and protects us from the assaults of the philosophies of Satan and men. We actually are to respond in love like Jesus. We must rearrange our priorities and our use of time. The things of God are to be first in our lives. We can never achieve this by the exercise of self-will, but only by yielding to our Lord Jesus. We are dependent upon the guidance and power of the Spirit, as He gives us the insight into the Word of God. We depend upon our Lord Jesus for the power from God to be responsible and follow the revealed will of God our Father.

QUESTIONS ON JOHN 1:1-5 AND 10-14

1. Who is the Word?
2. What has the Word done?
3. Why didn't the darkness understand Him?
4. Why didn't His own people receive the true Light?
5. What does He give power for?
6. What is the essence of the Word as He came like man?

Believers are not born again from kinship or natural descent, by the will of man, nor by their own will, but through the will of God, [98] to then do the will of God.

---

97. *Atonement*, Exchange, that is, restoration to divine favor: reconciliation. See Romans 5:10-11
98. John 1:12-13.

CHAPTER 12

JUSTIFICATION BY FAITH

Therefore being justified by faith [placed in Jesus to keep His promises], we have peace with God through our Lord Jesus Christ.   Romans 5:1 **[To Memorize]**

Justification is the binding cable woven throughout the Old and New Testaments. The Just and Righteous One offered us a free gift. Taking our sin-saturated offenses upon Himself, Jesus was delivered to the Romans, to die on our behalf and was raised again for our justification. [99] Jesus was willingly and freely offered, so that the grace of God could be imparted to us through faith placed in Him as Redeemer from the wrath of God.

Genesis 15:4-6 is part of a conversation that the Lord had with Abraham. This man was chosen by God to be the progenitor of the Jewish people. They were to be the channel through which the living God would deliver His only Son, to bring salvation to fallen men. Abraham had thought that because he did not have any children himself, the steward of his house would be his "adopted heir," to fulfill the promise given by God.

QUESTIONS ON GENESIS 15:1-7

And behold, the Word of Jehovah came to him saying, This one shall not be your heir, But he that shall come forth out of your own bowels shall be your heir. And He brought him [Abraham] outside and said, look now toward the heavens and count the stars, if you are able to count them. And He said to him, so shall your seed be. And he believed in Jehovah, and He counted it to him for righteousness.

Genesis 15:4-6

1. **What did Jehovah tell Abraham?**
2. **How did Abraham respond to this information?**
3. **How did Jehovah respond to Abraham?**
4. **What is the importance of this declaration?**

QUESTIONS ON ROMANS 4:1-25

1. **How are we justified by our faith?**
2. **What are the works that men do to gain merit before God?**

99. Romans 4:25 *"Who was delivered for our offences, and was raised again for our justification."* See also Romans 3:21-22, 25-26, 4:3 and 5-25

3. **Why do men believe it is possible to be justified by the various <u>works</u>?** [100]
4. **Why is it that we cannot earn salvation by works?**
5. **Why was Abraham declared righteous before the Covenant of Law was given at Sinai Mountain?**
6. **Was Abraham declared righteous before or after he was circumcised?**
7. **What are the sacrifices that God accepts and why does He accept them?**
8. **Why is faith nullified by works?**

There is a very significant fact given in these few verses that often passes unnoticed by the reader because most readers are concentrating upon the flow of the story rather than the details. This event happened four hundred and seventy years before the Law was given at Mt. Sinai. The Lord was aware that Abraham was a natural man, without righteousness, as we are. Nevertheless He declared Abraham's belief in Himself as righteousness. God counted Abraham's belief in (trust and dependence upon) Him and the promises made as being equal with goodness. This is earth-shaking information. A person whose trust is placed in the living God as having a trustworthy character and who speaks only the truth is counted as righteous.

Romans 4 takes the reader into the mind of Abraham, to explain how he thought about the promises God had made to him. He would be the father of many nations, and through his *"seed"* [101] the whole world would be blessed. God instituted the rite of circumcision at a later time, after Abraham already had children. And God's promises were made to Abraham four hundred and seventy years before He issued the Sinai Covenant to Moses, so that the promise of imputed righteousness for faith placed in God would apply to all who believed, both the circumcised and the uncircumcised. Through the righteousness of faith would flow the fulfillment of the promises of God, not through human efforts to keep the Law. Abraham believed absolutely that God would keep His promises of a son, but God waited to fulfill this promise until well after both Abraham and Sarah were able to naturally conceive children.

Paul explains to the reader that this history was written because it had a dual application. If we believe that the living God is able to keep His promised salvation through His Son Jesus, then, just like Abraham, our belief placed in God is imputed to us as righteousness, because this same Jesus, who was delivered to the Romans on our behalf, paid for our offenses by His blood and was raised to life for our justification.

He [Abraham] staggered not at the promise of God through unbelief; but was strong in faith, giving glory to God; and being full persuaded that, what He had promised, He was able also to perform. And therefore it was imputed to him for righteousness. Now it was not written for his sake alone, that it was imputed to him; but for us also, to whom it shall be imputed, if we believe on Him that raised up Jesus our Lord from the dead; who was delivered for our offences, and was raised again for our justification.

Romans 4:20-25

---

100. Work, to work; toil (as an effort or occupation); by implication an act: deed, doing, labor.
101. Seed, here is not plural but singular, meaning one particular person.

Abraham acted upon his faith in God and took his family on the road, following God's instructions. Abraham's actions proved that his trust in God was real. We must be like Abraham and put our trust in the worthiness and truthfulness of God. The Father's plan of salvation culminated in Jesus' sacrifice being sufficient to pay the debt of our sin, so that we might place our God-given gift of faith [102] in Jesus Christ and have it counted as righteousness. Believing our Lord's plan for redemption and reconciliation is perfect and necessary.

QUESTIONS ON ROMANS 3:9-20
OUR LORD DOES NOT CHANGE HIS PURPOSE. [103]

1. Which one of the three parts of the Sinai Covenant (Ten Commandments (moral law), religious sacrificial system or civil law) is this discussion about in Romans?
2. How do you know this?
3. What was the purpose of the Law and how does it apply to us today?
4. What does Romans 3 say in answer to this question, *"Can anyone keep the Law and justify himself before God"*? [104]
5. Why is this true?

It is impossible for anyone to keep the Law so as to accumulate merit and be able to say to God, "I did what You asked. See all the good things. Now, give me my reward."

For by grace are you saved through faith; and that not of yourselves: it is the gift of God: nor of works, lest any man should boast. Ephesians 2:8-9 **[To Memorize]**

QUESTIONS ON ROMANS 3:21-31

1. What is the righteousness of God that is revealed but not connected to Law keeping?
2. What does it mean that Jesus is a propitiation for our sin? [105]
3. What does Abraham's response have to do with faith?
4. What does Jesus Christ have to do with faith?
5. What does belief have to do with faith?
6. What is justification [106] by faith?
7. How do believers establish the Law?
8. What does circumcision or uncircumcision have to do with faith?

---

102. See Ephesians 2:8-9
103. I recommend an excellent book on the subject of the Law and its function in the life of the believer: *The True Bounds of Christian Freedom* by Samuel Bolton, published by The Banner of Truth Trust
104. See Romans 3:19-26 (NASB)
105. *Propitiation*, a expiatory (place or thing), that is, (concretely) an atoning victim, or (specifically) the lid of the Ark (in the Temple): mercy seat
106. *Justification*, to render (shown as or regarded as) just or innocent: be righteous, free, justified.

It is interesting to note that the Ark, which was carried by the priest on the days the Israelite people journeyed through the wilderness, continued to be carried for forty years. When Solomon, the son of King David, built the Temple in Jerusalem, the Ark was placed in the second most private room there called the Holy of Holies. The Ark had a gold seat that was its top lid, which was placed between two gold cherubs. This seat was called the Mercy Seat and was used only once a year, when a blood sacrifice was sprinkled there to cover the sins of both the priest and the people (see Leviticus16). Jesus is the sinless and perfect sacrifice that was slain, and it was as if His blood was sprinkled upon the Mercy Seat for us, that our sin might be paid for and removed forever.

The Law did impact the descendants of Abraham to some degree, but it had limited contact with the larger habitations of men, except perhaps the Babylonians, until Jesus came and the Gospel spread over the world, taking the Law with it. This caused some men's fluid definitions of evil and good to change, to reflect the truth of God's Word, as they became believers.

QUESTIONS ON GALATIANS 3:1-29

And the scripture, foreseeing that God would justify the heathen through faith, preached before the gospel unto Abraham, (saying), In thee shall all nations be blessed.　　　　Galatians 3:8

Therefore as by the offence of one (Adam) (judgment came) upon all men unto condemnation; even so by the righteousness of one (the free gift came) upon all men unto justification of life. Romans 5:19

But to the one who does not work, but believes in Him who justifies the ungodly, his faith is credited as righteousness, just as David also speaks of the blessing on the man to whom God credits righteousness apart from works: Blessed are those whose lawless deeds have been forgiven, and whose sins have been covered.　　　　Romans 4:5-7 (NASB) **[To Memorize]**

The sacrifices of God are a broken <u>spirit</u>: [107] *a <u>broken</u>* [108] *and a <u>contrite</u>* [109] *heart,* [110] *O God, you will not <u>despise</u>.* [111]　　　　Psalm 51:17 **[To Memorize]**

1. **What was the first question Paul asked in chapter 3?**
2. **Who are the children of Abraham?**
3. **What do the Gentiles have to do with Abraham?**
4. **Why are we under a curse if we try to keep the Law to earn "brownie points"?**
5. **What are the sacrifices that the Lord is pleased with?**
6. **How did Jesus Christ redeem us from the curse of the Law?**

---

107. *Spirit*, wind; by resemblance breath, that is, ... exhalation, ... by resemblance spirit, but only of a rational being.
108. *Broken*, to burst (literally or figuratively): to break (down, off, in pieces, up), broken (hearted), crush, destroy, hurt, quench, tear
109. *Contrite*, to collapse (physically or mentally): break (sore), contrite, crouch
110. *Heart*, also used (figuratively) very widely for the feelings, the will and even the intellect; likewise for the center of anything
111. *Despise*, to disesteem: disdain, contemn, think to scorn, vile person

7. When was the promise of Genesis 15 made to Abraham?
8. How long after the promise was the Law instituted?
9. Why does Paul call the Law our *"schoolmaster"*?
10. Why couldn't the Law give life?

We need to be prepared to defend ourselves against the evil one, who is the instigator behind evil men. These Galatians had been tricked, by false followers of Christ, into adopting what seemed to be a reasonable suggestion, that keeping the Law was a good addition to the original salvation. Paul wanted us to see that these men had left Jesus Christ when they substituted faith in Christ for faith in Christ + keeping the Law as the amended way of salvation. This lie is still one that Satan uses today, that adding some works to our faith in Christ Jesus enhances our salvation. Nothing we can do adds extra merit to salvation because it is already complete and finished in Christ. Adding anything to or subtracting anything from God's already-perfect work only puts us in grave danger, endangering the very souls influenced by the additions or subtractions.

With the further requirement of Law-keeping is added to "faith in Jesus," "free-grace salvation" has become "performance-based salvation," just as happened in ancient Israel. Remember that the standard of the Law is perfection, and not one human being (except Jesus Christ) can remain one hundred percent pure in action, word and thought. Therefore the Law's just condemnation for our failure to keep it is a curse upon men, not a pathway to salvation. Paul reminded the Romans that none of the works of the Spirit had been demonstrated through Law-keeping.

God is concerned with our hearts\minds, and we cannot hide our souls from His sight. God opened Abraham's heart\mind and revealed that He was God, the Holy and Living One. The Spirit opens our hearts\minds to receive the truths presented in both Testaments. Here Paul is proving that Abraham is our spiritual father. Remember, Abraham's belief in the truthfulness of God, his "faith," was counted as righteousness before the Law was given. The Law was and is different from faith.

Consider some of the things we all have thought or done that were or are ungodly. What could any of us do or say that could wipe the sin within away, for sin springs from our core nature. But God is full of mercy, and He opens our eyes to see our sterile internal darkness. Pray to the Lord for His bountiful mercy. Turn to the Lord, and He will give you new life.

Jesus said this about Himself:

All things are delivered to me of my Father: and no man knows who the Son is, but the Father; and who the Father is, but the Son, and he to whom the Son will reveal him. Luke 10:22 **[To Memorize]**

No man can come to me, except the Father which has sent me draw him: and I will raise him up at the last day. John 6:44 **[To Memorize]**

I am the way, the truth, and the life: no man comes unto the Father, but by me.   John 14:4

[To Memorize]

My husband and I were in France for a brief season and drove south to see an old church, a medieval site of worship. This particular site was unusual because of the "Black Madonna" carved from a very dark stone. But even more interesting to me were the steps leading to the church. They were very steep and irregular, having been worn down by the knees of many saints. Participants had been taught the false teaching that God was pleased with such sacrifices. Many kings and princes had apparently made the pilgrimage to this church, to gain a promised reward. They believed that entrance into Heaven was obtained by merit gained by ascending those steps on their knees.

The belief in the merit of good deeds or participation in rituals or various traditions providing the way for sins to be forgiven is false. This way of thinking, presented here in Romans 4:4, is implying that God owes Heaven as payment for man's good deeds, rituals or law-keeping. But Abraham was not justified because of his works (good deeds, obedience, prayer or various sacrifices), and neither can we be justified that way.

Traveling the long painful journey up the irregular steps of that church upon your knees is a clear picture of the uselessness of human effort (works). Rituals, sacrifices and dependence upon law-keeping may cause much suffering in the knees, but it cannot change our sin nature. If we are separated from the love of God by our sin, no such empty sacrifices can bridge the gap.

QUESTIONS ON ROMANS 5:1-21

But God commended his love toward us, in that, while we were yet sinners, Christ died for us. Much more then, being now justified by his blood, we shall be saved from wrath through him. For if, when we were enemies, we were reconciled to God by the death of his Son, much more, being reconciled, we shall be saved by His life.   Romans 5:8-10 **[To Memorize]**

And we know that God causes all things to work together for good to those who love God, to those who are called according to His purpose.   Romans 8:28 (NASB) **[To Memorize]**

1. **What does this prove about the Lord?**
2. **What has God done for us through faith?**
3. **What were we?**
4. **Why would we exalt in our tribulations?**
5. **What does the love of God have to do with hard times?**
6. **What are the implications for us of Romans 8:28?**

Paul is explaining that all men are condemned because sin has infiltrated all men, and the proof of this sin is our death. All men die through the offence of one man, Adam. But God has nullified this death sentence for those who believe, giving us abundant grace and the gift of righteousness through Jesus Christ. We had no merit, or righteousness, of our own because our soul and spirit were under the harness of sin. *"But we are all as an unclean thing, and all our righteousnesses are as filthy rags; and we all do fade as a leaf; and our iniquities, like the wind, have taken us away"* (Isaiah 64:6). Any "right" things we may have done before the Lord opened our hearts were not motivated by love for God or any desire to please Him. Therefore these "good deeds" were vain (useless, of no value). God called them *"dead works."* [112] They were saturated with the pollution of our sin and, therefore, *"dead,"* incapable of pleasing Him.

Justification by faith in God with its gift of righteousness is far more gracious than we deserve. Salvation granted through the abundant grace of God is worth much more than all other gifts we might receive throughout our entire lifetime.

---

112. See Hebrews 6:1 and 9:14

PART III

THE POWER OF PRIDE

PRIDE, A PATTERN OF THINKING

What do natural men think? How do they make decisions and guide their own lives? There are so many examples of pride available from the Scriptures that I decided to take pride as one pattern of thinking so that we could concentrate on the particular traits common in it.

Your terribleness has deceived you, and the pride of your heart ... . Though you should make your nest as high as the eagle, I will bring you down from there, saith the Lord. Jeremiah 49:16

The pride of your heart has deceived you ... . Obadiah 1:3 (MKJV)

The wicked, in pride does persecute the poor ... . The wicked, through the pride of his countenance, will not seek God: God is not in all his thoughts. Psalm 10:2-7 (NKJV)

They are not in trouble as other men; neither are they plagued like other men, therefore pride is as a circle of chain around their necks; violence covers them like a garment ... . Psalm 73:5-9 (ASV-1901)

When pride comes, then comes shame: but with the lowly is wisdom. Proverbs 11:2 (MKJV)

Only by pride cometh contention [strife-argument]: but with the well advised is wisdom. Proverbs 13:10

Pride goes before destruction and a haughty spirit before a fall. Proverbs 16:18 (MKJV)

Thus I will punish the world for its evil and the wicked for their iniquity; I will also put an end to the arrogance of the proud and abase the haughtiness of the ruthless. Isaiah 13:11 (NASB)

QUESTIONS ON PSALM 10:2-4, 73:5-6 AND PROVERBS 13:10
(READ THESE VERSES AND THE VERSES ABOVE AND THEN ANSWER THE FOLLOWING QUESTIONS IN YOUR NOTEBOOK.)

1. **What does a heart filled with pride think and do to others?**

QUESTIONS ON PROVERBS 8:13, 16:18, 11:2 AND ISAIAH 13:11

1. **What five things does the Lord hate?**
2. **What follows closely upon the heels of pride?**

QUESTIONS ON JEREMIAH 13:1-12 AND 15-17 (MKJV)

1. **What insight to you gain from these verses?**
2. **Write down one or more examples of a movie star or political figure that treated the people under them badly.**
3. **Have you seen someone close to you treat someone badly? What did you think?**

Give glory to the LORD your God, before he causes darkness, and before your feet stumble upon the dark mountains, and while you look for light, he turns it into the shadow of death. ...
But if you will not hear it, my soul shall weep in secret places for your pride; and mine eye shall weep sore, and run down with tears, because the LORD's flock is carried away captive.

Jeremiah 13:7 and 16 **[To Memorize]**

Pride, in its many forms, is a stumblingblock because pride barricades self against anything that would penetrate our carefully constructed world view, even if it is the truth. In our natural state, indwelling sin is permanently bonded to our heart\mind and focuses all attention upon self, producing the terminal selfishness we call "pride." Pride functions somewhat like a circular Interstate exchange, with all roads leading to self, so that anyone or anything is subordinated to our interest, our goals and our desires. Our pride is offensive to God, *"The fear of Jehovah is to hate evil; I hate pride, and arrogance, and the evil way, and the wicked mouth"* (Proverbs 8:13). [113] The Lord is well able to humble all of us, as He often must, for pride is our natural attitude, and one of the fruits of the love of God working within man is a humble and submissive heart\mind. *"For thus says the high and lofty One that inhabits eternity, whose name is Holy; I dwell in the high and holy place, with him also that is of a contrite and humble spirit, to revive the spirit of the humble, and to revive the heart of the contrite ones"* (Isaiah 57:15).

Mankind's choice for sin did not surprise our Lord. The blueprint of the Father's plan for the salvation of men was finished while the world was as yet unmade. He had already determined the requirements for redemption and how the demands of justice would be met through Jesus. Jesus came so that He could break our natural bent toward pride in self, by replacing this sinful core with His indwelling Spirit, thereby giving us a heart and mind bathed in real love for our God and our neighbor. The Lord Jesus' intention is for our being to be focused upon Him, with all roads leading outward, loaded with the grace of God, to serve our families and our spiritual kin and to preach the truth of Jesus and His ability to free those bound in sin.

---

113. See also Proverbs 14:3, 16:18 and 29:23, Isaiah 2:17, 5:14 and 14:11. Why not study the word *pride* in the entire Old Testament.

CHAPTER 14

THE LOVE OF THE WORLD

Love [114] not the world, neither the things in the world. If any man loves the <u>world</u>, [115] the love of the Father is not in him. For all that is in the world, the lust of the flesh, and lust of the eyes, and the pride of life, is not of the Father, but is of the world. And the world passes away, and its lust; but he that does the will of God lasts forever. 1 John 2:15-17 (NASB) **[To Memorize]**

The light of the Spirit uncovers a multitude of religions, philosophies, principles and mindsets which are all part of our world system and have, at their heart, visceral opposition to the living God. The world has our natural affection. It is our habitat, but Jesus came to sever the ropes that tied us into dependence upon the world. It is no longer to be our source for all things. Our trust and allegiance has changed because we have been transferred into another kingdom. The Lord warns us that the desire for the things of this world are short-lived, and so is our life. We cannot afford to continue to pursuit such things as prestige, power, wealth, pleasures and philosophies not of or from Jesus Christ. The things of the world are like a lead anchor attached to a swimmer. The hours we can spend just in the pursuit of entertainment lead us further away from seeking God. Pride never seeks God, and our world runs on pride.

QUESTIONS ON 1 JOHN 2:15-17 AND MATTHEW 6:19-33

For as a man thinks so is he. Proverbs 23:7 **[To Memorize]**

1. What is the *"lust of the eyes"* [116]?
2. What is the *"pride [117] of life"* [118]?
3. Pride has the ability to _____ you (Obadiah 1:3 and Jeremiah 49:16). [119]
4. What else has this ability? (See Ephesians 4:22 and Hebrews 3:12-13)
5. What is the *"lust of the flesh"* and what does Matthew add to your understanding concerning it?
6. What is the main point of John 2:19-25?
7. Pick a book or movie and select at least one character in it who was blinded by pride. Show how pride functioned within his or her character?

---

114. *Love*, to love in a moral or social sense
115. *World*, orderly arrangement, by implication the world (in a wide or narrow sense, including it inhabitants, literally or figurative (morally) decoration:-adorning
116. *Eyes*, vision (figuratively envy-from the jealous side glance).
117. Braggadocio, that is (by implication) self-confidence: boasting
118. *Pride of Life:* This phrase literally means "the present state of existence."
119. *Pride*: The word *pride* in the Obadiah and Jeremiah selections means "presumptuously with arrogance."

QUESTIONS ON COLOSSIANS 1:12-22 AND 2:6-10

Therefore as you have received Christ Jesus the Lord, so walk in Him, having been firmly rooted and now being built up in Him and established in your faith, just as you were instructed, and overflowing with gratitude. See to it that no one takes you <u>captive</u> [120] through philosophy and empty deception [vain deceit, that is, delusion], according to the <u>elementary principles</u> [121] of the world, rather than according to Christ, for in Him all the fullness of Deity dwells in bodily form, and in Him you have been made complete, and He is the head over all rule and authority. Colossians 2:6-10 **[To Memorize]**

1. **What are we warned about in these verses that relates to pride?**
2. **What do these verses teach us about Jesus Christ?**
3. **Why is Jesus superior to all men?**
4. **What has Jesus done for us that teaches us that pride is a useless and evil mindset?**
5. **What is different in Jesus' thinking?**
6. **Jesus had more reason than all the men who ever lived to have pride in His life, but He did not take this mindset. Why?**

The acceptance of the clear truths of Jesus Christ over our own perceptions is one part of faith. Christ's thoughts and ways are radically different from those of this world, and by the power and motivation of His indwelling Spirit, we are to follow His teachings. He gave us more than one way to keep dissolving pride. Participation in the Lord's Supper requires a realistic judgment of self for all our sinful deeds and attitudes. [122] Every man must examine himself so that he will not eat the bread and drink the cup in an unworthy manner, and thus put himself under discipline. Reading and studying the Word of God also helps in keeping pride at bay, as does daily reflection upon the things of Christ. Repentance and correction are both necessary whenever the Spirit brings up things that are wrong in our thinking or actions, and this humbles us before God.

"For if we would <u>judge</u> [123] ourselves, we should not be judged" (1 Corinthians 11:31). This is a promise to us to encourage us to look at ourselves realistically and take whatever steps are necessary to change our behavior or thinking, in order to reflect Jesus. If we refuse to address these things, we will be chastened by the Lord, so that we will not be condemned with the world. In effect, this means that we are to be objective with our evaluation of self, which is only possible if we trust Jesus' evaluations in the Scriptures. We are to stand apart from self and assess self with a mind set on the truth of our Lord. *"If we say that we have not sinned, we make him a liar, and His word is not in us"* (1 John 1:10).

---

120. Captive, to lead away as booty, that is, to seduce: spoil
121. *Elementary* and *principles* are from the same word, meaning something orderly in arrangement, constituent, proposition (figuratively): element, principle, rudiment. The various world systems of finding value such as the monetary systems, religious systems, morality systems, philosophical systems, etc.
122. See 1 Corinthians 11:26-32
123. *Judge* here means "to separate thoroughly, that is, (literally and reflexively) to withdraw from, or (by implication) oppose; figuratively to discriminate (by implication decide), or reflexively) hesitate: contend, make to differ, discern, doubt, be partial, stagger, waver

If we are using denial as a shield, to avoid facing the obvious, we need to repent and face the truth about ourselves. We may not murder, but we do produce ungodly thoughts and deeds. This denial of real sin in thought and behavior must change.

He that saith, I know Him [Jesus], and keeps not His commandments, is a liar, and the truth is not in him.   1 John 2:4

Again, if we knowingly live, allowing obvious sin which is addressed in the Ten Commandments, we need to repent and drop those sins. Jesus realistically expanded the Ten Commandments to include what we think and how we think. *"But I say unto you, that whosoever looks on a woman to lust after her has committed adultery with her already in his heart"* (Matthew 5:28). In fairness to the clear intention of Christ's words, we must include all sensuality in media under this indictment of mental adultery.

If a man say, I love God, and hates his brother, he is a liar: for he that loves not his brother whom he has seen, how can he love God whom he has not seen?   1 John 4:20

As we read and understand what is clearly said, we are to carry forth action against self that will change our state. We must repent of the hate, for neutrality cannot parade itself as love, and love with forgiveness and mercy must replace the hate. The Lord showed me, as I was reading the Scriptures one day, that I did not love a member of my family, and that revelation shocked me. After I considered the implications, I was convicted that His assessment was correct, for toleration is far from love. I repented of my lack of love, and, since I could find no love for this person in me, I asked the Lord to teach me how to love as He has commanded. The change in my attitude began that day, and many conversations, spread over two or three years, changed my outlook even more. I came to understand something of the difficulties that person had faced, and we developed mutual respect.

Many Christians must begin here, first addressing sin in these three obvious areas of our heart\ mind. We are commanded to love one another. We actively follow the Spirit's lead by believing Jesus' assessment, while we proceed with changes in our attitude and behavior. We depend upon the Spirit for the motivation and power to change and reflect the love of Jesus.

Jesus has set His heart upon us, and in Him we have all we will ever need to overcome the world, Satan and our propensity to gloss over our own failures and remaining sins. We all have to deal realistically with our sin after we are blessed with salvation. It takes time to retrain ourselves in all areas necessary before we are more secure in our faith.

Some professions of belonging to Christ are false ones. This is why we are admonished to test our faith. In Romans 11:17-33, Paul talked about his kin, the Jewish branches of the olive tree that were removed because of unbelief. He called the Gentiles *"a wild olive tree"* that was grafted into the cultured olive tree, to partake of the life-giving root. God had determined long ago to bring Gentiles to salvation through justification by faith, the same justification by faith by which God determined that Abraham was to be called righteous. But He warns the Gentiles not to take this for granted. We are not to boast, for it was by no merit within us that we could partake. We are not to discount or devalue the Jewish branches. Most of them are blinded for a season, but they are still under the protection of God, and one day many will return to the Father in faith. God took them out because of unbelief, and He will do the same to us if we fall into unbelief. *"Examine yourselves, whether you be in the faith; prove your own selves"* (2 Corinthians 13:5).

QUESTIONS ON ROMANS 11:17-33
(TAKE YOUR TIME WITH THIS MATERIAL. WHEN YOU FINISH READING IT, SUM UP WHAT YOU HAVE LEARNED BY WRITING IN YOUR NOTEBOOK AN EXPLANATION OF THE MATERIAL WITHIN EACH REFERENCE.)

What are we to use as the standard against which we compare our faith, to see if we are still in the faith? This section will help us see what our faith should look like and how it should function. As you read through the references, take notes on what or who we are to love, how are we to love and to what extent we are loved.

1. **Matthew 5:1-48:** [124] Using Chapter 5, including the Sermon on the Mount, identify those areas in which you are lacking the qualities of godly love that you need to have.
2. **Luke 6:27-46:** If we had the ability to accept and love others as Jesus did, what would change in our attitude and actions? Think about your real relationships and see what you could do differently.
3. **John 8:39-59:** If we had been in the audience listening to Jesus, what would we know about Him and His Father who sent Him?
4. **John 13:31-35 and 15:1-20:** How did Jesus define love?
5. **Romans 8:26-31:** Define the love described here.
6. **Romans 12:3-21:** Make a list of the qualities of love described here.
7. **Romans 13:8-14:** What does this discussion have to say about love?

Do you have someone you trust enough to ask them to reveal what they see in you, both the positive and the negative? Consider what they have said and figure out ways in which you could relate to others in a more gracious and loving way.

---

124. *Perfect*, complete (in various applications of labor, growth, mental and moral character, etc.); neuter (as noun, with G3588) Completeness, of full age

QUESTIONS ON GALATIANS 5:1-26

For God has not given us the spirit of fear [timidity], but of power and of love and of a sound mind [discipline, self-control].   2 Timothy 1:7

1. **What is the liberty in which we are to stand fast?**
2. **What would circumcision tell us about a Jewish man?**
3. **What is the link between circumcision and law-keeping?**
4. **Why is the distinction regarding circumcision no longer valid?**
5. **Explain how faith works by love?**
6. **What if we use the liberty given in Christ to please the "flesh"?**
7. **What fulfills the Law?**
8. **What is the fight we must win? How do we win this war?**
9. **How do we walk in the Spirit? And what does this walk look like?**

What are the fruits of the Spirit? Love, joy and peace are the first three, but we should begin to recognize, value and yearn for all of them to be in our character. The Spirit uses the words of God to encourage us to incorporate this list of virtues into our lives, and the Spirit makes this possible.

Love is the greatest fruit because love is the substance of the character of the Father, the Son and the Spirit. The Father is the core of Jesus, our Lord, and He is the core of the Spirit. They are of one essence but cooperate together in bringing men to new life and repentance. They are indivisible. Therefore, all parts of the Godhead have the characteristics of the Father. The Father instituted the plan to accomplish His will, that through Christ Jesus He would have a Kingdom of believers, those upon whom He had set His love before the world was as yet made.[125] The Lord God's love is the source of our love to Him. Our love for the Father, the Son and the Spirit has been seeded and watered from above. We have no such love from our own sin-bound core.

Jesus knows our deepest needs and the hurts of our mind, body and newly-awakened spirit. He loves us with a fierce love. The Father reveals to our mind, through His Word and by the work of His Spirit, this fact of His truthfulness and love. This love in the heart of Jesus from the Father is revealed to us and gives assurance of the fullness of joy to be found in Jesus. It is amazing that the holy, perfect and all-wise Lord of Creation[126] should choose to love us. The more we hold to and follow the Lord Jesus, the more we trust Him. We want to be changed to love Him as He loves His children.

Jesus has died for us and covered our trespasses with His blood as full atonement. He also covered us with His personal righteousness, thereby making us acceptable to the Father. We

125. See Ephesians 1:1-14
126. See Colossians 1

believe that Jesus has spoken only the truth, as the <u>truth is in Jesus</u>.[127] Just as Abraham's belief in the trustworthiness of God was counted as righteousness, so is our imperfect trust in God the Father and Jesus Christ as the complete and perfect sacrifice is counted as righteousness. But Jesus' perfect uprightness has been given to us only in our permanent union with Himself because apart from Him we would remain alien in mind. We have been sealed forever by His Holy Spirit because we are in union with Jesus, our Lord and Savior, as ordained by the Father. We are to pray for and exhibit this unselfish mind-set of the Son.

The study of the Word of God is the first step in the enlightenment of our mind[128] and newly-awakened spirit. Prayer as well as a growing knowledge of the Scriptures are both God's chosen method of communication with believers through the Son by the work of the Spirit. Both of these are necessary for our spiritual growth and without yielded implementation of prayer and serious Bible study you cannot come to know God. This is the beginning of your walk in the Spirit, and it must continue throughout your lifetime.

Jesus walked in the Spirit continually, by choice, and with a determined will to remain always under the will of the Father.[129] The Father made two other means by which His children develop godly character. One is to take the Lord's Supper, to be continually reminded of the purposes of God found illustrated in the Supper. Jesus is precious to the Father, and we must embrace the Son by the Spirit's presence as we worship the Father for His kindness to us through the horrible death of His Son.

We must keep the Sabbath as a holy gift to us who believe and keep the fellowship of believers and rest as part of the joys of this day. Men who know God and love Him keep His commandments,[130] as these commandments are the Son's also. These men who follow Jesus are gifts given to the Church in each place that has believers of the Truth.[131] No one can maintain a godly life without the prayers and input of likeminded worshipers who also have the Spirit and growing knowledge of the truth fulfilled by Jesus the Christ as ordained by the Holy Father.

Blessed be the God and Father of our Lord Jesus Christ, who has blessed us with all spiritual blessings in heavenly places in Christ: according as He has chosen us in Him before the foundation of the world, that we should be holy and without blame before Him in love: having predestined us unto the adoption of children by Jesus Christ to himself according to the good pleasure of His will, to the praise of the glory of his grace, wherein He has made us accepted in the beloved. Ephesians 1:3-7 **[To Memorize]**

---

127. See John 14:6 and Ephesians 4:21
128. Or renewing of our mind
129. He set His face like a flint.
130. See John 15 and Mark 10:19
131. See John 1:14-17 and 14:61, Ephesians 1:13 and 21 and Romans 9:11

CHAPTER 15

A SELF-RIGHTEOUSNESS AND CRITICAL SPIRIT

We need to look at another part of the pattern of pride, that of self-righteousness and its traveling companion, the critical spirit of judgment. This pattern of critical spirit and self-righteousness is very much intertwined with pride. I would call it pride's first cousin.

Jesus spoke this parable unto those who trusted in themselves that they were righteous, and viewed others with contempt. Two men went up into the temple to pray; the one a Pharisee, and the other a tax collector. The Pharisee stood and prayed this to himself, "God, I thank you that I am not like other men, swindlers, unjust, adulterers, or even as this tax collector. I fast twice in the week; I give tithes of all that I possess." And the tax collector, standing some distance away, would not lift up his eyes unto heaven, but hit his breast, saying, "God, be merciful to me a sinner." I tell you, this man went down to his house justified rather than the other: for everyone who exalts himself shall be humbled; and he that humbles himself shall be exalted. Luke 18:9-14 (NASB)

QUESTIONS ON LUKE 18:9-14
(WRITE THE ANSWERS IN YOUR NOTEBOOK.)

1. What was the Pharisee's mental assessment of his own heart?
2. How could he be so wrong?
3. Why was the tax collector so humble?
4. Do you know someone who is humble? If so, what is different about that person?

ELI'S CRITICAL THOUGHTS

Hannah rose up after they had finished eating and drinking in Shiloh. Now Eli the priest was sitting on the seat by the doorpost of the temple of the LORD ... . And she was in bitterness of soul, weeping sorely and prayed unto the Lord ... .

Now it came about, as she continued praying before the LORD, that Eli was watching her mouth. As for Hannah, she was speaking silently in her heart, only her lips were moving. Eli said to her, "How long will you make yourself drunk? Put away your wine from you."

But Hannah replied, "No, my lord, I am a woman oppressed in spirit; I have drunk neither wine nor strong drink, but I have poured out my soul before the LORD. Do not consider your maidservant as a worthless woman, for I have spoken until now out of my great concern."

Then Eli answered and said, "Go in peace; and may the God of Israel grant your petition that you have asked of Him."

1 Samuel 1:9-10 and 12-17

If one answered [judged or decided] a matter before he heard (the facts), it is folly and shame before him.

Proverbs 18:13 (MKJV) **[To Memorize]**

QUESTIONS ON 1 SAMUEL 1:1-18 AND 2 SAMUEL 10:1-19
(WRITE THE ANSWERS IN YOUR NOTEBOOK.)

1. What was happening in Hannah's life?
2. What did Eli believe he knew about her? [132] What was her attitude toward Eli?
3. What does 2 Samuel 10 reveal?
4. Have you seen pre-judgment before knowing the facts in action? If so, write a few sentences describing the incident.
5. How do we stop being judgmental of others?

QUESTIONS ON MATTHEW 7:1-5, LUKE 6:37 AND 18:9-14 AND JOHN 7:18, 24 AND 50-51

1. What did Jesus mean in verses 1 and 2 of Matthew 7?
2. Why can judging another make you a hypocrite?
3. What does Proverbs 18:13 add to your understanding on this subject?
4. What does self-praise like the Pharisee's used reveal about us?
5. What does John 7:51 say about our judgment of others?
6. What does this discussion have to do with the Lord Jesus in John 7?

To judge another means "to distinguish, that is, decide to make a determination and by implication to try, condemn, punish." The Pharisee actually put himself as the judge of the motives and life of a man he did not know, while condemning the man as a sinner. By this means, he exalted himself to prosecutor and judge, revealing his prideful conceit and critical spirit. Pride automatically puts others in a position below self because pride values no one above self and devalues all others.

Did the Pharisee love the sinner? Jesus does. The Lord Jesus said, *"... Love one another; as I have loved you ... . By this all [men] shall know that you are my disciple ..."* (John 13:34-35). *"Speak not evil one of another, brethren"* (James 4:11). What is the motivation for comparing ourselves to another or of condemnation of another? What is always the effect of comparing ourselves to others? We cannot know the internal motives of any man. Therefore, it is risky to be his judge! Jesus is the only righteous Judge, and He alone knows the internal motives of all men.

---

132. **This footnote was missing in the original manuscript.**

Why behold the speck that is in your brother's eye, but consider not the beam that is in your own eye? Or how will you say to your brother, let me pull the speck out of your eye; and, behold, a beam is in your eye? You hypocrite, first cast out the beam out of you own eye; and then shall you see clearly to cast out the speck out of your brother's eye.   Matthew 7:3-5 **[To Memorize]**

Jesus has left His Word in both Testaments, by which we are to evaluate the sin in self as evil and condemn it. Jesus gives us the power to overcome all sin through Himself.

QUESTIONS ON ROMANS 2:1-13
(READ THE TEXT AND ANSWER THE FOLLOWING QUESTIONS IN YOUR NOTEBOOK.)

The Lord takes a look at the heart of man:

Therefore you are inexcusable, O man, whosoever you are that judges, for wherein you judge another, you condemn yourself, for you that judges does the same thing. But we are sure that the judgment of God is according to truth against them which commit such things. And think you this, O man, that judges them which do such things, and does the same, that you shall escape the judgment of God?
                    Romans 2:1-4 **[To Memorize]**

1. What does Romans 2:1-6 have to say that fits in with our questions?
2. What does the phrase, *"There is no respect of persons with God,"* mean?
3. Do you know anyone who showed respect of persons? If so, what did it look like?
4. Who is justified before God according to verse 13?
5. What does the rest of the chapter discuss that gives us more understanding in this area?

QUESTIONS ON 1 CORINTHIANS 11:24-32

For if we would judge ourselves, we should not be judged. But when we are judged, we are chastened of the Lord, that we should not be condemned with the world.   1 Corinthians 11:31-32 **[To Memorize]**

1. What were the sins that brought this response from the apostle?
2. How are we to judge ourselves?
3. What other areas do we need to include in this judgment of self?
4. What is the outcome if we neglect this necessary part of the Christian life?

Therefore judge nothing before the time, until the Lord come, who both will bring to light the hidden things of darkness, and will make manifest the counsels of the hearts: … .
                    1 Corinthians 4:5 **[To Memorize]**

Pride always overestimates and overvalues self. Pride elevates self and devalues all others. Pride always short-circuits love for God and man because pride takes everything it can and gives little in return. Pride grows disrespect, contempt and hate for others. Pride is neither grateful nor thankful toward God or men.

QUESTIONS ON ROMANS 12:1-4
(WRITE YOUR ANSWERS IN YOUR NOTEBOOK.)

1. How does thinking soberly, as advised in Romans 12:1-4, counter thinking highly of ourselves?
2. How can we plan to prevent our natural pride from being the source of our thinking?

QUESTIONS ON 2 CORINTHIANS 12:1-10
(READ THE TEXT AND ANSWER THE FOLLOWING QUESTIONS IN YOUR NOTEBOOK.)

1. How was Paul able to function under the pressure of direct revelation from the Lord and not become filled with pride and self-righteousness?
2. Have you ever become filled with pride or self-righteousness? Write down several examples.
3. What must change in our thinking to check our own natural drive to be proud?
4. Describe someone from the media, politics or sports who exhibited pride. What was their life really like?

QUESTIONS ON ROMANS 12:5-18

We are warned by Paul not to value, or trust, men above God's Word, nor value ourselves above another. The Lord made each one of us exactly as He wished for His glory and for His own reasons. [133]

For who makes you different from another? What do you have that you did not receive from the hand of God? And if you did receive it, why do you boast as if you did not receive it.

1 Corinthians 4:7, MKJV **[To Memorize]**

1. What does this selection in Romans have to say about accountability to God within the Christian body that defeats pride and the critical spirit of judgment?
2. If the Pharisee of Luke 18 had become a disciple of Christ, what would have changed in his thinking?

QUESTIONS ON ROMANS 14:1-23

1. What kind of judgment is this chapter concerned with?
2. How does this form of judgment differ from the Pharisee's judgment in Luke 18?

133. See Isaiah 43:7

3. **What is important in verses 10-15?**
4. **What is meant by the phrase, *"whatever is not of faith is sin"*?**
5. **Can you describe someone in your life who is like the Pharisee in judgment of the motives of others without real knowledge?**

We are to cast a critical eye upon our own ways and thoughts, using the Scriptures to give us light into our motives, our wrong thinking and our desires, so that we can repent and drop the sin revealed. Repentance, which is a gift from God, [134] is not just a one-time realization of the huge moral and spiritual chasm between our hearts and the perfect purity and holiness of the living God. Repentance is also a lifetime yielded to Christ in daily introspection and repentance according to the Word of Truth. Chastening by the Lord is also a gift to keep us from becoming hardened toward Him by the deceitfulness of sin. King David admitted that the Lord's chastisement had brought forth good fruit in him. *"Before I was afflicted I went astray: but now have I kept thy word. ... (It is) good for me that I have been afflicted; that I might learn thy statues"* (Psalm 119:67 and 71).

We must put on Christ, that is, acknowledge Him, giving thanks for all our blessings, bringing all our concerns before the Lord, for He cares for us. Make the study of the Scriptures a priority by setting aside time for this purpose. Read the Word of the Lord carefully, looking to find His will. [135] Depend on the Spirit to keep Christ as your focus each day. We must actively fight our old tendencies, as well as actively pursue obedience and not leave undone the kindnesses due others. It is impossible to do these things in our own strength. Therefore, we must depend upon Jesus each day to get His things done.

Along with the gift of repentance comes a realization of a new hostility to the sin within. We yearn to be free of this cancer and begin to thirst after righteousness, and this leads us to the cross of our Christ, to see afresh the eternal love of the Father in the willing sacrifice of His only begotten Son for sinful men. The great love of the Son for His Father and His children is demonstrated through His willingness and His sacrifice. We will become a reflection of our Lord, for the Word of Christ is sure, and He will present us blameless and pure before His Father and our Father. *"Being confident of this very thing, that He which has begun a good work in you will perform (it) until the day of Jesus Christ"* (Philippians 1:6) **[To Memorize]**

---

134. See Acts 5:31, 11:18, 2 Corinthians 7:10, Romans 2:4 and 2 Timothy 2:25-26
135. Mark 3:35 *"Jesus said, 'For whosoever shall do the will of God, the same is my brother, and my sister, and mother.'"*

PART IV

ISRAEL AS AN EXAMPLE

CHAPTER 16

OLD TESTAMENT ISRAEL

We are now going to follow the lives and decisions of some of the religious men and leaders, as well as the people of the Kingdom of Israel to see what pride does to men and the country they inhabit. These people were just like us today, in that their lives reflected the fact that they, too, were natural men with sin natures. We will cover roughly five hundred years, to see the response of men to the living God. We will be concentrating upon sinful pride with its arrogance and conceit, seeing how that pride influenced the decisions made. We will also see the consequences of the carnal thinking of the people. These examples are not necessarily chronological in nature. Instead, use the eyes and the words of the prophets sent by God as binoculars to view a collection of factual accounts for information about the Lord and man's true nature. To do this requires a view of the people the Lord used when He called out the family of Abraham from among other men of the earth. Abraham was the chosen progenitor of certain descendants through whom God would bring salvation and reconciliation, healing the breach begun with the rebellion of Adam and Eve. God has left for us, out of His mercy, a wide field of behavior and their consequences to observe and learn from, as He takes us through the history of Israel.

God called Abraham out from the land of the Chaldeans and directed him to travel into a land He Himself chose. Abraham followed God all the days of his life and believed that the promises God made to him would come true. [136] Abraham believed that through his descendants the whole world would be blessed. God promised to protect Abraham's family, saying, *"I will bless those that bless you and curse those that curse you"* (Genesis 12:3, ASV-1901). [137] Isaac was the son of Abraham, and he also followed God, as did his younger son, Jacob. Jacob had twelve boys and a girl. Those boys would be the twelve patriarchs, whose descendants would comprise the twelve tribes of Israel. The priests to serve in the Temple would come from the tribe of Levi. The High Priest would come from the family of Moses and Aaron, also of the tribe of Levi. Moses, inspired by God, wrote the first five books of the Bible. [138]

THE 12 TRIBES OF ISRAEL

Reuben	Zebulun	Judah	Naphtali
Simeon	Joseph	Issachar	Gad
Levi	Benjamin	Dan	Asher

---

136. See Genesis 15 (MKJV)
137. For the full story, see Genesis 12:1-10 (ASV-1901)
138. See Exodus 17:14, 34:4-14 and 27 (ASV-1901)

The people of Israel asked to have a king like the nations around them. They thus rejected the direct rule of God. [139] God sent the prophet Samuel to anoint Saul to be the first king. When Saul was found unfit to be king, the Lord had Samuel find David, of the tribe of Judah, and anoint him to be the next king. David's son Solomon became the third king. Solomon's son Rehoboam became the fourth king, but he so angered the people that most of the tribes left, dividing the Kingdom into two parts. The Northern Kingdom was composed of roughly ten tribes, headed by King Jeroboam. It was often called Israel, Joseph, Ephraim or Samaria. The Southern Kingdom, called Judah, was composed of the tribes of Judah and Benjamin, along with some of the Levites who were loyal to David's God. There were also a mixed group of other tribes loyal to David. [140]

THE KINGS OF ISRAEL

Saul	1095 BC
David	1048 BC
Solomon (The split occurred after his son Rehoboam ascended the throne)	1015 BC
Jeroboam (He instituted the worship of idols in the Northern Kingdom.)	975 BC
The Northern Kingdom was removed permanently.	740-721 BC
The Southern Kingdom was carried away into Babylon.	610-588 BC

THE KINGDOM OF ISRAEL

Saul, the first king, was from the tribe of Benjamin.

David, the son of Jesse, the second king, was from the tribe of Judah.

Solomon, son of David, the third king, was also from the tribe of Judah.

THE SPLIT OCCURRED BETWEEN 930 AND 975 BC [141]

- The Kingdom of Judah was composed of Judah and Benjamin, plus the priests and a remnant of the other tribes. [142] Rehoboam, son of Solomon and fourth king of the newly separated kingdom called Judah,
- The Kingdom of Israel was composed of the ten other tribes. Jeroboam was its first king.

God made a promise to David, *"When your days are fulfilled that you must go to your fathers, I will set up one of your descendants after you, who will be of your sons; and I will establish his kingdom. He shall build for Me a house, and I will establish his throne forever"* (1 Chronicles 17:11-12)·

---

139. See 1 Samuel 8:3-7 and 12:1-17 (MKJV)
140. See 1 Kings 12:23 (NASB)
141. Scholars disagree on the exact date
142. See 1 Kings 11:29-35

Notice that the One spoken of by God was a male, a particular Person, One who was (and is) eternal. His purpose was to build a house, not a physical building, but in the sense of a permanently-fixed dynasty under His rule. David came from the tribe of Judah, and the Anointed One, or Messiah, would also be of that tribe and also of the house of David, [143] as God promised.

The Law of the Kings (1495 BC) was given roughly 450 years before the first king, Saul:

When you have come unto the land which the LORD your God shall choose: (One) from among your brethren shall you set as king over you: you may not set a stranger over you, which (is) not your brother. But he shall not multiply horses to himself nor cause the people to return to Egypt, to the end that he should multiply horses: forasmuch as the LORD has said unto you, "You shall henceforth return no more that way," nor shall he multiply wives to himself that his heart not turn away: neither shall he greatly multiply to himself silver and gold. And it shall be, when he sits upon the throne of his kingdom, that he shall write a copy of this law in a book out of (that which is) before the priests the Levites: and it shall be with him, and he shall read therein all the days of his life: that he may learn to fear the LORD his God, to keep all the words of this law and these statutes, to do them: that his heart be not lifted up above his brethren, and that he not turn aside from the commandment, (to) the right hand, or (to) the left: to the end that he may prolong (his) days in his kingdom, he, and his children, in the midst of Israel.

Deuteronomy 17:14-20

QUESTIONS ON ISRAEL
(READ GENESIS 49:10, DEUTERONOMY 5:31-33 AND 17:14-20, MATTHEW 1 AND LUKE 3 AND ANSWER THESE QUESTIONS IN YOUR NOTEBOOK.)

1. What tribe was Jesus from?
2. What is the history of Joseph and Mary, as revealed in Matthew 1 and Luke 3?
3. What was the promise God made to King David?
4. What five things does the Law of Kings cover?
5. What was the stated purpose of the King's Law?
6. What are the similarities you find in Deuteronomy 5?

The tribe of Judah was given a promise by the Lord that from its ranks a king would rule forever. [144] Jesus' father Joseph's linage was directly from the family line of King David, which made Him entitled to kingship. [145] Mary's line descended from Nathan, the son of David, according to Luke 3:31. The Lord left very interesting instructions for the kings of Israel, and their history would have been vastly different if they had listened to Him. Israel's kings would have been strengthened greatly in their heart\mind\spirit, and their pride would have been

---

143. *The house of,* meaning of the family or a descendant
144. Genesis 49:10 "*The scepter shall not depart from Judah, nor a lawgiver from between his feet, until Shiloh come; and unto him shall the gathering of the people be.*" Shiloh, meaning tranquil; an epithet of the Messiah.
145. See Matthew 1:1-23

dampened or purged. The study of God's Word continually works to dampen or purge our pride and keep us always aware of the power and purposes of God. Serious study of God's Word would have done the same for the kings.

Reading the Bible keeps us aware of our true position before God, and this increases the respect and value we place in Him. Our hearts\minds are kept from terminal pride, causing us to be more realistic in our self-judgment. If we choose not to read and study as God commands all believers, [146]we greatly increase the chance that our heart will be turned aside by pride, to then face discipline from the Lord.

---

146. 1 Peter 3:15 and 2 Timothy 3:14-17: You cannot defend your faith if you do not know what it says, nor can you prepare yourself for "good works" if you do not know how.

CHAPTER 17

THE KINGDOM SPLITS

We continue our study of pride within the Scriptures, picking up the history of Israel at the point when the kingdom split into two parts. We will follow Solomon, the son of David, as the third king, after Saul and David. Rehoboam was the fourth king, and he did not follow the Lord but made his own way. His harsh words and arrogant attitude were one of the crowbars that split the kingdom into the Southern Kingdom (Judah) and the Northern Kingdom (Israel), now ruled by Jeroboam. Rebellion against God exacts a terrible price. It affects you and your family, as well as your descendants.

QUESTIONS ON 1 KINGS 2:1-4, 3:1-15, 6:12-13 AND 8:12-40

1. **What did David tell his son Solomon?**
2. **With whom did Solomon make an alliance? Why?**
3. **What did the Lord tell Solomon?**
4. **What promise did the Lord make to Solomon and what were the conditions?**

QUESTIONS ON 1 KINGS 9:1-28, 10:1-11:13 AND 2 CHRONICLES 7:12-22 (1012 BC)
(FOR MORE INSIGHT INTO SOLOMON, READ CHAPTERS 1 AND 12 OF ECCLESIASTES.)

1. **What did God promise Solomon?**
2. **In the twenty years that Solomon spent building the Temple and his palace, [147] what had taken place almost unnoticed?**
3. **How did Solomon disobey the Law of Kings?**
4. **What did God say to Solomon? Describe what had happened to Solomon.**

It is sad to note the harness of sin that was being assembled within Solomon. All of his wisdom was applied to thinking about this natural world and how man fits into it. He shows much of his wisdom in the books of Proverbs and Ecclesiastes. He had unlimited wealth, collecting silver, gold, the treasure of kings and provinces. He built the Temple in Jerusalem, as well as beautifully-landscaped estates with pools of water to irrigate his crops and trees. He planted large fields, gardens, vineyards and orchards and had more flocks and herds than either Saul or David. Alas, Solomon pursued the pleasures of men, having wives, concubines and many children. He had many servants

---

147. See 1 Kings 9:10

and court officials who curried his favor. He sought to study the pleasures of the world. [148] He said, *"All that my eyes desired I did not refuse them, I did not withhold my heart from any pleasure"* (Ecclesiastes 2:10).

Solomon chose to disregard the King's Law in areas that affected his pleasures: women, [149] precious metals, and horses for his chariots from Egypt. He was called to meditate and study the Word of God, but Solomon also sought the wisdom of the world. He thought he could have the delights of sin and still maintain the wisdom given to him by God, in spite of God's clear warning to the contrary. [150] Solomon allowed his sinful heart to *"love strange [non-Jewish, heathen] women"* (1 Kings 11:1), just as his father David had done, even though this practice was forbidden to them by God. [151] Solomon bowed voluntarily to sensual addiction, thereby yielding mastery to sin. He was then bound by the straight-jacket of lust and placed the higher value upon the wishes of his wives, rather than God's Word. This thought process seems very similar to Adam's choice to hear Eve rather than delight in the things of the Lord.

Solomon's wives captured his heart and turned it after other gods, as God had said they would. This sin of putting his wives above God deceived and then harnessed Solomon, as it led him ever deeper into idolatry. Blinded by sinful pride, he then built in Jerusalem places for worship of Moab's god Chemosh and Ammon's god Molech. This promotion of idolatry helped ensnare the people of the Southern Kingdom. This was something David had not done. How could Solomon do such things? Sin deceives us, and it is impossible for us to evaluate the real costs or estimate the damage to our own soul or to the people around us. Godly wisdom will not pass over the barrier of prideful disobedience.

We are not to be like Solomon, who chose to ignore both God's commands and warnings, [152] giving himself over to sensuality. In the end, when his own death was sure and all the world's pleasures have turned to dust in his heart, Solomon was aware that God was the only one who mattered: *"Remember now thy Creator ... before the silver cord is broken and the golden bowl is crushed ... , and the spirit returns to God who gave it ... . Fear God and keep His commandments ... . For God will bring every act to judgment, everything which is hidden, whether it is good or evil"* (Ecclesiastes 12:1, 6-7 and 13-14 (NASB).

Early in Ecclesiastes, Solomon said something very radical: *"Thus I considered all my activities which my hands had done and the labor which I had exerted, and behold all was vanity* [153] *and striving after wind, and there was no profit under the sun"* (Ecclesiastes 2:11). According to Solomon, all that natural men seek in this world is full of vanity. Such sharp, clear comprehension of the vanity bound in the heart of men is a gift of truth to us. It is true that, without due consideration of the Living God, which only happens through the enlightenment of the Spirit of Christ in both worship and life we all are lost to vanity.

---

148. 1 Corinthians 1:21 *"For since in the wisdom of God the world through its wisdom did not come to know God, God was well-pleased through the foolishness of the message preached to save those who believe."*

149. See 1 Kings 9:14, 10:26-28 and 11:1

150. See 1 Kings 3:5-13, 4:29-30, 6:12, chapter 8, 9:1-9. See especially 11:1-9, God's specific warning to Solomon because of His sin

151. Nehemiah 13:27 *"Shall we then hearken unto you to do all this great evil, to transgress against our God in marrying strange wives?"*

152. Deuteronomy 17:17 *"Neither shall he multiply wives to himself, that his heart turn not away: neither shall he greatly multiply to himself silver and gold."* See also Judges 3:3-8

153. *Vanity*, emptiness: figuratively something transitory and unsatisfactory; often used as an adverb.

CHAPTER 18

JEROBOAM AND REHOBOAM AS EXAMPLES

Rehoboam, the son of Solomon, and Jeroboam, the first king of the Northern Kingdom, were men who had wrapped themselves in pride as a cape and pursued vanity instead of heeding the words of the Lord, men so filled with pride that the decisions they made were twisted and perverse.

QUESTIONS ON 1 KINGS 11:26-40

1. What was the message of the prophet of God? [154]
2. What became Jeroboam's concern? Why?
3. What was one effect of the prophecy upon Jeroboam? Why? (See verses 29-36)
4. What should Rehoboam have done? What influenced him?
5. What was the condition of Jeroboam's heart\mind? What was he thinking?
6. What would have happened to Jeroboam if he had followed God? (See verses 35-38)
7. What did this sin mean to the living God?

QUESTIONS ON 1 KINGS 14:1-31 AND 2 CHRONICLES 11:1 AND 12:21-31

1. What was Jeroboam's plan? Why didn't he go himself?
2. What was the attitude of Jeroboam? What was missing in his heart?
3. What was Rehoboam's attitude? [155] How was he repentant?

Prophecy is very often two-fold in its application. The message usually has an immediate effect (when first given) and then a second phase (to be fulfilled in the future). The Lord would send a prophet to give a message, as He did for Jeroboam at His altar. Immediate proof of authority was given (Jeroboam's shriveled arm and the split altar). The completion of the prophecy, which validated God's authority and His Word, could come generations later. Read the selection below to see how the Jeroboam prophecy was precisely fulfilled in 624 BC.

QUESTIONS ON 2 KINGS 23:13-20 AND 1 KINGS 13:1-6

1. What is happening here?
2. What fulfilled the prophecy given in 1 Kings 13?

---

154. See Numbers 18:1-22 (Gods plan for the priesthood) and Deuteronomy 4:1-40 (God's plan for His people).
155. For more insight, read 2 Chronicles chapters 11 and 12

Pride rendered Jeroboam terminally selfish, and he regarded no one else as important as himself. Therefore, his family suffered, as did his nation. Jeroboam was trapped by his own pride, melded with covetousness. His cold heart and dark thoughts destroyed his family and corrupted the Northern Kingdom.

It is said that David comforted Bathsheba when their illegitimate child was taken by God because of David's sin. David took Bathsheba from one of his favorite captains, Uriah, and had a close friend send Uriah into the front lines of battle so that he would die. Later, when Bathsheba became his wife, "... *she bare a son, and David called his name Solomon: and the* LORD *loved him*" (2 Samuel 12:24).

Solomon was trapped by his pride and sensual desires, so that he forfeited much of the gift of wisdom from the Lord and seemed to spend his life in the empty pursuit of pleasure. His wisdom could have helped his children in many ways, but ultimately his choices led them down into darkness. In his pride, Rehoboam did not follow his grandfather David's steps in the pursuit of God, nor his father's wisdom when it was bright, but put his trust in men and their words rather than preparing his heart to seek the living God. The result of his choice was a split kingdom, to the detriment of both kingdoms. None of these men learned anything from the example of King David, a man having far more regard for the person and wisdom of God than any of them. David, when rebuked by God, changed his ways and his life's direction in true repentance. But David's son Solomon half-heartedly followed the Lord, and his grandson Rehoboam, as far as we know, never repented of his self-will.

QUESTIONS ON 1 KINGS 12:1-33, 14:21-31 AND 2 CHRONICLES 12:1-16

1. What plan did Jeroboam make to control the ten tribes? Why? (See verses 28-33)
2. How did he use their history to support his rebellion? [156]
3. What should the people have done to the man who enticed them to leave God? [157]
4. Does God hold them responsible for yielding to the new king?
5. Whose advice did Rehoboam take? Why?
6. What was the result? And what part did the Lord play in this decision?
7. What was Jeroboam's part in the division of the country?
8. Who was Rehoboam's mother? [158] And what was her possible influence?
9. How did Rehoboam do evil by not preparing his heart to seek the Lord?

Jeroboam also showed disrespect for the living God in his thoughts and actions. He ignored the warning given by our gracious Lord. Jeroboam was a deeply covetous man, wanting the kingdom, but not willing to yield to God. Therefore, he lost the kingdom, his family, his life and his soul.

---

156. See Exodus 32, the history of the golden calf
157. See Deuteronomy 13:1-18 and 18:1-22 to see the fate of a false prophet
158. Rehoboam's mother was an Ammonite, distantly related to the Jewish people (See Genesis 19:30-38, Deuteronomy 2:19 and Judges 10:6 and 9)

For this you know, that no fornicator, nor unclean person, nor covetous man, who is an idolater, has any inheritance in the kingdom of Christ and of God. Let no man deceive you with vain words: for because of these things comes the wrath of God upon the children of disobedience.

Ephesians 5:5-6 **[To Memorize]**

Remember, God has no pleasure in the death of the wicked but wants him to turn away from sin and live. [159] The Lord gave these men time to repent, but sin would be served at the expense of their souls. *"But if you will not hear it, my soul shall weep in secret places for (your) pride; and mine eyes shall weep sore, and run down with tears"* (Jeremiah 13:17). This account illustrates the truth that the Lord never passes over sin. Consider how the Lord works behind the scenes to bring His will to pass. In his commentary, Matthew Henry made this observation, "God serves his own wise and righteous purposes by the impudences and iniquities of men and snares sinners in the work of their own hands." [160]

QUESTIONS ON 2 KINGS 11:1-43, 13:1-10, 14:1-20 AND ECCLESIASTES 1 AND 12
(REVIEW THE PREVIOUS LESSONS ON SOLOMON, REHOBOAM AND JEROBOAM AND ANSWER THE FOLLOWING QUESTIONS.)

I said, I will be wise; but it was far from me.   Solomon in Ecclesiastes 7:23

1. **What did pride do to all of these men? How did Solomon's wisdom fail?**
2. **How could these men have prevented their sad outcomes?**
3. **In whom or what did these men trust?**
4. **What did the rebellion of Solomon, Rehoboam and Jeroboam look like? List the character traits you find.**

Rehoboam was forty years old when this incident occurred. He showed his extreme arrogance by not seeking God and by ignoring the council of elders who had served his father, Solomon. Rehoboam leaned, instead, upon the counsel of men who had been his youthful playmates, men filled with pride, who were as without understanding, as was he. Listen to the raw pride in this proposed reply: *"My little (finger) shall be thicker than my father's loins, and now whereas my father did lade you with a heavy yoke, I will add to your yoke: my father has chastised you with whips, but I will chastise you with scorpions"* (1 Kings 12:10). Rehoboam exposed his deep lack of wisdom with the decisions he made and revealed a heart filled with vanity and pride. Remember that pride deceives you about your true state before God, and is a barrier over which godly wisdom cannot pass.

Satan rules the kingdoms of this world and, through the heart of prideful men, uses cruel hate to produce violence, oppression and a total disregard for all life—especially the Author of Life

---

159. See Ezekiel 33:11
160. Matthew Henry, study notes on 1 Kings 12:1-15

Himself. Satan embodies all the evil found within pride [161] and loves to foster pride within men. Pride deceives you about your true state before God and will not yield to God. Pride devalues all others and hates the truth of God. Jeroboam ignored the Word of God, the people in his kingdom and the members of his own family, and Rehoboam did the same.

Here in America, we are raised to have pride in self, our traditions, our heritage, our intelligence, talent or achievements, etc. This pride has nothing to do with the Kingdom of God, but it always interferes with the passage of godly truth into our hearts\minds.

Jesus was not like Solomon, Rehoboam or Jeroboam. He did not invest in sin or yield to sin [162] of any kind, nor was He self-indulgent. Jesus Christ did not pursue the world's storehouse of vanities. The love of our Lord Jesus Christ saves men and gives purpose to our lives, as the indwelling Spirit comforts us and gives quiet joy, even in the midst of the dark seasons of life, which will come to all, as they did to Solomon. Jesus Christ lived and sacrificed Himself for men who were, at heart, hostile to Him and, in mind, alien from Him. Jesus abhors evil, [163] and we are evil in heart\mind until His Spirit touches us with pure, piercing love. This love that Jesus has is a reflection of His pure character, a love different in kind, intensity and purity. It is not an admixture of anything in or of this world. His love flows like a stream through His sacrifice into the hearts of men, bringing forgiveness, reconciliation and peace with God.

Jesus Christ had more reason than any man to have pride in Himself. After all, He gave the blind sight, healed the sick and raised the dead. Still, he did not show pride or any of the traits that are found in pride. Jesus did not indulge in arrogance or conceit, but He did confront the pride-filled men of Jerusalem, exposing their ripe ungodliness. Jesus, our Lord, had pity, not contempt, for humble and contrite men. He did not devalue men, but valued them enough to die for them. His assessment of men was pure, and His thinking reveals the holy Son of God, whose mind was set on His mission to bring salvation to men, not indulging self. Jesus quietly depended upon the Holy Spirit and lived under the will of His Father, even though, as the Son of Man, He could have had or done anything He wanted. This amazing attitude of Jesus is such a contrast with the pride-filled minds of men.

A prideful person believes he is in control and immune from consequences. Jeroboam believed this, as did Rehoboam and, perhaps, even Solomon. What did pride cost Solomon? Sin ruled his heart\mind through His addictions to sensuality. His children grew up to be vain, prideful people seeming to have no respect for either their father or God. They lost the throne given to David by default and never repented. Solomon built a place to worship at least two false gods and helped lead his people into idolatry. He spent a bountiful treasury on building projects, horses and chariots from Egypt and his own pleasures, and this is just what we know. Jeroboam and Rehoboam related everything they did to themselves and showed no pity or remorse.

161. See Isaiah 14:1-32. The end of the king of Babylon is the main part of the chapter, but it is also used to identify the pride and fall of Satan because of verses 11-12.
162. Hebrews 4:15 "For we have not an high priest which cannot be touched with the feeling of our infirmities; but was in all points tempted like as we are, yet without sin."
163. See Hebrews 1:8-9

Do nothing from selfishness or empty conceit, but with humility of mind regard one another as more important than yourselves; do not merely look out for your own personal interests, but also for the interests of others. Philippians 2:3-4, [164] **[To Memorize]**

This is how we should be thinking of self, regarding others as more important. Do what is best for them and look out for their interest. This mindset is the opposite of the mindset found in people of pride.

---

164. I strongly recommend that you read the whole chapter. In fact, if you can, read all four chapters of Philippians.

CHAPTER 19

JEROBOAM TOOK OVER THE PRIESTHOOD

Jeroboam arrogantly took the priest's office for himself, so now we will study something of the priesthood. Jeroboam had contempt for the office of the priest and offered sacrifices on an altar he made himself. We need to know how the priests were to function in the sacrificial system given by God, for we cannot understand the degree of Jeroboam's sin unless we have some knowledge of the priest's office.[165]

QUESTIONS ON 2 CHRONICLES 11:1-17
(READ THE REFERENCES AND WRITE THE ANSWERS IN YOUR NOTEBOOK.)

1. Who had God appointed to be priest? [166]
2. What was the penalty for intrusion into the office of the priest? [167]
3. What had Jeroboam and his sons done to the Levite priest? (See verse 14)
4. Why did the people come into Jerusalem? (See verse 16)

QUESTIONS ON 1 KINGS 11:26-40, 13:1-10 AND 33-34

1. What was the message of the prophet of God? [168]
2. What became Jeroboam's concern?
3. What should Rehoboam have done? What influenced him?
4. What was he thinking? What was the condition of Jeroboam heart, his mind?
5. What did this sin mean to the living God?

It may be hard for some to understand how awful the things Jeroboam did really were. Today there is an atmosphere of irreverence and amplified individual rights permeating our culture and thinking, and they cloud the truth. This man did everything the opposite of God's prescribed way. Jeroboam set up idols to entice the people into sin, a perverse substitute for God's personal care of the people He loved. He put the worst men as priests to serve God with contempt and disrespect.

165, Read Leviticus 16 to understand how the priesthood was to function.
166. Numbers 3:5-13 (15:28-31 *"The soul that sins presumptuously, shall be cut off from among his people."*) (Deuteronomy 12, they were to destroy all strange altars and places of worship and set up sacrifices and worship in a place that God would show them to put His name there forever.) See also 1 Chronicles 23:25-32.
167. Numbers 3:10 (Aaron and his sons were to have the priest's office, the stranger who came close was to be put to death.
168. Numbers 18:1-22 (Gods' plan for the priesthood), Deuteronomy 4:1-40 (God's plan for His people). 1 Kings 13:30-34 (The lowest men were made priests by Jeroboam) Numbers 16 (No one who was not of the descendants of Aaron could burn incense.)

[169] The priests were to teach the people the Word of God. [170] Instead, they defiled the Word of God by speaking their own words, as if God had spoken to them. The altar was to be made by men following the plan designed by the Lord. [171] It was to be touched only by the designated priest of the tribe of Levi. [172] It was to be set up only in Jerusalem. [173] Jeroboam ignored all of these commands and made the altar himself. He then proceeded to offer sacrifices as a self-assigned priest to his man-made idol.

It is interesting that the Lord promised Israel a priest who would be far above natural men and have a permanent priesthood. [174] Jesus Christ has been appointed by God to be the final permanent Priest. Jesus also offered Himself as the perfect and complete sacrifice for sin. [175] He is the indwelling Teacher of truth, who uses the Scriptures to change the thinking of believers.

Jesus Christ is the only trustworthy High Priest, [176] the only permanent Intercessor appointed by God and the last needed between God and man. Our Lord Jesus has a nature full of righteousness and full of far more wisdom than Solomon to lead believers in this world. Jesus is worthy [177] of our trust and devotion, for He leads us in the ways of His holy Father, full of truth, love and everlasting joy. Why would anyone wait for some other time to seek the Lord? Do not be like Jeroboam, Rehoboam, Adam or Eve who did not seek God. Solomon did not seem to respond to the convicting words of God in his later life and did not seek Him. He became a sad old man who would not be admonished because of pride. It is better to seek the Lord when He is convicting us of our personal sin with the truth of His words. *Now set your heart and soul to seek the LORD your God* (1 Chronicles 22:19).

---

169. See 2 Chronicles 11:13-17
170. See 1 Chronicles 15:3 (the teaching priest) (final prophet, Deuteronomy 18, Hebrews 1:1-4)
171. In 1 Chronicles 28:9-19, David states that the Lord designed the plan and directed his understanding.
172. From Deuteronomy 18:1-7, Exodus 28:1-4, 28:40-44 and Exodus 2 and 9, get an idea of just how precise God's instructions were.
173. See 1 Kings 14:21
174. See 1 Samuel 2:35, Leviticus 7:34 and Exodus 40:15
175. See Leviticus 4:35, 5:6 and 10, the sin offering, atonement, forgiveness, Hebrews 2:14-17, 3:1-6 and 4:9-16
176. Hebrews 9:7-15 *"neither by the blood of goats and calves, but by His own blood He entered in once into the holy place having obtained eternal redemption for us."*
177. Revelation 5:9 and 12 *"... And they sung a new song, saying, Thou are worthy to take the book, and to open the seals: for you were slain, and has redeemed us to God by your blood ... . Worthy is the Lamb that was slain to receive power, and riches, and wisdom, and strength, and honor, and glory and blessing."*

CHAPTER 20

THE PEOPLE OF THE NORTHERN KINGDOM AS EXAMPLES
AMOS 4 THROUGH 7

We have been concentrating on Jeroboam of Israel in the Northern Kingdom, but now we will look at his people, to see how pride and arrogance also made them foolish. Men can and do regulate morals by law, but it is often true that the actions and speech of the leaders of a country actually have a bearing on how the people regard many issues, for either good or ill. Whole countries can be taken captive to pride, as were Israel and Judah in the Old Testament. A modern example would be Germany and Japan during World War II. Pride will not seek God. Pride will pass over the words of God. Pride deceives the heart.

Amos was a sheep herder from Tekoa, he saw visions concerning the northern kingdom of Israel in the days of Uzziah king of Judah.
Amos 1:1

The Lord spoke to Israel:

They hate him who reproves in the gate,
And they abhor him who speaks with integrity.
Therefore because you impose heavy rent on the poor
And exact a tribute of grain from them,
Though you have built houses of well-hewn stone,
Yet you will not live in them;
You have planted pleasant vineyards, yet you will not drink their wine.
For I know your transgressions are many and your sins are great,
You who distress the righteous and accept bribes
And turn aside the poor in the gate.
Therefore at such a time the prudent person keeps silent, for it is an evil time.
Amos5:10-13, NASB

QUESTIONS ON AMOS CHAPTERS 4 AND 5
READ THESE CHAPTERS AND THEIR CORRESPONDING FOOTNOTES AND THEN ANSWER THE FOLLOWING QUESTIONS IN YOUR NOTEBOOK

Remember, these citizens prided themselves on the fact that they were chosen by God as His people, and they had the living Word of God preached to them each Saturday. They also had the prophets, sent by God to give them up-to-date messages, which were very relevant to their situations. Bethel was where one of the golden calves was located. Gilgal and Beersheba were famous places in the history of Israel, and became places chosen to worship idols. Molock and Chium were two of the idols adopted from the nations surrounding Israel.

QUESTIONS ON AMOS 5

1. What does this phrase reveal, "<u>Seek</u> [178] me and you shall live"?
2. What else should the people seek? What did they seek?
3. What does the phrase mean in verse 24, "Let <u>judgment</u> [179] run down like water"?
4. What does it mean in verses 14-15 to "love the good and <u>hate</u> [180] evil"?
5. Why is this mindset so important? Why did they hate in verse 10?
6. What does it mean, in verse 15, to "establish <u>judgment</u> [181] in the gate"? [182]
7. What had they done? (See verses 7, 11 and 12) What does this have to do with justice? [183]
8. Why did the Lord refuse to accept the worship of these men in verses 21-23?

It was not long before the Jewish people failed to humble themselves before God and seek His face. The fact that they were the children of God, privileged beyond all people, began to mean, in their minds, that they were naturally superior to other peoples, in spite of God's clear assessment. [184] The seed of pride began to grow in their hearts, and they began to break the moral laws and multiply hypocrisy by worshiping idols, while still going to worship the Lord with sacrifices on feast days. God sent the prophets to warn the people of the consequences of their sin, *"Take heed to yourselves, that your heart be not deceived, and you turn aside, and serve other gods, and worship them ..."* (Deuteronomy 11:16). The consequences of corruption seeped into the fabric of their culture, as they grew cold and despised the Law of God. They were blinded by pride and believed lies, sacrificing their children to false gods, [185] even though God had warned the people not to practice this most awful sacrifice. During the siege of Jerusalem carried out by the Babylonian Empire, the people

---

178. *Seek,* to tread frequently, to pursue diligently, inquire, and search with the main goal being worship

179. *Judgment,* a formal utterance of authoritative Truth, particularly the Divine Law. (An obligation created by the decree of a court or, in this case, by God, through His covenant agreed to by His people) A verdict pronounced judicially, including the act, the place, the suit, the crime and the penalty.

180. *Hate,* intense personal hostility and aversion, a habitual mindset of enmity, to abhor, loathing all forms of evil.

181. Same as previous reference to judgment.

182. See also Ezra 7:10 and 21-26, Judges 4:3-9 and 2 Samuel 15:1-6

183. Exodus 23:2 "You shall not follow a multitude to do evil, neither shall you testify in a dispute so as to turn aside after a multitude in order to pervert (twist) justice"(NASB).

184. Deuteronomy 7:7 *"The Lord did not set his love upon you, nor choose you, because you were more in number than any people for you (were) the fewest of all people."* Deuteronomy 9:4-6 *"Speak not in your heart, saying, 'For my righteousness the Lord has brought me in to possess this land: but because of their wickedness the Lord does drive them out.' Understand therefore, that the Lord your God gives you this good land to possess it not for your righteousness; for you (art) a stiffnecked people."*

185. See Leviticus 18:21, 20:2-5 and Jeremiah 32:5

even turned to cannibalism. [186] The appointed armies surrounded Jerusalem and carried the people away. *"And among these nations shall you find no ease, neither shall the sole of your foot have rest: but the LORD shall give you there a trembling heart, and failing of eyes, and sorrow of mind"* (Deuteronomy 28:65).

Jesus was entirely different in His thinking than the people presented in the Amos selections. He was intimately connected to His Father and always had respect for the laws and precepts of the Scriptures. Therefore, Jesus' heart\mind did not join in the pursuits of men, but He glorified His Father by joyful and perfect obedience. Our Lord Jesus exhibited a pronounced hatred of evil and hypocrisy, and, instead, revealed a heart of pity to men in bondage to sin. Jesus was kind and full of mercy toward the poor, broken-hearted, sick and downtrodden. Our Lord Jesus was keenly aware of the sinful nature of men, but this knowledge did not change the purpose for which He came, nor did it make Him either bitter or impatient. He was not sentimental, but, rather, motivated out of pure love for His Father and for God's children.

Jesus commanded us, *"As the Father has loved me, so have I loved you: continue in my love; even as I have kept my Father's commandments, and abide in his love. These thing have I spoken unto you, that my joy [187] might remain in you, and that your joy might be full; this is my commandment, that you love one another, as I have loved you"* (John 15:9-12). *"Hitherto you have asked nothing in my name: ask, and you shall receive, that your joy may be full"* (John 16:24) **[To Memorize]**

QUESTIONS ON AMOS 6 AND 7

1. **Why does "being at ease" cause rebuke? [188]**
2. **What is meant in verse 6, *"but they were not grieved for the affliction [189] of Joseph"*? [190]**
3. **What do the last statements in verses 12-13 reveal about the people's hearts?**
4. **What did they really believe about themselves and what filled their minds?**
5. **What was routinely done to the destitute? (See Psalm 10:2-8)**
6. **How were they to treat the poor? [191]**
7. **How do the words *gall*, *hemlock* and *wormwood* [192] help to explain the actions of the wicked?**
8. **Why did Amos go the house of Israel? And what did his actions show us about his belief in the Lord?**

Each of the Israelites had oppressed his conscience by repeatedly refusing to hear the Word of God, and therefore, his will was hardened into rebellion. Each sought to pursue his own pleasures, therefore, pity and mercy had flown away. Prudent men know that when law is used to take away the necessary things of life by taxation, justice has seeped out of the culture. When the letter of the

---

186. See Jeremiah 19:1-15, Lamentations 2:20, 4:10, Ezekiel 5:10, 16:21 and 33:25 (Forbidden in Genesis 9:4) See also Isaiah 57:5

187. *Joy*, cheerfulness, that is, calm delight: gladness, exceeding joyful, joyous. See John 15:9-12 and 16:2.

188. See Deuteronomy 8:1-20

189. *Affliction*, a fracture, figuratively ruin: breach. The messages in Amos point out the terrible breach between God and the tribes. The poor are the destitute, afflicted by their own kinsmen, who take tribute.

190. Amos uses the name Joseph to indicate Israel in verse 8. Joseph was one of the sons of Jacob (Israel).

191. See Exodus 23:2, 6, Leviticus 19:15, 25:35-37, Deuteronomy 16:19, 15:7-8 and 11, 24:14 and Psalm 72:4

192. *Gall*, a poisonous plant, as poisonous as snake venom, *hemlock*; *wormwood* was used to curse, as it was regarded as poisonous and, therefore, accursed.

law is used to condemn the righteous or separate them from their property, justice is turned to poison. When justice sleeps, men of means give bribes to secure verdicts, and judges comply.

Amos mentioned another characteristic of the people, *"They hate him who rebukes in the gate, and they despise him who speaks uprightly"* (Amos 5:10).

QUESTIONS ON ISAIAH 10:1-3 AND DEUTERONOMY 16:19

You shall not wrest [twist, stretch, bend away] justice: you shall not respect persons; neither shall you take a bribe; for a bribe does blind the eyes of the wise, and pervert the words of the righteous.
Deuteronomy 16:19 [To Memorize]

Will the Lord be pleased with thousands of rams, or with ten thousand rivers of oil? Shall I give my firstborn (for) my transgression, the fruit of my body (for) the sin of my soul? He has showed you, O man, what (is) good; and what does the Lord require of you, but to do justice, and to love mercy, and to walk humbly with your God?
Micah 6:7-8 [To Memorize]

1. **Why are justice and judgment so important to God?**
2. **What does this phrase mean, *"you shall not respect persons"*?** [193]
3. **Why is this attitude important?**
4. **Using James 2:1-16, explain why this mindset of respect toward some is so wrong.**

A judge is to keep the law, not add to, subtract from or twist it to conform to his personal perceptions or the perceptions of the culture. Men, even in corrupt societies, crave justice, a place where no wrong is sanctioned and no one is denied his right. Natural man will pervert justice, whatever the court system. It is his natural bias against the restraint found in law. There can be no justice when the laws are twisted to benefit some and not others, or to penalize some and not others. We are not to champion either the rich or the poor, but both are to be equal before the judge. [194] The judge is to keep to the law, not add or subtract or twist it to conform to his personal perceptions. It was said of King David that he reigned over all Israel, and *"did judgment [195] and justice [196] to all his people"* (2 Samuel 8:15).

Christ is the <u>Righteous Judge</u>, [197] able to ensure that justice is the outcome, for He will judge all men, both living and dead. [198] No man can escape the authoritative truth of the Divine Law, which will hold all men accountable for what they think, how they speak, what they do and the fruit of

---

193. See Exodus 24:4-8, Leviticus 19:9-18, chapters 34 through 37 and James 2
194. See Exodus 23:3 and 6
195. *Judgment*, a formal utterance of authoritative Truth, particularly the Divine Law. A verdict pronounced judicially, including the act, the place, the suit, the crime and the penalty.
196. *Justice*, right (natural, moral or legal)—equity, fair, impartial, being just.
197. Righteous Judge *"Henceforth there is laid up for me a crown of righteousness, which the Lord, the righteous judge, shall give me at that day: and not to me only, but unto all them also that love his appearing"* (2 Timothy 4:8)
198. See 2 Timothy 4:1

those deeds. We come to Christ for mercy, for He shed His blood in payment for our sins, so that He could justly extend mercy to those whose sins are paid in full.

Those men who stand before the Lord, dependent upon their own righteousness and "good deeds" to garner mercy, will receive against their sins the full weight of the Law, but no mercy. Always remember, our sinful pride, with it arrogance and conceit, is offensive to God.

CHAPTER 21

PRIDE AND WEALTH (AMOS 8—787 BC)

There is another circumstance that tends to produce pride in the heart of man, and that is wealth. Wealth often isolates us from the struggles and realities of life and, because pride does not value others, pride often assumes wealth is deserved. The Law of Kings warned kings not to multiply gold and silver for themselves.

QUESTIONS ON DEUTERONOMY 8:1-20 (1451 BC)
(READ THE DEUTERONOMY SELECTION TO ANSWER THE QUESTIONS AND SEE HOW THE PEOPLE COULD HAVE SUCH A WRONG VIEW.)

1. Who makes you rich or poor?
2. Is it possible to worship both God and mammon? Why?
3. Describe the process that had taken place in the hearts of the people in the Amos 5 and 6 selections, plus the information given in this chapter. Read Amos 5:7, 10-12, 21-27 and 6:1-8.

QUESTIONS ON AMOS CHAPTER 8

1. What was the significance of the basket of summer fruit?
2. What was the concern of the business people?
3. What was their idol? What value did they place on their poor kin?
4. What does this kind of attitude reveal about the thinking of the people?
5. What were the common business practices? [199]
6. What was the most important famine that God sent? Why?
7. What did Amos think about the Lord and what did He believe?
8. In what light did the people regard the Sabbath?

Where were the hearts of the people of the Northern Kingdom focused? And what was their treasure? It is fair to say that the rulers and those ruled neither feared God nor had respect for His holy Word, neither had they any regard for their fellow citizens. Our Lord Jesus is nothing like the people chastised by Amos. Jesus cared for the apostles and the people under His teaching. He did not use these men to gain material advantage, but spent many hours patiently teaching them the ways of God. He paid attention to their needs, sharing everything with them. Jesus fed them, as well as

199. Read Leviticus 19:9-18 and 34-37 (1490 BC), Exodus 20:1-26 and 24:1-18 the Mt, Sinai-Law.

others on more than one occasion. He spent all of His time pursuing men and changing their focus so that, through Him, they might have life. Believers with newly-awakened hearts become heavenly minded for Jesus because He loves them deeply. Jesus told one of the disciples that He could call upon legions of angles to tend to His needs, but the mind\heart of Jesus Christ was focused upon the will of His Father to save the lost, not to serve Himself.

Jesus said some interesting things about collecting treasure and wealth. In Matthew 6, He said, *"Lay not up for yourselves treasures upon earth, where moth and rust does corrupt, and where thieves break through and steal: but lay up for yourselves treasures in heaven, where neither moth nor rust does corrupt, and where thieves do not break through nor steal: for where your treasure is, there will your <u>heart</u> [200] be also"* (Matthew 6:12).   [To Memorize]

No servant can serve two masters: for either he will hate the one, and love the other; or else he will hold to the one, and despise the other. Ye cannot serve God and <u>mammon</u>." [201]   Luke 16:13   [To Memorize]

Solomon also said some interesting things about wealth. Remember, he was the wealthiest man of his time and perhaps of all time. *"He that loves silver shall not be satisfied with silver; nor he that loves abundance with increase: this is also vanity. When goods increase, they are increased that eat them: and what good is there to the owners thereof saving the beholding of them with their eyes? The sleep of a laboring man is sweet, whether he eat little or much: but the abundance of the rich will not suffer him to sleep"* (Ecclesiastes 5:10-12).   [To Memorize]

QUESTIONS ON WHAT JESUS AND SOLOMON SAID ABOUT WEALTH

1. **What does the quote from Jesus tell you about our values?**
2. **What does this quote from Solomon add to your understanding of wealth?**

QUESTIONS ON 1 TIMOTHY 6:5-10 AND 17-19

But godliness with contentment is great gain. For we brought nothing into this world, and it is certain we can carry nothing out. And having food and raiment let us be content. But they that would be rich fall into temptation and a snare, and (into) many foolish and hurtful lusts, which drown men in destruction and perdition. For the love of money is the root of all evil: which while some coveted after, they have erred from the faith and pierced themselves through with many sorrows.

1 Timothy 6:6-10   [To Memorize]

---

200. *Heart*, that is, (figuratively) the thoughts or feelings (mind)
201. *Mammon*, **This footnote was incomplete in the original manuscript.**

1. How are we to judge our own behavior and thoughts in light of the previous selections of scripture and Timothy?

2. What else does the New Testament have to say about dishonest gain or <u>covetousness</u>? [202] (See 1 Peter 5:2-4 before you answer the question.)

3. What should our mindset be in regard to seeking wealth? Why?

4. What does *"the deceit of riches choke the Word"* mean? [203]

5. What does *"anxiety or cares of this world"* add to this lethal mix?

QUESTIONS ON PSALM 49

They that trust in their wealth, and boast themselves in the multitude of their riches; none of them can by any means redeem his brother, nor give to God a ransom for him: ... that he should still live forever, and not see corruption. Their inward thought is, that their houses shall continue forever, and their dwelling places to all generations; they call their lands after their own names ... . For when he dies he shall carry nothing away: his glory shall not descend after him.

Psalm 49:6-7, 9-11 and 17   [To Memorize]

1. What is meant by this phrase, *"none of them can by any means redeem his brother, nor give to God a ransom for him"*?

2. What are some reasons why men trust in wealth?

3. Why do people who trust in their wealth not see Heaven?

Jesus discusses the problem of riches and other things that have no eternal value in the Parable of the Sower, where He says that the seed is the Word of God. He goes on to describe the things that interfere with the passage of the Word into our hearts. Read the quoted selections from Matthew and Mark to understand how they fit into the picture.

QUESTIONS ON MATTHEW 13:22

[Jesus said,] He that received seed among the thorns is he that hears the word; and the care of this world, and the deceitfulness of riches, choke the word, and he becomes unfruitful.

Matthew 13:22   [To Memorize]

MATTHEW 6:19-21, MARK 4:14-20 AND LUKE 12:15-21

And the cares of this world, and the deceitfulness of riches, and the lusts of other things enter in, choke the word, and it becomes unfruitful.

Mark 4:19   [To Memorize]

---

202. *Covetousness*, See 1 Peter 5:2-4. Guide by example and make sure your motive is not for material gain
203. See Matthew 13:22 and Mark 4:19

Watch and keep yourselves from covetousness. For a man's life is not in the abundance of the things he possesses.
Luke 12:15 **[To Memorize]**

1. What ability do the cares of the world and the deceitfulness of riches have?
2. How do riches deceive you?
3. What has happened to the power of the Word?
4. How do we put a top priority upon the Word of God and the passage of His Word into our hearts\minds?

In His conversations, our Lord Jesus mentioned the things that lure men. Riches and the pursuit of wealth are hooks that snag men. Two more hooks mentioned are the concerns, or distractions, of the world and a lust for that which has been forbidden. None of these things are even close to the value of our salvation, so why would we place them before the heavenly Kingdom? What does that attitude or mindset say about us?

QUESTIONS ON JOHN 15:1-8

1. What does the discussion of the vine add to your understanding?
2. Who makes the branch fruitful?
3. What happens if some of the branches are not fruitful?

Jesus clearly valued heavenly things. Obedience grew from His devotion to His Father. Jesus had a heart filled with joy and a willingness of mind to go to the cross for men under bondage to sin, who were not even seeking Him or Heaven. Single-mindedness in Jesus' love to His Father flowed naturally to the divine mission as the intention of His heart. Jesus was never lazy or self-indulgent or forgetful as the people of the Northern Kingdom, nor did He spend time, as they did, plotting how to get the last nickel from the poor. Instead, our Lord showed kindness, gentleness and patience, while continuously transforming lives throughout His days upon the earth.

QUESTIONS ON JOHN 15:9-27, 16:1-33 AND 17:1-26
(READ THROUGH THESE SELECTIONS AND THEN ANSWER THE FOLLOWING QUESTIONS IN YOUR NOTEBOOK.)

1. What are the major truths given to us by Jesus?
2. Who was Jesus speaking to?
3. What applies only to the people of His day and what applies to us today?
4. What does hate have to do with how the enemies of God think?
5. What are the jobs of the Comforter?
6. What are the other names Jesus applies to this Person?

7. **What did Jesus say about the Father? What did Jesus say about Himself?**
8. **What promises did Jesus make? Why could He say these things?**

Here Jesus showed us how the Father would insure that the truth, the necessary information of the work of salvation through Christ, was delivered to the disciples, so that, through their writings and through the presence of the Spirit of Christ, men, those touched by God, would hear and believe the truth.

Remember Solomon and Jeroboam. Lusts and material treasures bind both mind and heart to the thing treasured, like a spider rolls an insect until it is cocooned and pinned to the web.

CHAPTER 22

PARALLELS

This was the end of the citizens of the Samarian kingdom in Northern Israel. The Assyrian army conquered then and those not killed were transported to other parts of the Middle East. The Assyrians were noted for their extreme cruelty. In spite of the warnings given by the prophets of God, the people of Israel still considered themselves to be good religious people.

QUESTIONS ON RECONSIDERING PAGES 60 AND 61

1. What had pride done to their hearts/minds?
2. How many of the traits found in pride do you find in these people?
3. What had God said all citizens would be held accountable for?

QUESTIONS ON 2 KINGS 17:1-23 AND DEUTERONOMY 18:9-14

1. What were the circumstances surrounding the Assyrian army's capture of Israel and their removal from Samaria?
2. What were the people's sins against the Lord and how many of the Decalogue did they break? [204]
3. What were the sins they committed against each other?
4. Who was sacrificed upon the false altars, [205] and what were the occult practices instituted? [206]

There were some poor (part-Jewish) people left by the Assyrians in the land. In His day, Jesus went to Samaria, [207] where these mixed peoples from many nations had lived for hundreds of years, melding religious practices with various gods from many countries. That was where Jesus met the woman at the well. She believed that He was the Prophet\Messiah and ran to tell her fellow inhabitants what He had said. When the people heard Jesus for themselves, the men committed their lives to Him. How gracious was God to these descendants of the rebellious people of the Northern Kingdom who lived in this city of Sychar by Jacob's well! Consider His words carefully when you hear them, for Jesus is reaching through all our barriers of sin to enliven our souls, that we might know Him, the Maker of all things.

---

204. See Exodus 20:1-26
205. See Leviticus 19:31, 20:1-6 and 27 and Deuteronomy 18:9-14. This happened about 1451 BC
206. *Enchantment*, to hiss, whisper a magic spell; to foretell from observation of signs, to prognosticate: divination, a lot; oracle, divination (which includes the fee), witchcraft. See 2 Kings 23:1-30. This happened about 624-588 BC
207. See John 4:4-40 and 2 Kings 17:24-41

PART V

THE SOUTHERN KINGDOM AS AN EXAMPLE

CHAPTER 23

THE FRAMEWORK FOR THE BEHAVIOR OF MEN

Judah was aware of everything that had happened to the Northern Kingdom. But remember that pride deceives us, and therefore we no longer are aware of our true condition. What were the consequences of choosing such blindness? Did the people of the Southern Kingdom learn anything of the cost of rebellion against God? Remember, the Lord had warned Israel in 1451 BC what would happen if they turned away from Him. [208] He had done only good for His people, showing them great mercy by sending prophets to warn them repeatedly and to restore them.

QUESTIONS ON ISAIAH CHAPTERS 1 AND 3
(READ THE REFERENCES BELOW SO THAT YOU HAVE A FRAMEWORK FROM WHICH TO UNDERSTAND ISAIAH BEFORE ANSWERING THE QUESTIONS IN YOUR NOTEBOOK.)

1. What was the pattern of men's choices apart from the influence of God? [209]
2. What was taking place in Judah and to the social, religious and legal structure? Why?
3. What were the choices made by the people? What was their idol? [210]
4. What is revealed about the hearts/minds of the women of Judah? What was their idol?
5. What did the faces, speech and actions of these people reveal about their hearts and minds?

QUESTIONS ON ISAIAH 1, 5 AND 6

1. In what ways was Israel like a vineyard to the Lord?
2. Write the 6 woe's in your own words, explaining how sinful behavior reflects the mindset?
3. What do you see in verses 12-30 of chapter 5?
4. What do you think happens to a people when the distinctions between good and evil are mixed?
5. Does this describe our nation in any way? Write down each example you see.
6. Why had the people refused and despised God and His Word?
7. What did Isaiah believe about the Lord in chapters 5 and 6?
8. What did Isaiah believe about himself in chapter 6?

---

208. Remind yourself of the warnings in Deuteronomy 28:45-68
209. See Romans 1:18-32, man's natural progression apart from God
210. See Exodus 20:1-26

QUESTIONS ON MATTHEW 21:33-41, MARK 12:1-11 AND LUKE 20:9-20

Jesus used the picture of the vineyard to illustrate many teachings in His earthly journey, but the one in Matthew is similar to the one found in Isaiah 5. Here Jesus began a conversation with the Chief Priest and elders.

1. Whom does Jesus use to be representative of the Chief Priest and elders?
2. To whom did the vineyard in Matthew (also Mark and Luke) belong?
3. Who was Jesus referring to as the husbandmen? And what would happen to them?
4. Who was the son? Who were the servants? What was the meaning of the answer Jesus gave these men?
5. What did the ordinary people know that the rulers did not know? Why?
6. What does the parable of Luke add?

"Jesus said unto them [the Jewish leaders], Did you never read in the scriptures, the stone which the builders rejected, the same is become the head of the corner; this is the Lord's doing, and it is marvelous in our eyes? Therefore say I unto you, the kingdom of God shall be taken from you, and given to a nation bringing forth the fruits thereof … . And when the chief priests and Pharisees had heard his parables, they perceived that he spoke of them. But when they sought to lay hands on him, they feared the multitude, because they took him for a prophet" (Matthew 21:42-46). Jesus said that the works He did testified to the fact that the Father sent Him, and they did. He healed the sick, the lame and the blind and raised the dead. The people heard the words of Christ and believed that He was a prophet, but many still did not respond with trust in the Person of Christ. They were without active faith.

QUESTIONS ON ISAIAH 7:1-25 AND 8:2-3 AND 18

1. Who was Rezin? And who was Remaliah?
2. Why did this confederacy cause Ahaz and his people such fear?
3. What did God say to comfort those bound up in fear?
4. Does having faith mean never having fear?
5. What is the nature of faith?
6. What was the sign? To whom was the sign given? Why was it given? And what was the meaning of his name?
7. Does this have a future fulfillment?

Fear can deceive us by blinding us to the trustworthiness of the Word\heart of our Lord. Jesus is a very different Shepherd. He alone is trustworthy and able to be the righteous King and Good Shepherd, as promised. He knows each one of His flock by name, and He knows what each of us needs. We hear His voice and follow Him. Jesus Christ does not lie, but tells us that in this world we will continually face tribulation. However, in Him, we can live in peace, in spite of our circumstances. [211] Jesus will never hurt, neglect, pass over, misuse or abuse any of His flock, but will give to each eternal life and eternal joy, as He gathers each of us to Himself in unselfish love.

---

211. See John 16:33. I can testify that this verse is true. In Christ, most of the time, you can have peace, no matter the circumstances.

CHAPTER 24

A TALE OF TWO SISTERS (EZEKIEL 23)

This lesson takes place about 145 years after Isaiah. It is a hard message, given to Ezekiel for the people of the two kingdoms. The living God set up a tale of two sisters, using the facts related to each kingdom. He had held His hands out to both, to deliver mercy, but neither would see or hear the truth. He compared the two kingdoms to women who sold their futures by giving themselves over to sin in three specific areas: (1) gross idolatry, (2) trust in the power of ungodly men and (3) confederacies of heathen saturated with wickedness.

1. **Write down what the people did in their gross idolatry.**
2. **What does this use of the things of God, the incense and oil, [212] tell you about their religious practices?**
3. **How did they defile the sanctuary and profane God's Sabbath on the same day?**
4. **How did they trust in the power of ungodly men? Why is this evil?**
5. **With whom did they make confederacies?**
6. **How much did they love their sons and daughters? [213]**
7. **What does God say are our responsibilities to our governments? [214]**

Men naturally look up to those in every culture who are considered to have value above ordinary people. The people of the kingdoms of Israel assumed that religious men and secular leaders who were successful were worthy of their trust. This natural trust that we place in such men is based upon the mistaken assumption that they are worthy. No man is worthy before God, and therefore we are not wise if we put our futures under the control of men.

Thus says the LORD; cursed be the man that trusts in man, and make flesh his arm, and whose heart departs from the LORD. Jeremiah 17:5 **[To Memorize]**

This verse is very strong in its declaration that trust placed in men equates with the heart's departure from trust in the Lord. Why do you think this is true?

Trust in the LORD with all your heart; and lean not unto your own understanding! Proverbs 3:5

---

212. See Exodus 30:22-38 and 40:9-16 for the prescribed use of the anointing oil
213. See Deuteronomy 18:9-22
214. See Matthew 22:21, Mark 12:17, Luke 20:25, Romans 13:7, Ephesians 6:7 and Revelation 22:12

(Oh) how great (is) your goodness, which you have laid up for them that fear you; (which) you have wrought for them that trust in you before the sons of men!   Psalm 31:19

It is better to trust in the LORD than to put confidence in man ... or princes.   Psalm 118:8-9 [215]

Blessed (is) that man that makes the LORD his trust, and respected not the proud, nor such as turn aside to lies.   Psalm 40:4

In God have I put my trust: I will not be afraid what man can do unto me.   Psalm 56:11

And the LORD shall help them, and deliver them: he shall deliver them from the wicked, and save them, because they trust in him.   Psalm 37:40

There shall be a root of Jesse, and he that shall rise to reign over the Gentiles; in him shall the Gentiles trust.   Romans 15:12 [216]

QUESTIONS ON TRUSTING IN MEN (REMEMBER SOLOMON'S SON!)

1. What happens to our heart when we put our trust in men?
2. What is the harm in respecting the proud or those who turn aside to lies?
3. Why is our own understanding suspect?
4. What happens to our heart when we trust in the Lord?
5. Why is it better to trust in the Lord rather than in men or ourselves?
6. Jesus did not put His trust in men, why not?

"But Jesus did not commit himself unto them, because he knew all (men). And needed not that any should testify of man: for he knew what was in man" (John 2:24-25). Jesus knows men in a far deeper way than we can know men, for Jesus knew their motivations and deepest thoughts. The Pharisees were saying that Jesus was casting out devils from within a man by Satan's power. *"And Jesus knew their thoughts and said unto them, every kingdom divided against itself is brought to desolation; and every city or house divided against itself shall not stand"* (Matthew 12:25) [217]

---

215. See also Psalm 146:3
216. Matthew 12:21 *"And in His name the Gentiles trust."*
217. See also John 6:48-66

Jesus entered the synagogue to teach, and there was a man present with a withered arm. The scribes and Pharisees watched Jesus and wondered if He would heal the man on the Sabbath, so that they could accuse Him of breaking the Sabbath regulations. *"But he knew their thoughts, and said to the man which had the withered hand, Rise up, and stand forth in the midst ..."* (Luke 6:8) and the man was healed before the assembly. The Jewish leaders and people could have dropped to their knees at that moment before the Son of God, asking for mercy, but they did not.

Remember, our Lord said something about how we serve Him: *"No servant can serve two masters: for either he will hate the one, and love the other; or else he will hold to the one, and despise the other. You cannot serve God and mammon"* (Luke 16:13). We cannot have multiple masters, as this creates divided loyalties. Either we trust, depend upon and follow men (and their perceptions of truth) or God, for we cannot serve both with our whole heart\mind. *"A double minded man is unstable in all his ways"* (James 1:8).

Our devotion to our Lord must be single-minded. It cannot be shared with any persons or any treasure of this world. In practice, this means you cannot serve your treasures or any other thing and God too. Devotion to self or any precious or highly-esteemed person or thing is idolatry, and God cannot share His heart with idols. No material or philosophical treasure will be in Heaven, and if your heart persists in grasping anything other than the living Lord, you will miss Heaven and an eternity with the Christ who loves us.

Paul said this about himself and those who follow Christ with him: *"... for therefore we both labour and suffer reproach, because we trust in the living God, who is the Savior of all men, especially of those that believe"* (1 Timothy 4:1). *"Now the God of hope fill you with all joy and peace in believing, that you may abound in hope, through the power of the Holy Spirit"* (Romans 15:13). Our Lord Jesus came to give us an abundant life and supernatural joy, even in the midst of tribulations because His love is active and will keep us close to Him, just as He kept the heart\mind of Jeremiah and the Ethiopian. *"Thou will keep him in perfect peace, whose mind is stayed on thee: because he trusted in thee"* (Isaiah 16:3). **[To Memorize]**

Now he which establishes us with you in Christ, and has anointed us, is God; who has also sealed us, and given the earnest of the Spirit in our hearts. That we should be to the praise of his glory, who first trusted in Christ. In whom you also trusted, after you heard the word of truth, the gospel of your salvation: in whom also after that you believed, you were sealed with that holy Spirit of promise, which is the down payment (earnest) of our inheritance until the redemption of the purchased possession ... .

2 Corinthians 1:21-22

Grieve not the Holy Spirit of God, whereby you are sealed unto the day of redemption.

Ephesians 4:30 [218]

---

218. See also Ephesians 1:13-14

We are transferred into Christ's heavenly Kingdom, [219] as believers have obtained an inheritance by grace granted through faith in Christ. We were also sealed with the promised Holy Spirit, for He is the down payment of our inheritance until we are redeemed. [220] He has made a way for us to receive His righteousness that renders us holy and blameless, so now we are able to love God and one another. Through Jesus, all those things that men seek after begin to lose their attractiveness. He has become our Lord and Husband. Therefore, we have put our love and trust in the Messiah.

What more could the Lord have done? He granted *"great goodness toward the house of Israel and Judah dealing with them according to his mercies, and according to the multitude of His loving kindnesses"* (Isaiah 63:7). But they refused every overture, and the Lord had to tell them, *"Your iniquities have turned away these things, and your sins have withheld good things from you"* (Jeremiah 5:25). [221] So they had to go into bondage. Even in justified chastisement, however, God showed mercy for this bondage would work *'for (their) good."* This terrible punishment had a purpose, to bring good to the people in exile.

The Lord is moved by our plight. He is complete within Himself, but out of mercy, love and pity, He sets His heart to deliver His people from Satan and sin. The Lord Jesus determined to pull His children up out of the firestorm of His wrath before our rebellious hearts knew we must yield to Him for life. He came that we would have an abundant life in Him, freed from the controlling pull of sin. This requires active dependence upon Jesus, to be alert to the weakness of our own flesh and to maintain awareness of the wiles of Satan. We will never be able to understand the Lord fully, nor the things He does, but He is in control. *"Trust in the LORD with all your heart; and lean not unto your own understanding"* (Proverbs 3:5). **[To Memorize]**

In Christ, we can have peace and joy, knowing that He loves us and will work out all things for our good. *"And we know that all things work together for good to them that love God, to them who are called according to his purpose"* (Romans 8:28). **[To Memorize]**

QUESTIONS ON ISSUES OF TRUST
(USE THE ENTIRE LESSON, INCLUDING QUOTED SELECTIONS AND REFERENCES TO ANSWER THE FOLLOWING QUESTIONS.)

1. How much of your time\life does Jesus want?
2. What is wrong with trusting men? And what would that mindset imply?
3. What does Jesus know about all of us?
4. What are two reasons that He saves men?

219. 2 Corinthians 1:21-22 *"Now he which established us with you in Christ, and has anointed us, (is) God; who has also sealed us, and given the earnest of the Spirit in our hearts."*
220. See Ephesians 1:11-14
221. *"... for (their) good."* See also Jeremiah 24:5-7

CHAPTER 25

BABYLONIAN BONDAGE (607 — 580 BC)

The book of Jeremiah contains the words of the prophet of God to the remnant—those Jewish peoples left in the lands surrounding Jerusalem after its destruction.

QUESTIONS ON JEREMIAH 37

Then Zedekiah the king sent, and took him out: and the king asked him secretly in his house, and said, Is there (any) word from the Lord? And Jeremiah said, There is: for, said he, you shall be delivered into the hand of the king of Babylon. Moreover Jeremiah said unto King Zedekiah, What have I offended against you or against your servants, or against this people, that you have put me in prison? Where (are) now your prophets which prophesied unto you saying, The king of Babylon shall not come against you nor against this land?

Jeremiah 37:17-19

1. In verse 2, no one believed Jeremiah. Why do you think they refused to acknowledge the truth? They had sufficient proof that Jeremiah spoke the true words of God.
2. Who was deceived? What did King Zedekiah really understand?
3. Why did the rulers keep putting Jeremiah in prison? What were they thinking?

QUESTIONS ON JEREMIAH 38

1. What did Jeremiah tell the people that would save them from death?
2. What did the princes do? What lie did they tell against Jeremiah? Why?
3. Who was Ebedmelech and what did he do? Why?
4. What message from God did Jeremiah relay to the king?
5. What does the phrase *"go forth to the Chaldeans"* mean?
6. What role did pride play in the king's failure to heed the message? (See verses 2 and 17-23)

When rebuked, we will go one of two ways: (1) We will accept the rebuke as valid and act upon what God has said, or (2) we will hate both the message and the messenger. Remember that the religious rulers hated Jesus for the true words He spoke, and here the civil and religious rulers, including the king, hated Jeremiah for the true words he spoke, words from the living God. In Jeremiah 36, a scroll was written that contained all that Jeremiah had preached to the people from

God concerning their sin and the coming destruction. The scroll was read to the people on the day of fasting so that all who came to participate would hear. Afterward, the scroll was read to the princes, and then, last of all, to the king. The king was in no way touched by these words of truth and directed the scroll to be cut into pieces and burned in the fireplace. He sent men to take Jeremiah and Baruch the scribe, but the Lord hid them and directed that they rewrite the scroll.

It was a brave act for Ebedmelech to go to the king to ask for mercy for Jeremiah. Ebedmelech could have been put to death. God had opened his heart to consider the prophet and the words he spoke. Ebedmelech believed that Jeremiah was speaking the truth; therefore he put his trust in God, just like Abraham! *Thus says the Lord, Let not the wise man glory in his wisdom nor the mighty man glory in his might, let not the rich man glory in his riches: but let him glory in this; that he understands and knows me; that I am the Lord, which exercises loving kindness, judgment, and righteousness in the earth: for in these things I delight* (Jeremiah 9:23-24).   **[To Memorize]**

QUESTIONS ON JEREMIAH 39 AND LUKE 2:1-9

1. **What did the king of Babylon say was to be done to Jeremiah?**
2. **What was the king of Judah told to do? What did he do? Why?**
3. **What did the captain of the guard do for the poor people? Why?**
4. **What did King Nebuchadnezzar say to the chief of the executioners?**
5. **Why did God take notice of the Ethiopian? And what does this reveal about the Lord?**

In Amos 9:7, the Lord asks this question of His people having no regard for Him, *"Are you not as the children of the Ethiopians unto me, O children of Israel?"* What He meant was that the Jewish people resembled the Ethiopians, a people whose minds\hearts were alienated from the Lord. It is interesting to note the care of the Lord for this Ethiopian, for the Lord shows mercy to anyone He chooses. The Ethiopian was from a heathen nation, separated from all of the blessing of God's chosen people, and yet God extended mercy and kindness to him because he responded to the truth. Believing that the prophet's words were from the living God, he put his trust in the Lord. This is faith.

Jeremiah the prophet and Ebedmelech the Ethiopian were both men who understood that the man of God speaks the Word of God. Both men put their trust and their hopes in the hands of the living God, for He cared for them. They would not be like the hypocrites [222] or cowards, who neither spoke nor followed the Word of God, while declaring themselves to be from God. While professing to be God's people, the princes, king and people clung to the sayings of the false prophets who pronounced what they wanted to hear, that the Babylonians would not breach the gates. Most of the leaders, being filled with pride, did not want to hear that they must submit to the Chaldeans in order to live. They were also filled with malice, wanting to destroy the man coming in the name of the Lord, just as did those religious rulers of Jerusalem who wished to destroy Jesus. To these

---

222. *Hypocrisy*—acting under a feigned part; that is, (figuratively) deceit: dissimulation, condemnation. One who wears a mask, creates a facade and pretends to be what he is not.

people, religion was just a cloak to mask pride-hardened souls and terminal selfishness. *"The Lord knows the thoughts of the wise, that they are vain.* [223] *Therefore let no man glory in men. For all things are yours"* (1 Corinthians 3:20-21).

These people had seen the army of Babylon come and destroy Jerusalem. Those left alive after the battle for the city witnessed most of the rulers, princes and artisans being carried away. The Babylonians put Gedaliah in charge of the remnant left in the land. What is amazing is the fact that Nebuzaradan, the captain of the Babylonian guard, knew more of Jeremiah and his God than did the Jewish people, and this man obviously respected Jeremiah as the messenger of God, while most of his own people did not.

The word that came to Jeremiah from the LORD, after that Nebuzaradan the captain of the guard had let him go from Ramah, when he had taken him being bound in chains among all that were carried away captive of Jerusalem and Judah, which were carried away captive unto Babylon. And the captain of the guard took Jeremiah, and said unto him, The LORD thy God hath pronounced this evil upon this place. Now the LORD hath brought it, and done according as he hath said: because ye have sinned against the LORD, and have not obeyed his voice, therefore this thing is come upon you. And now, behold, I loose you this day from the chains which (were) upon your hand. If it seems good unto you to come with me into Babylon, come; and I will look well unto you: but if it seems ill unto you to come with me into Babylon, forbear: behold, all the land (is) before you: whither it seems good and convenient for you to go, go. Now while he was not yet gone back, (he said), Go back to Gedaliah the son of Ahikam the son of Shaphan, whom the king of Babylon has made governor over the cities of Judah, and dwell with him among the people: or go wheresoever it seems convenient unto you to go.

So the captain of the guard gave him victuals and a reward, and let him go. Then went Jeremiah unto Gedaliah the son of Ahikam to Mizpah; and dwelt with him among the people that were left in the land.

Jeremiah 40:1-6

QUESTIONS ON JEREMIAH 41

1. Describe what took place in this chapter in your own words.
2. What was Ishmael's thinking?
3. Who was Johanan? And should he have feared the Chaldeans or someone else? Why?

QUESTIONS ON JEREMIAH 42

1. Why did God stress obedience? What should the people have done?
2. Why did the people promise to obey?

---

223. *Vain*—empty, useless, having no value

3. **Explain why Jeremiah's estimation of their motives was correct? (See verses 20-22)** [224]
4. **What did God say would be the penalty for disobeying Him?**

These people were in dire straights, and they sought Jeremiah the prophet and insisted that they would do as God said, if Jeremiah would just intercede on their behalf. They then gave themselves an excuse for "not knowing the will of God." Jeremiah prayed and then reported for the second time God's same negative answer. The people were to stay in the land of Judah. God would take care of the Babylon king, and death awaited them in Egypt. The people revealed themselves to be hypocrites and proved that Jeremiah's assessment of their true heart values was correct. They overruled the orders of the Lord and substituted their perception of truth, that Egypt would be a safe haven, in spite of Gods clear warnings. **Pride prevents us from heeding warnings.** *"Only by pride comes argument, but with those who take advice is wisdom"* (Proverbs 13:10, MKJV). **[To Memorize]**

We see that **pride will not allow us to understand or accept the truth spoken by God. Pride renders our hearts unteachable** and prevents us from listening to warnings. If we have a mind closed by sin, we will trust men over God and be captured by their lies. All of us, before God opens our minds, are self-deceived, like these Jewish people of the Southern Kingdom. We do not deal with ourselves or our perceptions according to the truth of the Scriptures. Instead, we follow the course of least resistance, covering our eyes from seeing and our ears from hearing. Pretending that all is well, we sear our conscience, which may well already be in its last struggles to warn. And if we prevail? Sin reigns in such darkness, and **we will believe in the lies of men and Satan,** just as these people, who were determined to go to Egypt, did.

QUESTIONS ON JEREMIAH 44

This chapter was written to those who had fled to Egypt for safety and is the most amazing chapter in Jeremiah. These people and their parents had seen the promised destruction coming to pass over a period of years. They had been warned repeatedly by God through Jeremiah and told in the beginning that Egypt was forbidden to them as a refuge. The Word from God given through Jeremiah had been demonstrated to be as sure as the nightfall. Still, **they did not yield to the truth,** but **suppressed it within their own minds,** so that **the false prophets' lies had become truth to them.** [225] **Seeds of spiritual darkness always bloom in the fertile soil of pride,** and **pride deceives us by blinding us to reality.**

Therefore now thus says the LORD, the God of hosts, the God of Israel; Wherefore do you commit (this) great evil against your souls, to cut off from you man and woman, child and suckling, out of Judah, to leave you one to remain; in that you provoke me unto wrath with the works of your hands, burning incense

---

224. *Dissimulation*—(in asking God's will and in disobedience after they were told God's will) to vacillate, that is, reel or stray (literally or figuratively): to deceive, (cause to, make to) err, pant, seduce, cause to wander, make to stagger
225. Spiritual Blindness See John 5, Luke 6:7, 13:14: 2 Corinthians 4:3-7 and 2 Thessalonians 2:7-12

unto other gods in the land of Egypt, where you have gone to dwell, that you might cut yourselves off, and that you might be a curse and a reproach among all the nations of the earth? Jeremiah 44:7-8

1. **Verses 1-14 highlight the truth of God's message. Had these people lost their minds? Or is there some other explanation?**
2. **What were the wives doing to dishonor the Lord?**
3. **If their husbands knew this was going on, why did they not stop it, as they should have?** [226]
4. **What was the argument and justification for worshiping *"the Queen of Heaven"*?**
5. **Explain how the people could have such a wrong view of cause and effect, giving the credit for good to *"the Queen of Heaven"*?** [227]
6. **How could the people not see the truth?** [228] **What was the truth?**
7. **How does pride relate to spiritual blindness?** [229]
8. **Why did the Lord let a few escape and make it back to Israel?** [230]

Following the reasoning of the people in verses 15-18, how could they come to this conclusion? They had seen the northern and southern kingdoms crushed under hostile civilizations. The majority of the people had been killed, captured or carried away, to never return, because they trusted men rather than God. *"From this place also you will go out with your hands on your head; for the LORD has rejected those in whom you trust, and you will not prosper with them"* (Jeremiah 2:37). **[To Memorize]**

To the people who wanted refuge in Egypt, the Lord said, *"Behold I am going to punish Amon of Thebes, and Pharaoh, and Egypt, along with her gods and her kings, even Pharaoh and those who trust in him"* (Jeremiah 46:25). God will not allow us to continue to commit to the person or precepts of men, for they become idols when we put our trust in them. Are they not only men, having no power except that which is given by God for His own reasons? The Lord gives hope to those who trust in Him. Every single warning given by God through the prophets had been fulfilled to the letter. There was something amiss, and it was spiritual blindness. Judah and Samaria were both so bound by pride that they could no longer see the truth. They were like mules with blinders, believing the road beneath their feet was the whole of reality.

QUESTIONS ON JOHN 5:1-47

1. **What did Jesus demonstrate to the Jews by the miracle?**
2. **What did Jesus say about His Father that added fuel to the hate of the Jewish rulers?**
3. **What powers did Jesus say His Father had given Him?**

---

226. See Numbers 30:1-16 (This concerned vows made to God for good, but the point is that God would still hold men responsible if they see an oath made to the "Queen of Heaven" and do nothing to prevent it.)
227. See Deuteronomy 8
228. See 2 Corinthians 4:1-6, 2 Thessalonians 2:7-14 (to happen in the future before Christ's Second Coming), Matthew 9:13, 21:27-32, Acts 5:30-31, 11:1-18 and 20:18-21
229. Review the verses on Pride on page 60.
230. *Mercy*—See 2 Chronicle 6:37-39

4. **What reason did Jesus give for His purpose?**
5. **What witness proved His contention of being the Life-Giver?**
6. **What was missing from these men that proved Jesus' contention about them?**

Being familiar with the Old Testament, these rulers knew that God had promised to send a prophet from among the people who would be like Moses and would speak the words given by the Father. Anyone who did not obey His words would be held accountable for what he had heard. *"The Lord thy God will raise up unto thee a Prophet from the midst of thee, of thy brethren, like unto me; unto him shall ye hearken ... and he shall speak unto them all that I shall command him. And it shall come to pass, that whosoever will not hearken unto my words which he shall speak in my name, I will require it of him"* (Deuteronomy 18:15 and 18-22).

A prophet was to be judged as worthy of death if He said something was "from the Lord," and it did not come to pass, or if his words undermined the Word or ways of God. Most of the Jewish leaders did not wait to see what would come to pass of the promises of our Lord Jesus, but totally rejected all of His words and their implications.

[Jesus said this], Verily, verily, I say unto you, he that hears my word, and believes on Him that sent me, has everlasting life, and shall not come into condemnation; but is passed from death unto life. Verily, verily, I say unto you, the hour is coming, and now is, when the dead shall hear the voice of the Son of God: and they that hear shall live.   John 5:24-25 [231]

Jesus, when he had cried again with a loud voice, yielded up the ghost, and behold, the veil of the temple was rent in half from the top to the bottom; and the earth did quake, and the rocks rent; and the graves were opened; and many bodies of the saints which slept arose, and came out If the graves after His resurrection, and went into the holy city, and appeared to many.   Matthew 27:50-53

The remnant of people left in Jerusalem refused to acknowledge the truth of the Word of God given by Jeremiah and the other prophets, in spite of having seen their dire predictions come to pass. Jesus Christ, our Lord, faced the same refusal to accept His words as valid. The Jewish leaders did not consider Jesus as being the foretold Messiah, in spite of His ability to perform miracles in public view, thereby fulfilling many of the Scriptures given to identify the Messiah.

And He [Jesus] came to Nazareth, where He had been brought up and, as His custom was, He went into the synagogue on the Sabbath day, and stood up for to read. And there was delivered unto Him the book of the prophet Isaiah. And when He had opened the book, He found the place where it was written, The Spirit of the Lord (is) upon me, because He has anointed me to preach the gospel to the poor; He has sent me to heal the broken hearted, to preach deliverance to the captives, and recovering of sight to the blind, to set at liberty them that are bruised, to preach the acceptable year of the Lord.

---

231. In John 11, Lazarus came to life and walked out of his place of burial at the command of Jesus.

And He closed the book, and He gave (it) again to the minister, and sat down. And the eyes of all them that were in the synagogue were fastened on Him. And He began to say unto them, This day is this scripture fulfilled in your ears.
Luke 4:16-21

Jesus then went out and proceeded to preach the Gospel to the poor, deliver men bound by Satan, heal the blind, the lame and the sick and raise the dead.

Skeptics focus on whatever fits within their own world view and reject those truths that do not conform to their thinking. Jesus deliberately did miracles on the Sabbath, to challenge their view. Here it was a feast day and a Sabbath, and this man had been there by the pool for thirty-eight years. The Jews focused on the fact that he was carrying his sleeping mat on the Sabbath, thereby violating the admonition to do no work on this day. When the man mentioned that he had been made whole, the Jewish leaders focused on the One who had dared do the miracle on the Sabbath, not on the undeniable fact that the man was healed and standing whole before them.

This is the pattern we see through the ages. Men refuse to acknowledge that the Word of God is the Truth. Now the Jews sought all the more to kill Jesus because they judged that He had broken the Sabbath and blasphemed God by calling Him *"Father."* [232] This is another demonstration of the power of self-deception generated by pride. Pride renders the heart unteachable and prevents us from heeding warnings. It is also a testament to the working of Satan in the mind of men through pride.

But if our gospel be hid, it is hid to them that are lost: in whom the god of this world has blinded the minds of them which believe not, lest the light of the glorious gospel of Christ, who is the image of God, should shine unto them. ... For God, who commanded the light to shine out of the darkness, has shined into our hearts, to give the light of the knowledge of the glory of God in the face of Jesus Christ.
2 Corinthians 4:3-4   **[To Memorize]**

232.See Matthew 12:1-23 and Luke 6:1-1

CHAPTER 26

"THEY WOULD NOT HEAR"

We have seen from all the scriptures studied that faith does not automatically come from seeing the Word of the Lord fulfilled. The Jewish people had more than a thousand years of God's messages of warning, His laws and testimonies for instruction in righteousness and His many promises to lead the way, and yet only a small remnant of them believed and followed the Lord. What more could He have done for such a rebellious people? [233] They had been chosen by the Lord to be a living testimony of the many perfections of our God for all the other nations to see. [234] The Lord had demonstrated to them time after time that His Word was true and that truth was spoken by the mouths of the numerous prophets He sent. The people heard the Word and saw the repercussions of non-compliance, but still they did not honor either God or His Word, reaping unto themselves the rewards of rebellion. [235] Pride is a great dam that holds our self-tailored perceptions, justifications and chosen beliefs. Pride will not heed warnings or acknowledge God's authority. It refuses to hear God's truth or keep any law but its own. Pride grows a heavy crop of self-deception, which does not allow reality to intrude.

Romans 10:17 states, *"So then faith comes by hearing and hearing by the word of God."* This is truly how God works, so what is missing? In Hebrews 3, the answer is found with which to solve the problem of those who hear but do not hear, who see but do not perceive. They have no faith. Why?

QUESTIONS ON HEBREWS 3:1-4:2

Wherefore, holy brethren, partakers of the heavenly calling, consider the Apostle and High Priest of our profession, Christ Jesus; who was faithful to him that appointed him, as also Moses (was faithful) in all his house. For this (man) was counted worthy of more glory than Moses, inasmuch as he who has built the house has more honor than the House ... , and Moses was faithful in all his house, as a servant, for a testimony of those things which were to be spoken after; but Christ as a son over his own house; whose house are we, if we hold fast the confidence and the rejoicing of the hope firm unto the end.

Wherefore as the Holy Ghost says, (To day if you will hear his voice, harden not your hearts as in the day of temptation in the wilderness: when your fathers tempted me, proved me, and saw my works forty years, wherefore I was grieved with that generation, and said, They do always err in their heart; and they have not known my ways so I swear in my wrath, they shall not enter into my rest. Hebrews 3:7-11

233. See Isaiah 43
234. See Deuteronomy 7:6-15
235. See Roman 1:18-32, the downward course of men who suppress the truth and will not hear God

Take heed, brethren, lest there be in any of you AN EVIL HEART OF UNBELIEF in departing from the living God. But exhort one another daily, while it is called to day; lest any of you be HARDENED THROUGH THE DECEITFULNESS OF SIN. For we are make partakers of Christ, if we hold the beginning of our confidence steadfast unto the end; while it is said, To day if you will hear his voice, harden not your hearts, as in the provocation … . But with whom was God grieved forty years? Was it not those who had sinned, whose carcasses fell in the wilderness? [236] *And to whom did he swear that they would not enter into his rest, but to those that believed not? So we see that THEY COULD NOT ENTER IN BECAUSE OF UNBELIEF. Therefore let us fear, lest, a promise of entering into his rest is missed, should we seem to come short of it. For unto us was the gospel preached, as well as unto them: BUT THE WORD PREACHED DID NOT PROFIT THEM, NOT BEING MIXED WITH FAITH IN THEM THAT HEARD.*

Hebrews 3:7-19 and 4:1-2, Emphasis added

1. *What did the writer mean by "harden not your heart"?*
2. **What took place in the wilderness?**
3. **How are we *"hardened by the deceitfulness of sin"*?**
4. **What is the condition in verse 6?**
5. **What truth applied to men in Moses' time? To men at the time of Christ? And still today?**
6. **What does this phrase mean, *"but Christ as a son over His own house: whose house we are"*?**
7. **What is this *"rest"*?**
8. **How do you enter into this rest? How do you choose not to enter into the rest of Christ?**
9. **Where are we to go in time of need? Why?**

The explanation given in Hebrews 3 for the unbelief of the people aids our understanding of the results of sin-hardened hearts. Before the period of the kings, earlier in Jewish history, God had called His people into Egypt, and they stayed there for four hundred years. God then instructed Moses to bring His people out of Egypt and into the Promised Land, to live and worship Him. Remember that they refused to go into this land because they trusted their own judgment over God's command. Therefore, He let them wander in the desert wilderness for forty years. [237] The writer of Hebrews was underscoring the importance of our Lord Jesus and the importance of having an opened mind. A mind that is receptive to the Gospel gives a response of trust, believing in the Lord to the point of obedience, just as Abraham did. This is what active faith looks like.

It was just as necessary for those in the Old Testament to keep their hearts open, responding with trust and obedience to the promises of God. The people had seen miracles in Egypt and throughout those forty years in the desert. [238] But pride worked as a shield against the truth, and the people did not heed the warnings of the prophets sent by God.

236. See Exodus chapters 16-17 and 19-20, Numbers chapters 13-27 and Deuteronomy chapters 1-12
237. See Numbers 11-14, to see the reason for the forty years of wandering in the wilderness
238. Read the book of Exodus to see the various responses of the people to our Lord

Therefore, God called the Assyrian armies to carry away the Northern Kingdom. The people of the Southern Kingdom knew what happened to the North, and still they persisted in their sin, refusing to turn to God with repentance from their evil.

The conditions confronting all true seekers after God are the same throughout both Testaments. Men must come to God through faith placed in God and His Word. Repeated refusals to respond to the true words of God always harden our hearts\mind, because sin deceives us, and we will not see or value the truth any longer. Repentance is not a separate step in faith. It is the response of our heart\mind to the revelation of divine truth. [239] Remember that our perceptions have been molded by us. We modify all that we hear, see and read. Sin influenced and filtered everything that went into our minds. Repentance is the process whereby the false perceptions of our sin-hardened heart\mind are broken up, causing us to see and believe the truths of God. Much like a Troy-built tiller breaks up clay, our home-made perceptions are broken up as we are changed by the Holy Spirit. Repentance is the active response of faith in God.

QUESTIONS ON HEBREWS 11:1, 3 AND 6

Now faith is the substance of things hoped for, the evidence of things not seen ... . Through faith we understand the worlds were framed by the word of God, so that things which are seen were not made of the things which do appear. But without faith it is impossible to please him: for he that comes to God must believe that he is, and that he is a rewarder of them that diligently seek him. [240] These [the old prophets and the believing remnant] all died in faith, not having received the promises but having seen them afar off and were persuaded of them and embraced them and confessed that they were strangers and pilgrims on the earth.   Hebrews 11:1, 3, 6 and 13   **[To Memorize]**

1. **What is faith?**
2. **Why is it impossible to please God if we have no faith?**

"Faith is being persuaded of, giving credence to, having assurance of, a moral conviction of biblical truth, and the inward assurance of the absolute <u>truthfulness</u> [241] of God."[242] We hear the Word of God concerning salvation, and we believe to the point of giving our complete trust and our futures into the hands of God. Through the Spirit, we are bonded to our Lord Jesus with a powerful glue, and it will not be undone. Do you see that the Word of God did not profit the people of the two kingdoms because it was not mixed with any faith in them that heard it? Why? Because they were deceived by sin, and their hearts were hardened by the repeated refusal to heed the Word and respond with submission to the will to God. Do

---

239. Ephesians 2:8 *"For by grace are you saved through faith; and that not of yourselves: it is the gift of God."*
240. Read Hebrews 11:1-6 to understand the "faith that has feet."
241. *Truthfulness*—Veracity, being devoted to the Truth, having power to convey and perceive the Truth
242. Strongs, under the explantation of faith.

you see what Jeremiah and the other prophets sent by God had that most of the rulers and people did not have? Jeremiah believed God, and he believed that every word spoken by God was true, every promise He made would be fulfilled and that every decision God made was right. He trusted God with his very life. Job said, "... *though He slay me, yet will I trust in Him ...*" (Job 13:15).

Let us labor therefore to enter into that rest, lest any man fall after the same example of unbelief. For the word of God (is) quick, and powerful, and sharper than any two-edged sword, piercing even to the dividing asunder of soul and spirit, and of the joints and marrow, and (is) a discerner of the thoughts and intents of the heart. Neither is there any creature that is not manifest in his sight: but all things (are) naked and opened unto the eyes of him with whom we have to do.

Hebrews 4:11-13   **[To Memorize]**

The Lord is fully aware of our lack of faith and will give us the faith to act. Jesus said this to give us hope: [243] *"All that the Father gives me shall come to me; and him that comes to me I will in no wise cast out"* (John 6:3). Submit; place your complete trust upon Jesus, the One sent and sealed by the Father. Jesus has already demonstrated how much love He has for us through His death on the cross, and He will never abandon us.

---

243. See Mark 9:24

Chapter 27

FALSE SHEPHERDS VS. TRUE SHEPHERDS

... Hearken not unto the words of the prophets that prophesy unto you: they make you vain: they speak a vision of their own heart, and not out of the mouth of the LORD. They say unto them that despise me, The LORD has said, You shall have peace; and they say unto every one that walks after the imagination of his own heart, No evil shall come upon you.   Jeremiah 23:16-17

It is important to realize that all men are to give an account of their lives before the Lord. However, religious leaders will be judged without mercy if they violate the precepts of the Lord, particularly in worship and teaching the Word. Why? The false religious leader holds the souls of the others in his hands. The Lord has given His Word as the means by which men are taught the character of God, along with His absolute truth and His principles, which guide His people. The Word serves also to warn all people of the firestorm of the wrath of God.

QUESTIONS ON JEREMIAH 23 (740 BC)

1. What had the shepherds done to the people who followed them?
2. The *"righteous Branch of the house of David"* will reign. What will He do differently? What did Jeremiah know about the Lord?
3. What did Jeremiah know about the priests and prophets?
4. What was the state of Jeremiah? And what was his message to the people?
5. What were the lies that leaders spoke? [244]
6. What did they pervert?
7. If they had been faithful, what would have been the outcome?

And the Word of Jehovah came to me, saying, Son of man say to her: ... A plot by her prophets in her midst, like a roaring lion tearing the prey. They have devoured souls; they have taken the treasure and precious things; they multiplied her many widows in her midst. Her priests have broken My Law and have defiled My holy things. They have put no difference between the holy and the common, and have not taught between the unclean and the clean, and have hidden their eyes from My Sabbaths, and I am defiled among them.   Ezekiel 22:23 and 25-26

---

244. See Jeremiah 9:1-9 and 2 Peter 2

QUESTIONS ON EZEKIEL 22:1-31
(AGAIN THE LORD SENT A PROPHET TO WARN THE PEOPLE OF COMING DESTRUCTION. USE ALL OF THE REFERENCES TO ANSWER THE FOLLOWING QUESTIONS.)

1. Make a list of the evils done by the prophets, [245] princes, priests and people.
2. How were the poor to be treated? [246] What does verse 7 imply?
3. Had they been warned? [247] Which laws of the Decalogue had they broken?
4. Ideally how are leaders to function? Which components failed in this case? [248] And why did they fail?
5. What does verse 31 mean when it says, *"I have brought their own way upon their heads"*? [249] And how is this fulfilled?
6. Read Micah 3:1-12 and consider what is said there that adds understanding.

QUESTIONS ON EZEKIEL 34

1. Write down all the ways in which the shepherds used their flock.
2. How did these shepherds rule?
3. In verses 18-19, what does the word image help you to see?
4. What did these shepherds think within themselves? [250]
5. What shepherd will God put in charge of His flock? [251]
6. How will this Shepherd treat God's flock?
7. How does the thinking of God's Shepherd differ from these shepherds?

Remember, these profane [252] and false shepherds (pastors, priests, princes or prophets) in Jeremiah and Ezekiel were full of vanity and cursing, bound up in pride and covetousness and full of sexual and spiritual immorality. They perverted the Word of God, betrayed the trust given them and used the flock of God to keep themselves warm and fed. Neglecting to care for those under their rule, as they had been given charge, they caused the people to be scattered into harm's way. The weapon used against the people by the false prophet was lies coming continually out of their hearts\minds into their mouths. Remember also that if these false leaders had stood and pronounced only the Word of God, the people would have been turned from their evil ways. [253]

---

245. See Deuteronomy 13:1-18
246. See Deuteronomy 15:1-18 and Leviticus 25:35-55
247 See Deuteronomy 17:1-13
248. See Micah 3:1-13
249. A principle of cause and effect, see Jeremiah 2:19-37
250. See Jeremiah 8:1-12
251. See John 10:1-30
252. *Profane*—to soil, especially in a moral sense: corrupt, defile, pollute
253. See Jeremiah 23:22

2 PETER 2
TO ADD TO YOUR UNDERSTANDING, MAKE A GROUPING OF THE CHARACTERISTICS OF THE FALSE PROPHETS AND TEACHERS.

1. What do they preach?
2. How do they speak?
3. What do they believe?
4. What are they really after?
5. What do they think of the people and resources of the Church?
6. What are they in bondage to?
7. What do they despise and have contempt for?

QUESTIONS ON JOHN 8:28-58

If God were your Father, you would love Me, for I proceeded forth and have come from God, neither came I of myself but He sent Me. Why do you not understand my speech? (Even) because you cannot hear my word. You are of (your) father the devil, and the lusts of your father you will do. He is a murderer from the beginning and abode not in the truth, because there is no truth in him. When he speaks a lie, he speaks it of his own: for he is a liar, and the father of it. And because I tell (you) the truth, you believe me not. Which of you convicts of sin? And if I say the truth, why do you not believe me? He that is of God hears God's words: you therefore hear (them) not, because you are not of God.

John 8:42-47　**[To Memorize]**

1. What did Jesus mean when He said, *"Whosoever commits sin is the servant of sin"*?
2. What is the truth that will make you free?
3. Who was the real father? Why?
4. What does the love of Christ have to do with this discussion?
5. What particular sins does Jesus focus on in dealing with these men?
6. What are the major truths found here in this discussion?
7. What proof did they have that Jesus spoke the truth?
8. Why did Jesus respond with such sharp accusations against these leaders of the people?
9. In verse 24, what was Jesus referring to when He said, *"I am (he)"*?

Jesus spoke, *"If you continue in my word, (then) you are my disciples indeed; and you shall know the truth, and the truth shall make you free"* (John 8:32). The Word of Christ Jesus sets you free from the lies of Satan and the misconceptions and false perceptions found within us, as well as the philosophies of men. In order to live comprehending that truth, we gratefully bend to God's will. *"Love does not rejoice in unrighteousness but rejoices in the truth"* (1 Corinthians 13:6). Jesus Christ's truth emanates from the Father, and this truth is valid. Salvation is found in none other than the living Christ. All men can tell you only of their own perceptions of reality, just as did the false prophets. *"How blessed is the man who has made the Lord his trust, and has not turned to the proud, nor such as turn aside to lies"* (Psalm 40:4). **[To Memorize]**

The self-deceived, false shepherds of Jesus' day routinely corrupted the words of the living God, twisting the Holy Word as a cover over the preaching of their own perceptions or traditions, [254] rather than the holy teachings of God. Promising liberty to others, they were controlled by various lusts of the flesh. They were men who despised the rule of the godly, speaking against them. When their hate was perfect, they murdered the Lamb of God and later His followers.

There was no shadow of sin that marred the heart\mind of our Lord Jesus. He loved righteousness and hated iniquity. [255] His desire was always to love the Father and accomplish His will, the redemption of the lost. Jesus in no way resembled these men who wished to use the things of God for material advantage and for power over other men. Our Lord Jesus used the things of God to give men understanding of the majesty of the living God and His amazing and abundant love. The Son of God brought the ancient truth to full light, the truth that freedom from all of the enslaving sins of men comes through His blood. He came speaking the eternal truth, which leads men into an everlasting loving relationship with the Son and Father. Jesus did not seek His own glory, but spoke the truth that the Father honored Him, and men dishonored Him. *"That all men should honor the Son, even as they honor the Father He that does not honor the Son does not honor the Father which has sent him"* (John 5:23). Contrary to the belief of many, Jesus is the only way to the Father and the only One through whom salvation comes unto men. Jesus spoke the truth that He existed before Father Abraham. The cold hearts\minds of the Pharisees and scribes reached peak fury, and they determined to kill Him. [256] Sin-enslaved men with dead hearts and hostile minds often respond to Jesus with fury. Jesus Christ guided men to the Father who had sent Him, to worship Him in spirit and truth through Jesus. *"Jesus said unto him, I am the way, the truth, and the life: no man comes unto the Father, but by Me"* (John 14:6). *"No one can come to Me unless the Father who has sent Me draw him, and I will raise him up at the last day"* (John 6:44). **[To Memorize]**

Jesus also made it clear that His words were equal to those of the Father. [257] *"For He whom God has sent speaks the words of God; for He gives the Spirit without measure. The Father loves the Son and has given all things into His hand. He who believes in the Son has eternal life; but he who does not obey the Son will not see life, but the wrath of God abides on Him"* (John 3:33-36).

Jesus pointed out that people who hear Him, that is, with careful attention, leading to a response of obedience and worship, are, in fact, people of God. These false leaders could not and would not hear Jesus' words because they had very different hearts\minds. Their characters mirrored their

---

254. Matthew 15:2-3 *"Why do your disciples transgress the tradition of the elders? For they do not wash their hands when they eat bread? But He [Jesus] answered and said to them, why do you also transgress the commandment of God by your tradition?"* Mark 7:9 *"And He [Jesus] said to them, Do you do well to set aside the commandment of God, so that you may keep your own tradition?"*
255. See Hebrews 1:9
256. See John 8:58-59
257. See John 8:31-59

spiritual father and mentor, the evil one, who continually constructs lies, as did those men who were denounced by the prophets Jeremiah, Ezekiel, Amos and Isaiah. This was still true after Christ ascended into Heaven. *"Also men shall arise from your own selves, speaking perverse things in order to draw disciples away after them"* (Acts 20:30).

QUESTIONS ON JOHN 10:1-16

1. Why do the sheep hear only the voice of the true Shepherd?
2. How do the sheep know the true Shepherd? In what way is Jesus *"the Door"*?
3. What is in the mind\heart of the false shepherds?
4. What do we learn in these verses about Jesus?

Jesus came as the Good Shepherd of the sheep, and never was He unfaithful in His care of His flock. He prayed for them continually and fed them when they were hungry and exhausted. Our Lord Jesus was skillful in His handling of each one, using speech empowered through the Holy Spirit to open the mind, bring comfort and heal those He encountered. How are we to discern the true teacher from the false today?

QUESTIONS ON 1 JOHN 4:1-21
(BEFORE YOU READ THIS LESSON, WRITE DOWN A DEFINITION OF LOVE, MAKING IT AS CLEAR AS YOU CAN.)

Ye are of God, little children, and have overcome them: because greater is He that is in you, than he that is in the world.   1 John 4:4 **[To Memorize]**

1. What is in the confession of a true believer?
2. What is to be the overcoming character trait of a true believer'?
3. How far does the limit of love reach?

QUESTIONS ON 1 TIMOTHY 4:1-3

Now the Spirit speaks expressly, that in the latter times some shall depart from the faith, giving heed to seducing spirits, and doctrines of devils; speaking lies in hypocrisy; having their conscience seared with a hot iron; forbidding to marry, and commanding to abstain from meats, which God has created to be received with thanksgiving of them which believe and know the truth.   1 Timothy 4:1-3

1. How do you identify seducing spirits, which bring false doctrines?
2. What does it mean *"to speak lies in hypocrisy"*?
3. What does it mean that their conscience was seared?

4. **What is the correct teaching or doctrine for marriage and food?**
5. **If we don't know the correct teaching on a subject, how do we find it?**

There was no shadow of sin that marred the heart\mind of our Lord Jesus. Again, He loved righteousness and hated iniquity. Jesus said, *"Greater love has no man than this, that a man lay down his life for his friends"* (John 15:13), and He proceeded to demonstrate the truth of that statement. Jesus did not seek His own glory. He delivered us from sin, that we might really love our families and neighbors and pity even the enemies of good. Jesus has become our hope and desire, and to know Him more intimately than we know ourselves has become our goal.

The Scriptures are to be the standard by which we judge the teachings of anyone who comes in the name of the Lord or whoever comes in his own name. Our Father has given believers both Old and New testaments as the record of God's eternal and inerrant truth, to stand against the philosophies and precepts of men. The indwelling Spirit uses the truth of the Scriptures to help us sift through the teachings of men and to alert us to false or twisted principles parading as the truth. We must heed these warnings today, for many a wolf hides in the shadows of the woods which surrounds the Christian. If Satan cannot have our soul, he will distort the truth and send evil men to bring lies, speculations and false doctrines into the Body of believers. Jesus warned us to judge the fruit of those who might be false prophets or teachers. *"A good tree cannot bring forth evil fruit; neither can a corrupt tree bring forth good fruit"* (Matthew 7:15 and 18). Jesus spoke to the Pharisees, *"O generation of vipers, how can you, being evil, speak good things: for out of the abundance of the heart the mouth speaks"* (Matthew 12:34).

I remind myself of this truth often. We have in our hands the ancient records of the two judgments of Israel and the truth of the third judgment sometime in the future, to come upon the whole world system. There is no reason to doubt Jesus. We know His truth and learn through Him how to love the living God, our families and our neighbors. God has made us like the shepherds in this sense: we are called to do what they did not do. We are to love our Lord, and following His commandments demonstrates that our love is real. Out of a new heart and renewed mind we are to love our brothers and sisters in Christ and pray for them, according to the words of prayer and exhortation found in the Scriptures. We are to come along side others, to help carry their burdens, bind up their wounds and comfort them in their distresses. We love our fellowmen and even our enemies and show it by praying for them, as well as speaking to them the truth in love. Jesus did all of this and also gave His life for us who were His enemies. Therefore, from Jesus we learn something of the scope of godly love and what unselfishness really entails.

PART VI

THE GENTILE KINGDOMS AS EXAMPLES

CHAPTER 28

THE CRUEL ASSYRIANS

We have been studying pride within mankind in general and in the Jewish people in particular. However, prideful thinking is the universal trait of all kingdoms. Prideful mindsets occur when men incorporate their personal perceptions and prejudices into their minds, while deliberately refusing to hear the truth of God. They rationalize choices, striving to do whatever is considered necessary to meet or exceed the desires of mind and body.

Now let us consider the pride-dominated thinking of the most powerful Gentile kings and overlords. The Assyrian and Babylonian civilizations came into contact with the Jewish people and their God. In what ways did pride manipulate the thinking of these Gentile rulers?

During the reign of Hezekiah, the King of Judah, Sennacherib, King of Assyria, came against all the fortified cities of Judah and seized them and surrounded Jerusalem. God had great mercy, delivering Jerusalem and the Southern Kingdom, giving the Jewish people more time to turn away from their willful choices to do all that God had warned them against.

QUESTIONS ON 2 KINGS 18 AND 19

A representative from the Assyrian king was speaking to King Hezekiah of Israel: "Hear you the words of the great king of Assyria. Let not Hezekiah deceive you: for he shall not be able to deliver you. Neither let Hezekiah make you to trust in the LORD saying, The LORD will surely deliver us: this city shall not be delivered into the hands of the king of Assyria. Don't listen to him make an agreement with me, come out to me and I will let you stay on your land until I come and take you to a land much like your land. Have any of the gods of the other countries been able to deliver his land from the hand of the king of Assyria?

2 Kings 18:28-33

1. **What was the Assyrian king's attitude toward the Jewish people?**
2. **What did the Assyrian king believe about himself? And how did he die?**
3. **What was the Assyrian king's assumption concerning the Jewish God? And how was he used by God?**
4. **What can we learn about our own assumptions from this?**
5. **What kind of man was Hezekiah?**
6. **What was the Lord's answer? Why? (See Isaiah 37:28-29)**

[Hezekiah prayed to the Lord, It is true, O LORD, the kings of Assyria have laid waste to all the nations, and cast their gods into the fire: for they were the work of men's hands. Now therefore, O LORD our God, save us from his hand that all the kingdoms of the earth may know that you are the only true LORD.   2 Kings 19:17-19

[The Lord answered by Isaiah to the King of Assyria, Whom have you offended and blasphemed, and against whom have you exalted your voice and lifted up your eyes, against the Holy One of Israel! I know where you sit, when you go out and come in, and your rage against me. Because you rage against me and your noise has come to my ears, I will put my hook in your nose, and my bridle in your lips, and I will turn you around and send you back. The king of Assyria shall not come into this city, nor shoot an arrow there nor come before it with shields, nor build a bank against it … . I will defend the city … . Behold, he shall hear a rumor and return to his own land; where I will cause him to fall by the sword in his own land.   2 Kings 19:22, 27-28, 32 and 34-35

Then the angel of the LORD went forth and smote the camp of the Assyrians and when Israel arose the next morning there was one hundred eighty-five thousand corpses.   Isaiah 37:36

So Sennacherib king of Assyria departed and dwelt at Nineveh. As he was worshiping in the house of his god, two of his sons killed him with the sword.   2 Kings 19:26-37

The Assyrian view of the incident is what you would expect. There was a tablet found in Assyria which says that King Hezekiah would not bow down, so he was bound to his city like a bird in a cage. [258]

In our text the Lord is speaking to Isaiah, and He lets us see the pride within the heart\mind of the Assyrian king. The Assyrian kings and warriors were men of great cruelty.

However he does not mean so, neither does his heart think so but it is in his heart to destroy many nations I will punish the fruit of the stout heart of the king of Assyria, and the glory of his high looks, for he says, BY THE STRENGTH OF MY HAND I HAVE DONE THIS, AND BY MY WISDOM; FOR I AM PRUDENT: AND HAVE REMOVED ALL THE BOUNDARIES OF THEIR OWNERSHIP, I HAVE PUT DOWN THE INHABITANTS LIKE A VALIANT MAN; THERE ARE NONE THAT CAN MOVE THE WING, OR OPEN THE MOUTH, OR PEEP?
                          Isaiah 10:7 and 12-14, Emphasis added   **[To Memorize]**

It is certain that successful and powerful men believe that they have accomplished everything by their own will. It is interesting to note that this king had no idea of the depth of

---

258. This information was gleaned from a series presented on the History channel about "Mesopotamia."

cruelty to which he was capable of sinking. The king also had no idea that he was a pawn in the hand of God, being called out of the boundaries of his country to accomplish God's will.

> *For he flatters himself in his own eyes, until his iniquity be found to be hateful. The words of his mouth are iniquity and deceit: he has left off to be wise, and to do good.*   Psalm 36:2-3

Out of mercy the Lord chose to wait to chastise Israel, until evil had reached saturation, and then retribution began. It is interesting to note that the principle found here has been in effect for some time. God told Abraham that his descendants would serve another nation for four hundred years but would not come out of captivity until the iniquity of the Amorites was complete. [259] The Lord had warned repeatedly, but His people had deliberately chosen to commit iniquity for generations and were now ripe for destruction. King David spoke this truth, *"If I regard iniquity in my heart, the Lord will not hear (me)"* (Psalm 66:18) **[To Memorize]**

There is never a time that God is unaware of our thoughts and motivations, just as He was well aware of the thoughts of Judah. If we have regard for evil within, as they did, and will not turn in repentance, then the Lord will not hear us.

The Lord sent this message to Ezekie1 [260] the prophet to speak against the Ammonites, an enemy of Israel:

> *For so says the Lord Jehovah: Because you have clapped your hands and stamped the foot, and rejoiced in heart with all your spite against the land of Israel; behold, therefore I will stretch our My hand on you, and will give you as a prize to the nations. And I will cut you off from the peoples, and I will cause you to perish out of the lands. I will destroy you, and you shall know that I am Jehovah.*
>
> Ezekiel 25:6-7

In this message, the Lord promised to punish the pride and arrogance of the self-righteousness exhibited by the enemies of Israel.

We Christians are not given the option of hating others, even our enemies. Love demands that we always deal with people, remembering it is only the mercy and the grace of God that pulled us out from under the wrath of God. The Lord has said, *"Dearly beloved, avenge not yourselves, but rather give place unto wrath: for it is written, Vengeance is mine; I will repay, saith the Lord"* (Ezekiel 25:12 and 15). [261] Christ Jesus is the only one without sin and the only one able to accurately read the mind, as well as the motives, of men.

---

259. See Genesis 15:7-16
260. See the entire account in Ezekiel 25:1-10
261. See also Deuteronomy 32:35, 41 and 43 and Jeremiah 51:6

QUESTIONS ON ROMANS 12

It is time we got over the pride and prejudices that bind all of us to some degree. Godly love requires us to lay down selfishness and self-absorption. Jesus cultivates within our hearts\minds those qualities that shine through His pure character. His thinking reflects a radically different understanding of love and how it is to operate in the heart\mind of men. Read Romans 12, for it is one of many chapters that urge us, as believers, to follow Jesus without pretense or mask. The Lord wants all of us. He does not hire part-time laborers. *"I beseech you therefore, brethren, by the mercies of God, that you present your bodies a living sacrifice, holy, acceptable unto God, which is your reasonable service"* (Romans 12:1)   **[To Memorize]**

QUESTIONS ON ROMANS 12:1-21
(MAKE A LIST IN YOUR NOTEBOOK OF EXACTLY WHAT WE ARE TO ENGAGE IN AND WHAT WE ARE NOT TO ALLOW OURSELVES.)

1. What is a living sacrifice?
2. Why is conformity to this present world so dangerous?
3. Why is it necessary for our minds to be transformed?
4. What are the gifts God has given the Church?
5. What are we to do? Why?
6. What are the things we should never do?
7. Why are we forbidden to do certain things?

Chapter 29

THE BABYLONIANS

This is the last example of pride that we shall study. Take note of the fact that pride does the same thing to these people as it does to us. Pride is universal, present in the heart\mind of all men. Daniel and three of his friends were in the crowd of people carried away from Jerusalem as prisoners of the Babylonian army. He became famous among the Chaldean soothsayers because God had given him the gift of interpreting dreams. He spent the rest of his life in Babylon and, for many years, advised the king and his descendants.

QUESTIONS ON DANIEL 2

1. What was the situation in this chapter?
2. What did Daniel say about God?
3. What were the gifts God had given Daniel? Why these particular gifts?
4. What did Daniel tell the king about his dream?
5. What did King Nebuchadnezzar now believe about the Hebrew God?

QUESTIONS ON DANIEL 3

1. How did King Nebuchadnezzar show his arrogance and pride?
2. How did God reveal Himself? Who saw this?
3. How did the kings view of the God of Israel change?

QUESTIONS ON DANIEL 4

1. What had the king learned about God up to this point?
2. What did he miss? What part did pride play in his decisions?
3. Why didn't he understand the implications of his own insight gained twelve months earlier?
4. What was God's purpose in this punishment? Who knew about all of this?
5. What did Nebuchadnezzar finally understand after his ordeal?

Daniel was called out of retirement to interpret a miraculous handwriting that had appeared upon the wall of the king's banquet hall. Daniel had been living in obscurity in the city. The current king, Belshazzar, said to have been the grandson of Nebuchadnezzar, called for Daniel to come interpret the writing and promised to shower him with gifts if he did. Daniel was about ninety years old at this time.

Daniels' reply to Belshazzar, the king of Babylon, was this: *"Let your gifts be for yourself, and give your rewards to another; yet I will read the writing to the king, and make known to him the interpretation. O king, the Most High God gave Nebuchadnezzar, your father a kingdom and majesty, glory and honor. And because of the majesty that He gave him, all peoples, nations, and languages trembled and feared before him. Whomever he wished, he executed; whom he wished, he kept alive; whomever he wished, he set up; and whomever he wished, he put down. But when his heart was lifted up, and his spirit hardened in pride, he was deposed from his kingly throne, and they took his glory from him. Then he was driven from the sons of men, his heart was made like the beasts, and his dwelling was with the wild donkeys. They fed him with grass like oxen, and his body was wet with the dew of heaven, till he knew that the Most High God rules in the kingdom of men, and that He appoints over it whomever He chooses."*

"But you his son, Belshazzar, have not humbled your heart, although you knew all this. And you have lifted yourself up against the Lord *of heaven. They have brought the vessels of His house before you, and you and your lords, your wives, and your concubines, have drunk wine from them. And you have praised the gods of silver and gold, bronze and iron, wood and stone, which do not see or hear or know: and the God who holds your breath in His hand and owns all your ways, you have not glorified. ... You have been weighed in the balances, and found wanting. Your kingdom has been divided, and given to the Medes and Persians"* (Daniel 5:17-23 and 27-28). That very night, Belshazzar, King of the Chaldeans, was slain.

QUESTIONS ON DANIEL 5:1-31

1. **How does the pride of Belshazzar show up in his actions?**
2. **What did he know?**
3. **What did he learn from his own family's experiences with God?**
4. **Who rules the kingdoms of men? What does this have to do with 1 John 2:15-17?**

QUESTIONS ON MATTHEW 20:25-18 AND LUKE 22:24-27

1. **What is Jesus teaching in these verses?**
2. **What is the position of the world on ruling over men?**

Our Lord Jesus not only thinks differently than men, but He also responds differently. His Kingdom has principles that are entirely different from those of the kingdoms of men. The King who owns all the treasures of the universe is serving sinful men, so we should have this same heart attitude of serving. Godly love is the essence of the narrow way, love is the currency of this eternal Kingdom, and this love was expressed through our Lord and Savior, as He sacrificed Himself to save the children of His Kingdom.

QUESTIONS ON LUKE 10:17-37

Men operate out of pride and prejudice, just as did the ancient Gentile kings, who ascribed no value whatsoever to their enemies. With their minds set in pride, the Hebrew people did not remember their servitude to the Assyrians and Babylonians, but devalued the peoples surrounding their land, especially the mixed people of Samaria. Jesus reminded the disciples that they were to keep a close guard upon their hearts, for pride could overshadow the effects brought about through the Spirit. The personal power granted to them from Jesus came with a warning, *"Yet do not rejoice in this, that the evil spirits are subject to you, rather rejoice because your names are written in Heaven"* (Luke 10:20, MKJV). The disciples' spiritual understanding emanated from Jesus Christ, so there was no reason for pride, and yet Jesus revealed that pride had indeed captured them.

1. How long was it before joy turned to natural pride?
2. What two things did Jesus say work against the poison of pride?
3. Jesus has the power to reveal the Father, so why is this important in dampening pride?
4. How was the lawyer trying to justify himself before Jesus?
5. Who is our neighbor?
6. What do the actions of the priest and Levite teach us about pride, personal perceptions and prejudice?

The Scriptures are very clear, and human history agrees that human reason is not sufficient, in and of itself, to order our lives or the lives of others. Successive waves of cruel armies have killed millions on their way to fulfilling the desire of men to have empires. These men, full of pride in themselves and their accomplishments, had no sorrow or pity for the thousands of people they killed or those put in harm's way. The history of the earth is a sad and dirty secret, when viewed from the past or the present. There is no good reason to think that those thousands of years are not actually a reliable predictor of the future. The civilizations which have been admired or romanticized, when viewed realistically, were governments of unlimited cruelty run by pride-filled men of spiritual emptiness and corrupt desires. The Egyptians, Assyrians, Babylonians, Romans, Incas, Mayan, Chinese Dynasties, Indus Valley cultures and the cultures of Indonesia, have had different degrees of skill in manipulating their environment. They had different languages, religious and civil differences and varying artistic expression. But one terrible thing has been truly held in common: pride-grown contempt brings violent force and cruelty, held together with cords of vanity and deceit. We see the same pride, cruelty and lack of compassion that killed millions of men in ancient history still being repeated today.

Jesus gives us peace of mind as we focus on His many truths and promises. The tribulation surrounding us is part of the permanent flux that courses through all cultures. Our response of calm is His work within our heart and is one mark of a follower of Christ. Another marked trait of a follower of Jesus is the fact that we trust the Lord over the passage of many years. This exhibits the strength of the promised Spirit in our heart\mind. I used to think that the Lord had put something, some spiritual steel, into my heart\mind that functioned like a backbone, causing me to stand. But one day I realized that the Lord *was* the steel dwelling within that caused me to stand in peace and joy. Our gracious Lord causes us to stand against the tide that comes rolling in to drown us. We are not the author of any of those things which are the marks of a Christian, but we gain in love for God and man through each gift. Jesus laid down His life to accomplish our salvation, so that we would be changed. His sacrifice was needed to pay the penalties incurred by our law-breaking and cleanse us from sin's corrupting effects. We have been divorced from the world systems of competing values, and we are free from the compulsion within sin that destroys. The Lord Jesus is our joy and sure hope. He broke the most terrible bond, with the heart of sin, freeing us from being part of the pattern of mankind's endless cruelty. Jesus, in whom we trusted after we heard the words of truth, becomes the focus of our life.

PART VII

THINKING DIFFERENTLY

Chapter 30

HOW ARE WE TO THINK?

God who at various times and in various ways spoke in time past to the fathers by the prophets, has in these last days spoken to us by His Son, whom He has appointed heir of all things, through whom also He made the worlds; who being the brightness of His glory and the express image of His person, and upholding all things by the word of His power, when He had by Himself purged our sins, sat down at the right hand of the Majesty on High ... .   Hebrews 1:1-3, NKJV[1]

Hebrews has the most amazing and comprehensive unfolding of the purposes of God in Christ Jesus. In the Old Testament system of the Law that the Lord set up, the High Priests were to be descendants of the house of Aaron and from the tribe of Levi. Their job was to present gifts and make sacrifices to atone for their sins and the sins of the people.[2] Certain animals were sacrificed, and their blood was sprinkled upon the altar,[3] for without the shedding of blood of the perfect Lamb there is no removal of sin. The priest did this until he died, and then another priest was appointed to take his place as high priest, and this went on more or less for generations. The Law and the sacrifices of the first covenant at Sinai were to be done *"with all your heart with all your soul."*[4] But these practices could not make sinful men good,[5] so what was the Lord doing? Many things. He wanted the people under this system to recognize their sins before Him and to understand the high cost of disobedience to His words, which required the eternal death of the sinner. The Lord was also setting apart a people for Himself.[6] God, in His mercy, set up the sacrificial system to temporarily cover the sin of those who believed and obeyed His words ... until the promised Messiah had come and purged the sin of those who obeyed Him. These believed that God keeps His promises and can be trusted. Believe and obey ... this is what faith looks like. Abraham believed this, and His faith in God was counted as righteousness.

Because this Sinai covenant could not make men good, God promised an everlasting second covenant. Through Jeremiah, He said, *"Then I will give them one heart and one way, that they may fear Me forever, for the good of them and their children after them. And I will make an everlasting covenant with them, that I will not turn away from doing them good; but I will put My fear in their hearts so that they will not depart from Me.*[7]

---

1. Jesus, as the permanent Son, is of the same essence as the Father and the Spirit. This unique relationship within the Godhead is what men have called the Trinity (see Colossians 2:6-10)
2. See Hebrews 5:1-4
3. See Hebrews 9:1-10
4. Deuteronomy 26:16-19, NKJV
5. See Hebrews 10:4, 6, 8 and 11
6. See Genesis 12:1-3, 13:14-17, 15:4-20, 17:1-27 and 18:1-15
7. Jeremiah 32:39-40, NKJV

The prophet Ezekiel also wrote down what the Father promised: *"Then I will give them one heart, and I will put a new spirit within them, and I will take the heart of stone out of their flesh, and give them a heart of flesh, that they may walk in My statutes and keep My judgments and do them; and they shall be My people, and I will be their God."*[8]

Jesus was not of the tribe of Levi, with its high priests and sacrifices. He was from the tribe of Judah and was appointed by God to be the permanent High Priest, made perfect through His sufferings. Jesus did not appoint Himself to this position. He is the one exalted by God as the finished atoning sacrifice,[9] offered once, not many times as in the Old Testament. The apostle John said this of Jesus, *"Behold! The lamb of God who takes away the sin of the world!"*[10] Listen to this description in Hebrews, where Jesus' suffering is described: *"who, in the days of His flesh,[11] when He had offered up prayers and supplications, with vehement cries and tears to Him who was able to save Him from death, and was heard because of His godly fear,[12] though He was a Son,[13] yet He learned obedience by the things which He suffered. And having been perfected, He became the author of eternal salvation to all who obey Him."*[14]

This *fear* was not the fear of men who have knowingly transgressed God's Law and are filled with iniquity in their minds and hearts. Our body is, to a degree, us, and it is hard to separate from this earthly physical framework. Everyone fears the destruction of their physical body—whether by assault, accident, disease or age—but this was not the primary fear that Jesus had in His heart. Jesus had set His will to glorify His Father and to accomplish everything His Father had sent Him to do.[15] Jesus, our Lord, was not terminally selfish or self-indulgent; He was a humble man and spent much time in prayer away from the crowds, alone with His father. He tells us that the words He spoke and the miracles He performed were from the Father. Jesus was gracious, kind, longsuffering, gentle, and acutely aware of the people around Him. He focused His attention upon the person who was speaking to Him. He was concerned always about individual salvation. He did not talk about the weather, the latest fashions, food, sports, nor various religions, politics, government, or policy either locally or in Rome. We are to set out wills, through faith, to follow Christ, with obedience to His Word, with humble hearts and humbled minds, because we love Him and His Word is truth.[16]

Jesus went into the garden to pray,[17] knowing that this was the time His ordeal was to begin. He took Peter, James and John. He began to be very distressed and troubled and said to them, *"My soul is exceedingly sorrowful, even to death. Stay here and watch."*[18] Jesus went again and fell to the ground, praying that if it were possible, this hour might pass away. Confronting Him was death, separation

---

8. Ezekiel 11:19-20, NKJV. See also 1 Peter 2:4-6 and 9-10. God has become our God through Jesus.
9. See Hebrews 4:14 through 5:9
10. John 1:29, NKJV
11. Jesus had a human body like ours, except without a sin nature. When He arose, He had a glorified body fit for eternity, and we will also be given this new body (see Philippians3:20-21).
12. The NASB uses the word piety instead of godly fear and defines it as being "devotion and reverence to God."
13. See 2 Corinthians 5:21, 1 Peter 2:20-25 and 1 John 3:5
14. Hebrews 5:7-9
15. See Colossians 1:9-27 and 2:1-10, John 8:28-32 and Psalm 40:8
16. See John 1:14-18, 4:19-26, 8:28-32, 16:6-16 and 17:14-26
17. See Mark 14:32-42
18. Mark 14:34, NKJV

from His Father and the guarantee of becoming sin for His people. And yet with courage and extraordinary grace He prayed, *"Abba! Father! All things are possible for You. Take this* cup *away from Me; nevertheless, not what I will, but what You will."*[19] His call was answered during the third prayer, as He received strength, renewed courage and grace to continue in the path that had been ordained from before the Garden.

Jesus was heard, because in His soul's anguish and fearful deep grief over the taking of this *"cup of suffering,"* He trusted His Father and reverenced Him above all—His character and absolute trustworthiness, His mighty power and creative mind, His never-ending love, grace and glory. Therefore, Jesus gladly and with great humility accomplished His Father's will.

Jesus was acquainted with grief[20] and endured many things. His family did not fully accept the fact that He was the Messiah ... until He rose from the dead. His people glorified Him when they thought He might be a prophet or take power from the Romans as their king. Soon after He was arrested, put on trial and pronounced guilty, He was given to the Romans for execution. His disciples soon left Him alone, and Peter even denied Him. Many were calling for His death in spite of the fact that He was innocent, and all of this was a gross injustice. Jesus' suffering was deeply agonizing in His spirit, His mind and His body.[21]

What is so amazing is that our Lord never once resorted to blaming others, cursing men or using His innate power.[22] Instead, He depended upon His Father's Holy Spirit, as we must. Our Lord knew that He could be delivered[23] but deliberately put His pain, sorrow and dread aside to accomplish His desire for His people within His Father's will.

Many times we find ourselves in various difficulties, and we know the Lord could stop these trials. Instead, He has chosen the same general pathway for Jesus' sons and daughters. Why? Because our hearts and minds have patterns of thinking and responding that are the remaining footprint of sin. Jesus always honored the will of His Father, but we must learn obedience to the will of the Father.[24] Adversity opens our eyes, but do not forget that the Father disciplines us out of love and grace.

Jesus, our Lord, never leaves us or forsakes us during these times. We may call upon Him for wisdom, strength and courage and the ability to endure, and Jesus graciously answers those prayers. Lean upon Him and trust Him fully because His love is so complete that He gave His life to purge our sin. Remember that He has been where we are now, and Jesus, our Lord, set His face like flint for the joy set before Him.[25] Consider this: we are His joy. It gives the Father, the Son and Spirit great joy each time a sinner repents and is saved. Believers enter into the everlasting Kingdom,[26] where

---

19. Mark 14:36
20. Read Isaiah 53 to see the fullest description of Jesus.
21. Please read Philippians 2:1-17
22. See Matthew 26:50-52, Luke 8:40-55, 22:47-49 and Luke 24:19-27
23. See Matthew 26:53-54
24. See Ephesians 2:1-10
25. Read Isaiah 50:4-9 to understand this better.
26. See 2 Samuel 7:12-17 and Genesis 49:8-10

Jesus is the everlasting King.[27] Jesus is the everlasting High Priest who is continually interceding for us before His Father.[28] He is the final Prophet[29] who has given us the final message of His Word, and He is the final sacrifice to atone for the sins of men. We need no more priest or sacrifices or prophets, but we need Jesus, for He is all things for us, and we need His Word because it is the eternal truth. Jesus said: *"These things I have spoken to you, that in Me you may have peace. In the world you will have tribulation; but be of good cheer, I have overcome the world."*[30]

QUESTIONS ON HOW WE ARE TO THINK

Jesus sets us apart for the Father through the offering of His body, once as the final sacrifice, and this begins sanctification, the transforming of a believers' minds and hearts, to think and behave like Jesus. Jesus prayed for the Father to send the Holy Spirit,[31] the Spirit of truth, to live within those who had believed Jesus Christ and the apostles. The Scriptures are used by the indwelling Spirit to change how we think and what we think.

God's people should be living mirrors, reflecting the mind and heart of Christ. Jesus completes His work within our minds and hearts during our lifetimes through the Holy Spirit. We are to become like Jesus in our character, heart and mind.

QUESTIONS ON HEBREWS 1:1-4 AND 8-12

1. **What does the Father tell us about Jesus?**
2. **Why is this information important to understand?**
3. **List all the information that is given in verses 5-9.**

QUESTIONS ON COLOSSIANS 1:9-29

1. **Why was the apostle Paul praying for these particular people?**
2. **What things did Paul pray for the believers (here called saints) in Colosse?**
3. **What did Paul say about Jesus?**
4. **What did Jesus deliver all believers from? (Verses 13-14)**
5. **Describe Jesus. (Verses 15-18)**
6. **What does it mean that we were *"once alienated and hostile in our mind,"* engaged in evil deeds?[32] (Verse 21)**

---

27. See John 17:1-17
28. See Hebrews 10:19
29. See Deuteronomy 18:15-22
30. John 16:33, NKJV. See also Isaiah 26:3 and Hebrews 13:20-21
31. See John 14:15-18
32. Wicked works—calamitous, evil in effect or influence, morally culpable, responsible for evil, derelict, vicious, mischief, malice, grievous, harmful, lewd, malicious.

7. How did Jesus reconcile[33] the people to God? (Verses 19-23)

8. What is the mystery that was hidden in the Old Testament? (Verses 26-27)

QUESTIONS ON COLOSSIANS 2:1-10

1. What is hidden within the Father and the Son?

2. Why was Paul so concerned? (Verses 4-9)

3. What did Paul want us to understand about Jesus?

4. What did Paul encourage believers to do?

QUESTIONS ON COLOSSIANS 2:8-23 AND JOHN 3:1-21

1. Why did Paul warn us to be on our guard?

2. Jesus came to give us new life, and *"in Him"* what things are true? (Colossians 2:11-15)

Except for some of the Jewish people who held tightly to the Lord, there were only cults in the world for thousands of years. The hearts and minds of men were enslaved by the belief system of each cult. After Jesus ascended back to Heaven, the truth began to spread out into the neighboring kingdoms. Even as the apostle Paul preached the truth of salvation through Jesus Christ, some men camouflaged their particular beliefs under the lie that they were "believers," just to gain followers. Some were persuaded to worship angels. Today, we are pressured on all sides to mold ourselves to be a part of various philosophies and traditions that are part of the world's belief system.[34]

Paul spoke about men making rules that formed some sort of self-imposed religion that tried to make men appear to be humble. The leaders imposed very strict regulations that were harsh, but men complied. These would-be leaders had "visions" and were zealous to recruit men into their groups. Paul preached against the various cults and alerted Christians not to be drawn away from Christ by deceived men practicing deceit. This, he said, produces, *"false humility, and neglect of the body which seem to be real wisdom but these things are not of any value against the indulgence of the carnal nature."*[35] Why?

QUESTIONS ON JOHN 3:1-21

1. How can we be connected to Jesus? (Read John 3:1-21)

2. What does it mean to be born of water and the Spirit to enter God's Kingdom?

3. How does the illustration of the action of *"wind"* explain the work of the Spirit?

4. What does it mean *"believes in Him"* and what is the result of this belief?

---

33. Reconciliate: to reconcile, to atone for sin, to be merciful or make reconciliation for, to unite, overcome the hostility, propitiate.

34. See Colossians 2:4-9

35. Colossians 2:16-23

QUESTIONS ON HEBREWS 2:1-18

1. What should we pay close attention to and remember? Why?
2. What three things testify to the truth concerning the Messiah?
3. Why was it necessary for Jesus to be made like the people He was sent to save?[36]

QUESTIONS ON HEBREWS 8:1-13

1. Why did the Old Covenant fail?
2. Using verses10-12, state the properties of the New Covenant?
3. What is the power found in the New Covenant that was not present in the Old?

QUESTIONS ON HEBREWS 9:1-10

1. How many times could the Old Covenant priest inter into the Holy of Holies?
2. He would die if He did not bring _____ with Him into the Holy place? (Verse 6-7)
3. Exactly what sins were covered by the yearly sacrifice?
4. What was God teaching His people through the sacrificial system?
5. What furniture was in the Holy of Holies?
6. What was under the Mercy Seat?
7. What three things were in the Ark of the Covenant?[37]
8. What truth did these three things reveal about the people?

QUESTIONS ON HEBREWS 10:1-16 AND 19-25

1. Why is it true that the sacrifice of the animals did not make men perfect? (Verses 1-2)
2. What was the sacrificial system intended to do? (Verses 3-4)
3. How did God fulfill the promises He had made under the Old Covenant?
4. How does Jesus sanctify[38] believers? (Verses 9-10)
5. What are the consequences of not being sanctified by the Lord Jesus? (Verses 19-25)

Jesus actively sought to do the will of the Father every minute of His time on earth. He did not have a separate agenda, other than humbling Himself, and He lived to glorify His Father and God. *"For I did not speak on My own initiative, but the Father Himself who sent Me has given Me commandment, what to say, and what to speak. And I know that His commandment is eternal life; therefore the things I speak,*

---

36. See Hebrews 2:10-18
37. See Exodus 25:10-22, Deuteronomy 9:6-18 and 10:1-5 and Numbers 17:5-11
38. Sanctify: to make holy, purify, or consecrate. (Strong's G37)

I speak just as the Father told me."[39] We are to actively remake our lives to suit Jesus' agenda. He said, *"Take My yoke upon you and learn from Me, for I am gentle and lowly in heart, and you will find rest for your souls. For My yoke is easy and My burden is light."* As we love the Lord and become filled with the fruit of the Spirit, over time we can know that this change within us is from the Lord, for without Him we can do nothing.[40]

For the word of God is living and powerful, sharper than any two-edged sword, piercing even to the division of soul and spirit and of joints and marrow, and is a discerner of the thoughts and intents of the heart and there is no creature hidden from His sight, but all things are naked and open to the eyes of Him to whom we must give account. Hebrews 4:11-13

QUESTIONS ON JOHN 1:1-5 AND 8-18

1. What does it mean when the Scriptures say that John was a *"witness"*?
2. Why did the Jewish people choose not to believe what Jesus preached?
3. How are believers made?
4. What does it mean to say that *"The law was given through Moses, but grace and truth came through Jesus Christ?"*

If the Father and the Son have all the treasures of wisdom and knowledge, why would you trust the reasoning and speculation of the men of the world and not Jesus Christ? *"For in Jesus dwells all the fullness of the Godhead bodily, and we are complete in Jesus."*[41]

QUESTIONS ON HEBREWS 3:1-19, 4:14-16 AND 5:1-10 AND PSALM 95

1. Why do you think Paul quoted Psalm 95 here in Hebrews 3:12-19?
2. Why was Paul warning us again, as God also warned His people in Psalm 95?
3. How does sin deceive us?
4. Jesus has been appointed by God to be the last High Priest, so what is He doing now? (Read 1 Timothy 2:5)
5. Why can we trust Him? (See Hebrews 4:14-16)
6. How can Jesus, our Lord, help us when we are in great need?
7. Hebrews 5:9 points out that Jesus, having been perfected by His suffering, became the Author of eternal salvation to *all who obey Him.* Why is it necessary to obey Christ, our Lord?
8. Why are we to set our mind on the things of Jesus as He sits on the right hand of God in Heaven?

---

39. John 12:49-50
40 John 15:5
41. Colossians 2:9

QUESTIONS ON COLOSSIANS 3:5-17

1. What parts of our natural thinking must we destroy?
2. How are we to put on the characteristics seen in believers discussed in verses 10-17?
3. Why is it necessary to obey Jesus?

QUESTIONS ON COLOSSIANS 3:1-17 AND HEBREWS 8:7-13

1. What was wrong with the first covenant and the priests that served it?
2. What is the everlasting covenant that Jesus fulfills?

QUESTIONS ON DEUTERONOMY 18:15-22 AND MATTHEW 21

1. The Lord spoke to Moses, a prophet of God, and gave him a description of another Prophet to come. How does Jesus fulfill this prophecy?

There is an old saying that you cannot know a man unless you walk in his shoes. Jesus walked in our shoes for thirty-three years, and He was without sin. He knows us all completely, as He knows how Satan's lies and deceptions are used to pull us away from the truth. The Lord has given us a great weapon in His Word against Satan's mental assaults. The Scriptures renew our mind as we believe, learn and accept the thinking of God as our own.[42] We can seek Jesus to help and to give us wisdom and strength not to follow temptation into sin. As His child, you can trust Him to fortify your internal being against the strongest temptations. Jesus is still within us during our time of testing. Through His Word and by the indwelling Spirit, we receive understanding, motivation and power to stand against Satan's wiles.

---

42. See 1 Peter 2:1-2

CHAPTER 31

THE REPENTANCE OF KING DAVID

With all of these scriptures fresh in your mind, this is a good time to bring to your attention a man whom God did hear. This man was a sinner, just like the other people we have studied, but he did what was right in the eyes of God [262] most of his life.

QUESTIONS ON 2 SAMUEL 11:3-27 (DAVID'S SIN)

1. Write down an outline of the events as they happened.
2. What was David doing sleeping that late in the day?
3. What should King David have been doing that day?
4. What was he thinking?
5. What should David have been concerned about?

QUESTIONS ON 2 SAMUEL 12:1-24

1. What was the result of David's "being at ease"? Why?
2. What is repentance? What does it look like in real life?

King David is an example of a person who repented of the evil he had done. The word *repent* means "to think differently about your life and values, to reconsider your thinking, and morally to feel compunction to turn away from thoughts and actions contrary to the biblical view." This means that we are to renounce and turn from all of those things practiced by men with unconverted hearts because they offend a holy God. This includes things like worshiping idols, being greedy, occult practices, murder, lies, evil thoughts, adultery, selfishness, strife, anger, deception and manipulation, in other words, whatever fulfills all the desires of our heart and mind. [263] Whatever it is in our life that separates us from God is a symptom of the disease of sin that has infected us. Remember the penalty for sin. [264] So it is not just a problem of the identification of various sins, but also the acknowledging that we produce them. Therefore it is our "self" which must be given a new heart. What did David say? *"The sacrifices of God are a broken spirit; a broken and contrite heart, O God, You will not despise"* (Psalm 51:17). *"The LORD is nigh unto them that are of a broken heart; and saves such as be of a contrite spirit"* (Psalm 34:18).

David set his heart, asking for forgiveness, restoration and guidance. Psalm 51 was written when the prophet Nathan was sent by the Lord to confront David. David had taken Bathsheba from Uriah

144

and then ordered Uriah to the frontlines to be killed. God was gracious to expose the mind of this man, as he went through his life, that we might learn from him the hard lessons he had to learn.

PSALM 51:1-17

Have mercy upon me, O God, according to your loving kindness: according unto the multitude of Your tender mercies, blot out my transgressions. Wash me completely from my iniquity, and cleanse me from my sin, for I confess my transgressions; and my sin is ever before me against you, you only, have I sinned, and done evil in your sight; that you might be justified when you speak, and be clear when you judge.

Behold, I was brought forth in iniquity, and in sin did my mother conceive me. Behold, you desire truth in the inward parts, and in the hidden part you shall make me to know wisdom. Purge me with Hyssop, and I shall be clean; wash me, and I shall be whiter than snow. Make me to hear joy and gladness; that the bones which you have broken may rejoice. Hide your face from my sins, and blot out all my iniquities. Create in me a clean heart, O God, and renew a right spirit within me. Cast me not away from your presence, and do not take your Holy Spirit from me. Restore to me the joy of your salvation, and uphold me with a willing spirit. Then will I teach transgressors your ways; and sinners shall be converted to you. Deliver me from the guilt of shedding blood, O God, O God of my salvation, and my tongue shall sing aloud of your righteousness. O Jehovah, open my lips, and my mouth shall show forth your praise. For you do not desire sacrifice; for else I would give it; you do not delight in burnt offering. The sacrifices of God are a broken spirit; a broken and a contrite heart, O God, You will not despise.

Choose at least one verse from this psalm to memorize.

QUESTIONS ON REPENTANCE FROM PSALM 51

1. Considering Psalm 51 as a model, how do we think when we are brought to godly repentance? [265]
2. When we truly repent, how do our actions reflect this change? Why?
3. Why do we need to repent daily of thoughts, deeds and attitudes which occur?
4. What does the word *repentance* mean?
5. What does the sorrow of the world produce? Why? (See 2 Corinthians 7:10)
6. What does your mental judgment against another cost you? And how is repentance reached? (See Romans 2:1-4)
7. What has Jesus done? (See Hebrews 12:1-4)
8. Why does the Lord discipline His children? (See Hebrews 12:5-14)
9. Why does the Lord rejoice when a sinner repents? (See Acts 5:30-33)

---

265. See also Matthew 22:37, Luke 10:27 and Romans 12:2

QUESTIONS ON PSALM 119:59, 67 AND 71

1. **In Psalm 119:59, David says,** *"I thought on my ways, and turned my feet."* **What does this mean?**
2. **In Psalm 119:67 and 71, what did David learn about suffering? Why is being at ease so dangerous to all men?**

Satan will try to convince us that there is nothing but peace for us, even if we give in to temptations. David committed these sins when he was roughly fifty years old, and He spent about a year refusing to repent, even though, in his deepest soul, he knew what he had done. Satan deceives us to keep us from serious repentance, just as he worked in David's mind. Often this happens at the same time the Lord's Spirit is giving us insight into our danger. Heed any red flags and listen to the Lord's convicting Spirit. Don't be like David and pretend that all is well. Repent daily so that sin does not suppress your conscience or pull you from active obedience onto the sideline or deeper into sin or into more sin. The consequences for David were truly awful. *"Now therefore the sword shall never depart from your house; because you have despised me, and have taken the wife of Uriah the Hittite to be thy wife … . I will raise up evil against you out of your own house …"* (2 Samuel 12:10-11).

David was grieved in his heart, for he had allowed his desires to darken his mind and suppress his conscience. He was no child in the things of God, and yet he allowed himself to be deceived by lust. He coveted Uriah's wife and chose openly to sin against his Lord. Then, he committed murder and provided the occasion for the enemies of the Lord to blaspheme. David asked God to create in him a clean heart and renew a right spirit within him, and he asked God not to remove His Spirit from him. David knew that the ugliness he felt inside was real, and he had no capacity to remove the sin himself. Nor could David change the spiritual and moral damage which was the result of his evil choice. He was heart-sickened and turned to the only Source of hope, the Lord, for help in His time of greatest need. True repentance is not a superficial response that lasts for a moment and has no lasting fruit. It is life-changing.

King David did spend much time in the Word, [266] as the Law of Kings commanded. David believed God would teach him, through His Word empowered by His Spirit, all that he needed to know. He also believed that God's power was great enough to keep him from evil desires in his mind and soul. He trusted God. He trusted God's Word. David worshiped the Lord and was grateful and thankful for all of God's mercy and care. He prayed often when the waters of life overflowed, his heart crying out, knowing that his glorious God would hear his prayers and give him hope in the darkness.

The Psalms are full of God's great wisdom, truth and mercy, as seen and experienced by King David. David's way of thinking was not hard, like Jeroboam's. Except in the matter of the murder of Uriah, David's heart remained sensitive, even when he rightly suffered because of evil choices. David knew the charges were true. He had taken the Word of God lightly and despised the Lord. He had brought the sword upon his own house, as did Jeroboam. David accepted rebuke from the

Lord's hand. [267] David was brought to repentance, when he realized the greatness of his sin before God. *"For I acknowledge my transgressions: and my sin (is) ever before me"* (Psalm 51:3, David's psalm of repentance).

It is necessary to acknowledge our sin and the fact that our sin is against God. For a while David was blinded by his sin and did not seek God, nor ask for forgiveness. But he repented after God had the prophet rebuke him for his adultery and murder. Through the work of the Spirit, David saw the depth of his rebellion and what advantage he had given the enemies of God. Then his pride-filled heart was broken, and he became genuinely contrite. As David was brought into a state of repentance, he was forgiven for his transgressions, but he had to live with the ugly fruit of the consequences which shadowed the rest of his life. The sword of rebellion broke up his family and his heart. Listen to his lament, *"Before I was afflicted I went astray: but now have I kept thy word .. . It is good for me that I have been afflicted; that I might learn thy statutes. I know, O LORD, that thy <u>judgments</u>* [268] *are right, and that thou in <u>faithfulness</u>* [269] *has afflicted me"* (Psalm 119:67, 71 and 75).

The Lord, in His kindness, has left us means whereby we can seriously address needed change in ourselves. *"Watch and pray that you enter not into temptation: the spirit indeed is willing, but the flesh is weak"* (Matthew 26:41). *"There has no temptation taken you but such as is common to man: but God is faithful, who will not suffer you to be tempted above that you are able; but will with the temptation also make a way to escape, that you may be able to bear it"* (1 Corinthians 10:13). **[To Memorize]**

This is a promise to remember, especially when we face any temptation. The mind is the first place temptation is wrestled with, and if we remember the power of the indwelling Spirit, we will not fall into the trap of believing we can only yield to temptation, for that is a lie. David set himself up to be taken captive by sin because He chose to be in the wrong place at the wrong time. Many times we let our guard down during vacations or periods of ease. We need to be alert and careful of self-indulgence, for it is the doorway into a room of desire. Through the Spirit, we can say "no" to temptation as it presents itself to us. *"Let us behave properly as in the day, not in carousing and drunkenness, not in sexual promiscuity and sensuality, not in strife and jealousy" But put on the Lord Jesus Christ, and make no provision for the flesh in regard to its lusts"* (Romans 13:13-14, NASB). **[To Memorize]**

We can immediately focus on the Scriptures from our Lord Jesus, to give us renewed strength and time to reconsider and stop the wrong thinking. The word *provision* means "to have or take forethought for a supply or provision." In other words, don't have a back-up or store of whatever it is you desire, nor put yourself in places or with people where temptations comes easily. We are also admonished to *"bring every thought in to captivity to Christ"* (2 Corinthians 10:5) before we are tricked by the desire of the flesh or mind into committing ourselves to following sin, as David did. Sin saved in the heart always leads to weakness in other areas, leading to more sin. Sin unchecked multiplies like rabbits in a field of clover. *"For though we walk in the flesh, we do not war according to the flesh, for the weapons of our warfare are not of the flesh, but divinely powerful for the destruction of*

---

267. See 1 Chronicles 21:1-30 and 2 Samuel 12:1-25

268. *Judgments*—a verdict (favorable or unfavorable) pronounced judicially, a sentence (to include the act and penalty that suits the crime)

269. *Faithfulness*—literally firmness; figuratively security; moral fidelity: faith (-ful, -1y, -ness,); stability, truth, verily. steady, set office

fortresses, We are destroying speculations and every lofty thing raised up against the knowledge of God, and we are taking every thought captive to the obedience of Christ, and we are ready to punish all disobedience" (2 Corinthians 10:3-6).

God chastened David for his sin, and He will do the same for us. Jeroboam, still wrapped in his pride, received the full wrath against himself, which included his family. This difference in outcome reveals that mercy is extended when repentance is real. Part of the Lord's love extended to all believers is that He disciplines us as a Father does his own children, to bring serious change in our attitudes and behavior.

> *... my son, do not despise the discipline of the Lord, nor faint when you are rebuked by him ... , for whom the Lord loves He chastens ... . This he does for our profit, that we might be partakers of his holiness ... afterward it yields the peaceable fruit of righteousness to those disciplined by it.*
>
> Hebrews 12:5-14 **[To Memorize]**

We learn and must continue learning righteousness.

This is what repentance looks like. Our ears are opened, and we hear the words of God, as did David, and we are convinced, persuaded of the truth that Christ is the promised Messiah, and our sins separate us from God. We consider our ways of sin, in light of this truth and turn our feet away from following self, as David did. Instead, we follow the living God, acting upon the understanding He gives us through His Word by the Spirit. This is not just being sorry for some deeds that have caused harm; this sorrow is over our heart\mind being estranged from God, when, for the first time, we see our sin as being a part of our nature, not just a random wrong.

Repentance is the response we make after God opens our heart\mind to understand His truth. *"The preparation of the heart in man, and the answer of the tongue, is from the Lord!"* (Proverbs 16:1). It is God's will alone that is the determining factor in our salvation. He must remove the stranglehold of sin on our heart and mind, so that we might hear the truth, believe the truth and put our trust in Jesus Christ as the Son of God. We have been walking in the darkness, believing the lies of men and Satan, and the Lord must bring us to the Light, to remove our spiritual blindness. Jesus said, *"All things are delivered to me of my Father: and no man knows who the Son is, but the Father; and who the Father is, but the Son, and he to whom the Son will reveal him"* (Luke 10:22). *"I am the way, and the truth, and the life; no one comes to the Father but through Me"* (Matthew 11:27). We are motivated by the Spirit to begin to actively engage our mind to search the Scriptures, to see how to follow the Lord. Everything has changed inside. Our goals change, what we value changes and we are moving to lay aside anything that is not of God. This change of life direction demonstrates repentance and active faith in God. This is a gift of God. It is not out of our will that we believe, trust and obey, but out of God's will. *"For by grace are you saved through faith and this is not of yourselves it is the gift of God"* (Ephesians 2:8).

CHAPTER 33

OUR NEED FOR REPENTANCE

Were they ashamed when they had committed abominations? No, there were not at all ashamed, neither could they blush: therefore shall they fall among them that fall ... . Jeremiah 8:12 **[To Memorize]**

Godly sorrow is very different from the worldly sorrow of being caught and exposed in some sin. Paul wrote in his second letter to the Corinthians, *"... I rejoice, not that you were made sorrowful, but that you were made sorrowful to the point of repentance; for you were made sorrowful according to the will of God,...which produces a repentance without regret, leading to salvation; but the sorrow of the world produces death"* (2 Corinthians 7:10). Repentance must be brought into being by the power of God, so that your sorrow will lead to a genuine turning away from sin and a turning toward God, which leads to salvation. We cannot understand the need for repentance unless we have some idea of the holiness of God and, finally, see ourselves through His eyes. Isaiah saw a vision of the Lord, and then he said, *"Woe is me! For I am a man of unclean lips, and I dwell in the midst of a people of unclean lips: for mine eyes have seen the King, the LORD of Hosts"* (Isaiah 6:5). [270]

QUESTIONS ON ROMANS 2:1-16, 3:9-23 AND MATTHEW 23

1. Who was the writer addressing here?
2. How do you know this?
3. What was the greatest sin displayed in the people discussed?
4. Who will judge the secrets of men? And what will be the standard for judgment?
5. Who is a child of God?
6. What is the purpose of repentance? Why do we repent? How often do we repent?

When the scribes and Pharisees saw Jesus eating with publicans and sinners, they asked His disciples how He could eat and drink with tax collectors and sinners. Jesus said to them, *"Those that are healthy do not need a doctor, but those who are sick do need him; I did not come to call the righteous, but sinners unto repentance"* (Mark 2:16-17, NASB). Jesus also spoke to the scribes and Pharisees about the joy a shepherd feels when one lost sheep of his flock is found. He said, *"I say unto you that there is joy in heaven over one sinner that repents more than 99 just persons, which need no repentance"* (Luke 15:7). *"And He spoke this parable unto certain which trusted in themselves that they were righteous, and despised others"* (Luke 18:9). *"Who is righteous and does not need repentance? As it is written, There is none righteous, no, not one: There is none that understands, there is none that seek after God"* (Romans 3:10-11).

QUESTIONS ON HEBREWS 1:1-4, EPHESIANS 1:1-14 AND COLOSSIANS 1:1-29
(READ THE SELECTIONS IN EACH CHAPTER AND THEN ANSWER THE THREE QUESTIONS FOR EACH SELECTION OF VERSES.)

1. Make a list of what the Father has done by and through the Son.
2. Write a few paragraphs detailing all that is discussed in each section of verses.
3. What does the Lord use His power to accomplish within us?

THE PSALM 119 SELECTIONS

As you read the selections from Psalm 119 on the next two pages, take notes on the things King David prayed. He prayed daily, and his thoughts were upon the Lord continually. When you see the span of David's life through his prayers, you see a heart and a mind vastly different from men like Jeroboam and Rehoboam. The Scriptures expose these kings as being corrupt and sin-hardened men because of their continual rebellion against the living Word. Study these selections until you know how David's thinking was different.

CHOOSE 10 VERSES AND MEMORIZE THEM.

1. *"Blessed are the undefiled in the way, who walk in the Law of the Lord."*

2. *"Blessed are they who keep the testimonies of the Lord."*

7. *"I will praise you with uprightness of heart when I shall have learned your righteous judgment."*

9. *"How can a young man keep his way pure? By keeping it according to Your word."* (NASB)

10. *"With my whole heart have I sought you; O let me not wander from your Commandments."*

11. *"Your word have I hid in my heart, that I might not sin against you."*

12. *"Blessed are you, O Lord; teach me your statutes."*

14. *"I have rejoiced in the way of your testimonies, as much as in all riches."*

15. *"I will meditate in your precepts and have respect unto all my ways."*

16. *"I will delight myself in your commandments: I will not forget your word."*

18. *"Open my eyes, that I may behold wondrous things out of your law."*

24. *"Your testimonies are my delight and my counselors."*

27. *"Make me to understand the way of your precepts, so I shall talk of your wonderful works."*

28. *"My soul melts for heaviness: strengthen me according unto your word."*

29. *"Remove from me the way of lying: and grant me your law graciously."*

30. *"I have chosen the way of truth: your judgments have I laid before me."*

32. *"I will run the way of your commandments, when you shall enlarge my heart."*

34. *"Give me understanding, I will keep your law, I have observed it with my whole heart."*

35. *"Make me to go in the path of your commands; for therein do I delight."*

36. *"Incline my heart into law and not to covetousness."*

37. *"Turn away my eyes from beholding vanity and quicken me in your way."*

43. *"Do not take the word of truth utterly out of my mouth, for I have hoped in your Judgments."*

46. *"I will speak your testimonies before kings and will not be ashamed."*

47. *"This is my comfort in my affliction: for your word has quickened me."*

59. *"I thought on my ways, and turned my feet."*

63. *"I am a companion of all them that fear you, and of those that keep your precepts."*

66. *"Teach me good judgment and knowledge; for I have believed your commandments."*

67. *"Before I was afflicted I went astray: but now I have kept your word."*

71. *"It is good for me that I have been afflicted; that I might learn your statues."*

72. *"The law of your mouth is better to me than thousands of gold or silver."*

73. *"You hand has made me and fashioned me; give me understanding, that I may learn Your Commandments."*

95. *"You have made me wiser than my enemies through your commands; for they are always with me."*

104. *"Through your precepts I get understanding, therefore I hate every false way."*

105. *"Your word is a lamp unto my feet and a light unto my path."*

130. *"The entrance of your words gives light: it gives understanding unto the simple."*

133. *"Order my steps in your word: and let not any iniquity have dominion over me."*

134. *"Deliver me from the oppression of man: so will I keep your precepts."*

142. *"Your righteousness is everlasting righteousness and your law is the truth."*

The influence of the Holy Spirit is clearly seen here in these thoughts of David. Consider how sensitive he was to his sin. Consider how strong his faith. Remember what the people said, that he brought justice to every man. Consider the great respect that David had for the Lord and for His Word (except for his season of sin). Consider David's trust in the power of the living Lord to bring to pass every promise He had made. See the difference in David's thinking. It is more like the thinking of Isaiah, Jeremiah and Ezekiel than the thinking of the other kings.

QUESTIONS ON PSALM 119
(AGAIN, PAY ATTENTION TO DAVID'S THINKING.)

1. List how many times, in the above selections, David mentioned directly or indirectly the Word of God being of value.
2. List all the ways in which the Word of God benefits the believer.
3. List the ways in which David expected help from God when he prayed.
4. What did David think about God? What was his attitude toward Him?
5. What characteristics of God can you identify from these verses?
6. Can you tell me why David's thinking was so different? [271]

---

271. See 1 Samuel 16:13

We have considered these patterns of pride, with their arrogance and conceit, so that we could see the ruin pride brings upon men. Natural men serve themselves at the expense of the good of others. Natural men make no room for God in their choices and, by this, we see the corruption and the terminal self-absorption exhibited in both heart and mind. [272] How does a mind that is corrupted by sin get from self to God? We are just like the people of Jerusalem. We can't do it on our own. We have a paradox presented to us. The One we need the most we don't naturally think of or go to. But if we have been convicted at various times by our conscience, we must respond, for repeated denial of truth renders the conscience unable to convict. Every conviction of wrong-doing of any kind or degree is the Spirit's call upon our soul to repent of sin and come to God in humility. Call out to God, asking for mercy, to send His Spirit into your mind, so that you can hear and understand the things of God and value them as precious.

And we know that the Son of God is come, and has given us an understanding, that we may know him that is true, and we are in him that is true, even in his Son Jesus Christ. This is the true God, and eternal life.
1 John 5:20 **[To Memorize]**

How does this happen? Remember Jesus' illustration in John 3. The wind travels as it wills, going here and there. We do not see the wind, but we can see the effects of it upon the landscape. So also is the work of the Spirit within the minds of men, changing the hearts of men. A spiritual rebirth is the only way our thinking can be changed. This alone makes the difference in thinking patterns between men who follow God and men who don't. Jesus said we cannot serve two masters because it divides loyalties and makes men double-minded and unstable. [273] The Scriptures make it very clear that God seeks those who love Him with their whole heart and mind. [274] He wants all of our devotion. The Lord has not left us wandering in the dark. His Word is clear: Hell exists, and those who do not love Him will forfeit Heaven. [275] Why? Because the Lord is just. Therefore He holds everyone accountable for what they do, think and say, as well as the results of those deeds. Since He is the Creator, it is fitting that He holds us to His standard, for His Word is Truth. [276] God does not lie as men do. He is the Source of pure love and pure truth. He has said that our minds do not naturally seek Him, nor can the natural man do good, [277] as this state of mind reflects spiritual darkness. Does this describe you? Do you have no natural thought of God?

God's Word gives us insight into the darkness of our hearts. We are the problem of sin, and we need to see our sin from the Lord's eyes. As natural men, we have no capacity to diagnose our disease, nor do we have the power for spiritual rebirth, nor can we muster up repentance that leads to salvation.

QUESTIONS ON LEVITICUS 26
(READ THIS CHAPTER AND THEN DISCUSS IT WITH YOUR PARENT/TEACHER.)

1. What good things did God promise the people if they walked in His way?
2. What things did God promise the people if they chose to walk in their own way?
3. What would be the outcome if the people turned to follow the ways of the Lord and away from following their own perceptions?
4. When did God have this word given to the people?

We are wise if we turn to God in repentance and ask for mercy as soon as we are aware of our sin because "time does not wear out the guilt of sin. Nor can we hope for impunity if judgment is delayed." [278]

QUESTIONS ON COLOSSIANS 1 AND HEBREWS 1:1-4

1. What was included in Paul's prayer for believers?
2. How is Jesus Christ defined?
3. How are we to increase in the knowledge of God?
4. How are we filled with the knowledge of God's will?
5. How do we gain wisdom and spiritual understanding?
6. How are we strengthened?
7. How do we become fruitful in every good work?
8. What has God made us fit for?
9. Whom or what are we delivered from?

What is so precious about the sin nature that we would want to keep it? We can see, from the lives we have followed, that the sin nature will never make us whole, but it degrades those who are ruled by it. Pride in sinful self is a great stumblingblock between us and the living God. Submission to the Lord Jesus is not a comfortable or reasonable move for our sin-nature, which values, above all things, a false perception of independence. Natural man cannot see that autonomy is an illusion. But if this resistance is present, then it is a good indication of the condition of our heart. It is important to the Lord for us to recognize and turn from deeds and attitudes which harm and devalue others. The Lord is aware of our deepest sinful attitudes, and the quality of our repentance is never sufficient within self. Unless our eyes and hearts are opened to hear the truth and believe it, we are forever lost. We are granted grace to repent when the indwelling Spirit has begun His work in us.

---

278. Matthew Henry (paraphrased)

Only acknowledge your iniquity, that you have transgressed against the Lord your God ... and you have not obeyed my voice, says the LORD.

Jeremiah 3:13

We acknowledge, O LORD, our wickedness, (and) the iniquity of our fathers: for we have sinned against thee.

Jeremiah 14:20

All of our encounters with the Lord God demand transparency and accountability to the greatest degree. Jesus requires that we look Him in the eye and speak the truth. Remember that pride has the ability to hide the real condition of our heart from self. Pride will barricade self against even the truth. Pride, if left unchecked, renders us terminally self-absorbed, self-deceived and unteachable.

Humble yourself and submit to our gracious and merciful God. The sacrifices that please the Lord are a broken, contrite heart and a broken spirit. [279] We bow before our Lord to have life, asking for mercy, as we desire freedom from bondage to sin. Following the Lord is the only place of hope and light. He keeps His promises. The Lord will draw us to Himself, and He will teach us to put aside self and love others, even our enemies, as He intended. Our Lord Jesus is the means we have been given to overcome the world, to live in peace and to truly love others. He is our strength, our hope, our life and our peace. The Lord Jesus has given us wonderful promises. *"All that the Father give to me shall come to me; and him that comes to me I will certainly not cast out"* (John 6:37, NASB). *"Come unto me all that labor and are heavy laden, and I will give you rest. Take my yoke upon you, and learn of me; for I am meek and lowly in heart: and you shall find rest unto your soul. For my yoke is easy, and my burden is light"* (Matthew 11:28-30). [280]

The first purpose of repentance is to honor our Lord Jesus, to glorify Him, for He is God. Out of His mercy, the Lord Jesus applies His cross in propitiation for our sins, thereby making it possible for our manifold sins to be forgiven and removed. We submit to the Lord Jesus as the One who purchased us through His blood, bringing us reconciliation with the living God. *"In whom we have redemption through his blood, the forgiveness of sins, according to the riches of His grace"* (Ephesians 1:7). *"Him hath God exalted with his right hand (to be) a Prince and a Savior, for to give repentance to Israel, and forgiveness of sins"* (Acts 5:3). Our sin created the separation from God, but through Jesus we receive reconciliation with God and a relationship that garners fellowship with Christ Jesus for eternity. Such mercy is far greater than we deserve!

Jeroboam never repented, even when he knew what would happen to his family. He never acknowledged God or God's Word, nor showed any awareness of having any obligation to be kept as a Jewish man under God's authority. Rather, he showed contempt for God and His Word. His actions, particularly the disregard for his family, revealed a visceral hardness. Jeroboam did not acknowledge his transgressions, and his heart remained as cold as granite.

---

279. See Psalm 51:17
280. See also Acts 2:29-31

CHAPTER 34

SAVED BY GOD'S GRACE

Grace is the umbrella that covers all things imparted to us by the Father through the Son by the indwelling Holy Spirit.

(READ THE FOLLOWING VERSES IN CONTEXT AND THEN ANSWER THE QUESTIONS FOUND UNDER EACH VERSE. PUT THE VERSES, THE QUESTIONS AND THEIR ANSWERS IN YOUR NOTEBOOK.)

QUESTIONS ON JOHN 1:1-14 AND 17 AND ACTS 15:11

And the Word was made flesh, and dwelt among us, (and we beheld his glory, the glory as of the only begotten of the Father,) full of grace and truth. John 1:14

For the law was given by Moses, (but) grace and truth came by Jesus Christ. John 1:17

But we believe that through the grace of the Lord Jesus Christ we shall be saved, even as they.
Acts 15:11 **[To Memorize]**

1. **Who is the Word?**
2. **What is the grace and truth that John speaks of here?**

QUESTIONS ON ROMANS 5:1-2

Being justified freely by His grace through the redemption that is in Christ Jesus: whom God has set forth (to be) a <u>propitiation</u> [281] *through faith in his blood, to declare his righteousness for the remission of sins that are past ... . Therefore being justified by faith, we have peace with God through our Lord Jesus Christ: by whom also we have access by faith into this grace wherein we stand.*
Romans 5:1-2 **[To Memorize]**

1. **How do we have access to this grace?**
2. **Why are we justified by the grace of God?**
3. **Why is the righteousness of Christ of such great value?**
4. **What are the benefits of being justified by faith?**

QUESTIONS ON ROMANS 5:15 AND 17

For if through the offence of one (Adam) many be dead (because of the curse of sin), how much more the grace of God, and the gift by grace which is by one man, Jesus Christ, has abounded unto many. For if by one man's (Adam's) offence death reined by one; much more they which receive abundance of grace and the gift of righteousness shall reign in life by one, Jesus Christ.

Romans 5:15 and 17   **[To Memorize]**

1. **What did Adam bring upon mankind?**
2. **What did Jesus Christ bring to mankind?**

QUESTIONS ON ROMANS 5:1-12 AND 15-21

God, out of His abundant grace, gave us the Law that we might identify our sins against each other and against our Lord.

Moreover the law entered, that the offence might abound. But where sin abounded grace did more abound: that as sin has reigned unto death, even so might grace reign through righteousness unto eternal life by Jesus Christ our Lord.   Romans 5:20-21   **[To Memorize]**

1. **Why did condemnation come upon men?**
2. **How does the righteousness of One bring into being the justification of life?**
3. **When the Law was made, what happened to men?**
4. **Where does sin lead?**
5. **How does grace operate? And where does it lead?**

QUESTIONS ON JOHN 14 AND 15 AND ROMANS 6:1-18

Do you not know that when you present yourselves to someone as slaves for obedience, you are slaves of the one whom you obey, either of sin resulting in death, or of obedience resulting in righteousness.

Romans 6:16, NASB [282]

But thanks be to God that though you were slaves of sin, you became obedient from the heart to that form of teaching to which you were committed, and having been freed from sin, you became slaves of righteousness.   Romans 6:17-18, NASB   **[To Memorize]**

1. **What happens within a man when he is indwelled [283] by Jesus Christ?**
2. **Why was circumcision important to the covenant made at Sinai?**
3. **What is the mark of men who follow Christ?**

We glorify the Lord by honoring His eternal Son. We are to serve the Lord Jesus Christ and, through Him, the eternal Father. Remember the promise of Romans 8:1-2, *"There is therefore now no condemnation to them which are in Christ Jesus, who walk not after the flesh, but after the Spirit. For the law of the Spirit of Life in Christ Jesus has made me free from the law of sin and death."* This new life of grace has set us free to love one another without selfish motives or false expectations, even our enemies. This is done by living in dependence upon Christ alone each day. We read His Word very often, for it will keep us on the straight way of real love. Reading the Word as commanded in the Law of Kings would have kept the Hebrew kings close to God by undermining pride and keeping their minds thinking in the straight way of God. This is the picture the words in Romans 6 form: our old man is crucified with Christ so that our sin nature dies. We have an iron-clad promise that our sin nature is destroyed and our attachment to the sin nature has been severed. [284] Therefore sin is no longer our Master.

QUESTIONS ON ROMANS 8:1-2

1. **What does it mean to walk after the Spirit?**
2. **How do men walk after the flesh?**

Therefore if any man be in Christ, he is a new creature: old things are passed away; behold all things are become new.
2 Corinthians 5:17

For in Christ Jesus neither circumcision availeth anything, nor uncircumcision, but a new creature.
Galatians 6:15

Sin shall not have dominion over you, for you are not under law, but under grace.
Romans 6:14   **[Memorize these three verses]**

God has also enlarged our hearts so that we might have a fuller comprehension of His love and joy for us. And not only this, the Lord has given His children abundant grace [285] so that we might think differently and bring our mind into conformity with the mind of Christ explained in His Word.

---

283. See John 14 and 15
284. See Romans 6:6
285. 2 Corinthians 10:5: *"Casting down imaginations, and every high thing that exalts itself against the knowledge of God, and bringing into captivity every thought to the obedience of Christ."*

GRACE

*Bless the L*ORD*, O my soul: and all that is within me, (bless) His holy name. Bless the L*ORD*, O my soul, and forget not all His benefits: who forgives all your iniquities; who heals all your diseases; who redeemed our life from destruction; who crowned you with loving kindness and tender mercies; ... . The L*ORD *(is) merciful and gracious, slow to anger, and plenteous in mercy.*

*He has not dealt with us after our sins; nor rewarded us according to our iniquities. For as the heaven is high above the earth, (so) great is his mercy toward them that fear him. As far as the east is from the west, (so) far has he removed our transgressions from us. Like a father pities (his) children, (so) the L*ORD *pities them that fear him. For He knows our frame; He remembers that we (are) dust. (As for) man, his days (are) as grass: as a flower of the field, so he flourishes. For the wind passes over it, and it is gone; and the place thereof shall know it no more. But the mercy of the L*ORD *(is) from everlasting to everlasting upon them that fear him.*   Psalm 103:1-4, 10-17, Ver?   **[To Memorize]**

We have gained faith, and everything that attends this faith, through the unfathomable grace found in the heart of our God and Savior. We have peace with the living God, and we are no longer aliens from the promise of grace. By God's grace we are redeemed, set free from the bondage to self in sin, and we are justified and sanctified. We are given an inheritance of sonship, as well as a place in Heaven through this abundant grace! We gain understanding and strength to stand through this gracious and powerful grace, as it weaves the Word of truth into our heart. By grace we have the righteousness of Christ accredited to our account. The Scriptures give ample testimony to this grace of God, teaching us to respond in gratitude for so great a gain in our Savior and God.

AMEN!

JESUS AS PROPHET, PRIEST AND KING

PRIEST OF GOD (HEBREWS 7:1-26)

Melchizedek was a king, and high priest of God Most High who lived in the city of Salem.[1] He came out of the city carrying bread and wine (used in the worship of God) and blessed Abraham and then blessed God for putting the soldiers from four city-states into the hands of Abraham. Abraham was a wealthy man who was highly respected in this land. He gave tithes (10% of his increase) to this king-priest as an offering to God.

Melchizedek resembled the Lord Jesus in at least two ways: Jesus, our Lord, is King, Prophet and High Priest appointed by God, and Jesus has a life without end. Melchizedek was also spoken of as having no beginning and no end. Why? No information is available to determine his history either before or after this incident. That is why the apostle Paul said that Melchizedek had no beginning or end. The apostle, led by the Spirit, brings up these interesting parallels between this king-priest Melchizedek and the Lord Jesus. No one else seemed to have made the connection. The argument made in Hebrews 7 is that, not only did Abraham give tithes to this high priest, but all the people who would come from Abraham's line of descendants were represented here, as if they, too, had given this tithe to Melchizedek.

Abraham's son was Isaac, and to Isaac were born two boys, named Jacob and Esau. Jacob had twelve boys, and these great-grandsons of Abraham would become the twelve tribes[2] of Israel. The writers of the Bible often used Jacob to represent all the tribes of Israel. Jacob lived in the land for years, but there came a serious drought, and the whole family of Jacob, seventy people, were forced to go to Egypt in search of food. Sometime later, as Jacob was dying, he gave a prophecy to each son concerning his particular tribe. Judah was called a lion, and the tribe was given a promise of having a future king and lawgiver.[3]

Abraham's people continued to live in Egypt about four hundred years after the death of Jacob. Jacob told his sons to carry his body out of Egypt and bury him in the same place where Abraham and Sara had been buried. Joseph had his father's body embalmed according to Egyptian custom. God called Moses, of the tribe of Levi, to go back into Egypt to bring the people of Abraham out of bondage and into the lands God had promised them. God made Aaron, the brother of Moses, to be Moses' prophet, relaying what was said by Moses to the Egyptians. Later, Aaron was designated the first High Priest unto the Lord, and all of Aaron's descendants were to be priests.

---

1. See Hebrews 7:1-3, This king was *"king of righteousness"* and *"king of peace."* Jesus is both our righteousness and our peace. This city later became Jerusalem (see Psalm 76:1-3).

2. See Genesis 35:22-29.

3. See Genesis 49:8-10. Before Jacob died in Egypt, he gave each son a prophecy related to the future of the tribe he represented.

After the first three months in the wilderness, the Lord spoke through Moses to the people. He gave them the Ten Commandments to live by and civil law to govern the people. The Lord also gave all the instructions needed to set up the priesthood with it various duties.[4] He also gave complete instructions on how to build the wilderness Tabernacle. It would serve as a portable Temple, where the priests could offer the various sacrifices to the Lord. The people agreed to do all that the Lord had said. This is what the Lord promised, *"Now therefore if you will indeed obey My voice and keep My covenant, then you shall be a treasure to Me above all people; for all the earth is Mine. And you shall be to me a kingdom of priest and a holy nation."*[5]

Jesus came to fulfill all the prophecy about Him and to do the work He was sent to accomplish. He came to make His followers into *"a kingdom of priests and a holy nation."* The Church was created to be the Holy nation of priests who offer up to the Lord the sacrifices of prayer and praise continually. The Church is also to be charitable to those inside and outside, when help and guidance are needed.

The Scriptures are filled with everything necessary for worship, obedience and instructions in the things of the Lord. If you do not read this living document sent from Heaven to men, you cannot truly be of the Lord. Why? Because the indwelling Spirit has the same objective as the Father and the Son. We are to be a holy people, like Jesus in our thoughts and deeds. The Lord Jesus is interceding for all His children continually. Therefore, we are to be serious intercessors for our brothers and sisters in Christ, as well as for our families, neighbors, state and nation. The Scriptures are both spiritual food and instructions for a life with Christ, without which the Spirit is hampered, and we stumble to follow Christ or love Him.

PROPHET OF GOD (DEUTERONOMY 18:15-22)

Abraham's descendants were now about a million people, and they found the wilderness to be a harsh and unforgiving land. Moses was the prophet called by God to relay His messages exactly as they were given to him. Moses was devoted to the Lord and His agenda and to the descendants of Abraham.

God revealed to Moses that in the future He would raise up another Prophet from the people like Moses. *"Him you shall hear ... . I ... will put My words in His mouth, and He shall speak to them all that I command Him. And it shall be that whoever will not hear My words, which He speaks in My name, I will require it of him."*[6] Our Lord Jesus is the fulfillment of this prophecy[7] because He is the true Prophet of God. Jesus always took the messages of God[8] and was careful to deliver only those messages, but He was much more that just a Prophet of God.

---

4. Exodus chapters 19 to 40 contain the necessary laws and their applications which served to create a culture that was strong enough to stand alone if the people seriously followed the Lord.
5. Exodus 19:5-6. Exodus 3:4-22 Jesus used the phrase, *"before Abraham was, "I Am"* to identify Himself basically as the living God. See also John 8:53-59
6. Deuteronomy 18:15 and 18-19, NKJV
7. See John 5:45-47
8. See John 8:28-29, 12:49-50 and 14:9-11

God said this to Moses, *"I AM WHO I AM."* And God said, *"Thus you shall say to the children of Israel, 'The LORD God of your fathers, the God of Isaac and the God Jacob, has sent me to you. This is My name forever, and this is My memorial to all generations.'* "[9]

The Jews accused Jesus of having a demon, saying, *"Abraham is dead and the prophets. And you say, 'If anyone keeps My word he shall never taste death.' Are you greater than our father Abraham, who is dead? And the prophets are dead? Who do You make Yourself out to be?"*

"Jesus answered, 'If I honor Myself, My honor is nothing. It is My Father who honors Me, of whom you say that He is your God. Yet you have not known Him, but I know Him. And if I say, 'I do not know Him,' I shall be a liar like you; but I do know Him and keep His word. Your father Abraham rejoiced to see My day, and he saw it and was glad.'"

"Then the Jews said to Him, "You are not yet fifty years old. And have You seen Abraham?"

"Jesus said to them, 'Most assuredly, I say to you, before Abraham was, I AM.' "

"Then they took up stones to throw at Him" because they knew Jesus was saying that He was indeed the living God who spoke to Abraham.[10]

KINGS OF KINGS

King David was told by the Lord that one of his descendants would be a king forever and have an everlasting kingdom: *"I will set up your seed after you, who will come from your body, and I will establish his kingdom. He shall build a house for My name, and I will establish the throne of his kingdom forever. I will be his Father, and he shall be My son. ... And your house and your kingdom shall be established forever before you. Your throne shall be established forever."*[11]

Both Joseph and Mary were descendants of King David. On the first page of the Gospel of Matthew, we can read Joseph's linage. *"The book of the genealogy of Jesus Christ, the Son of David, the Son of Abraham ... ."*[12] Luke further related, *"The angel Gabriel was sent by God to a city of Galilee named Nazareth, to a virgin betrothed to a man whose name was Joseph, of the house of David."*[13]

"Then the angel said to her, 'Do not be afraid, Mary, for you have found favor with God. And behold, you will conceive in your womb and bring forth a Son, and shall call His name Jesus. He will be great and will be called the Son of the Highest; and the Lord God will give Him the throne of His Father David. And He will reign over the house of Jacob forever, and of His kingdom there will be no end."[14]

"The angel ... said to her, 'The Holy Spirit will come upon you, and the power of the Highest will overshadow you; therefore also, that Holy One who is to be born will be called the Son of God."[15] His name is Jesus!

9. Exodus 3:11-15, NKJV
10, John 8:52-59, NKJV
11. See 2 Samuel 7:11-16, God's covenant with King David
12. Matthew 1:1, NKJV
13. Luke 1:26, NKJV
14. Luke 1:30-33, NKJV
15. Luke 1:35, NKJV

Think No Evil

The Parent-Teacher Guide

CONTENTS

NOTES ON SPECIFIC LESSONS

INTRODUCTION TO THE PARENT/TEACHER

I have written an explanation of some of the biblical principles covered and given references to be discussed in detail with the student. This is necessary because the student will generally not stop to read and consider the references. If desired, the student can read the parent-teacher material, but it is important for the parent-teacher to take the time to discuss the material and share the scriptures in the references with the student. The time spent in pre-lesson study (especially the wealth of information sited in the footnotes) in preparation for teaching is necessary in order for the parent-teacher to lead the student into a greater understanding of what Christianity is based upon and how real faith functions.

The adult reader should study all the information in order to get a fuller view, just as if he were the parent-teacher. We are building a framework for the Christian faith so that the student will understand what he believes (the tenets of the Christian faith) and why he believes them.

The various definitions are taken from the Hebrew and Greek dictionaries found in *Strong's Exhaustive Concordance of the Bible.* [1]

I have used the King James Version of the Bible more then any other for the references. Other versions used are listed and documented on the copyright page. The ones I particularly like are the ASV-1901 (the American Standard Version of 1901), the NASB (the New American Standard Bible), the MKJV (the Modern King James Version) and the NKJV (the New King James Version). [2]

---

1. *Strong's Exhaustive Concordance of the Bible* by James Strong, S.T.D., LL. D. (Peabody, Massachusetts, Hendrickson Publishers: 2007)
2. See the copyright page for details

ABOUT THE MEMORIZATION

After developing this series of lessons to guide students to faith in Jesus Christ, I added the extra step of the memorization of scripture because the Spirit uses the Word of God to inform, correct and generally guide the heart\mind. These memory verses can easily be reduced if it is difficult for the student to memorize. But I have found that even students who have never memorized can do this exercise, given enough time and encouragement. It helps if the parent-teacher also memorizes the verses, while working with the student.

Some students prefer verses out of other translations, so, by all means, let them use the translation that is easier for them to remember. I recommend that you open or close each lesson with five minutes spent on reciting the current memory verses. Then, once a month, review the verses the students have studied so far in all of their lessons.

The apostle John encouraged believers to *"test the spirits"* of all men because many false prophets are in the world. Every spirit confessing that Jesus Christ is of God and came in living flesh is of God. Every spirit that says that Jesus Christ is not of God and did not come to earth in the flesh is not of God. And then John said something to believers to give us sure hope: *"You are of God, little children, and you have overcome them, because He who is in you is greater than he who is in the world. They are of the world, therefore they speak of the world, and the world hears them. We are of God. He who knows God hears us. The one who is not of God does not hear us. From this we know the spirit of truth, and the spirit of error"* (1 John 4:1-6, MKJV).

Urge your student/s to remember the Word that they have memorized and remind themselves of their content often, so that they can keep their thinking in line with the words of the living God. His view of the world of men is the truth.

THE TIMING OF THE STUDIES

The material covered in these lessons is not time sensitive and can be taken at a fast or slow rate, depending upon the needs of the parent-teacher, the student or an adult reader. A few lessons are long and can be broken into two lessons if need be.

HOW TO APPROACH THE SCRIPTURES

When studying the Bible, approach it with the care and reverence it deserves because it is God's truth that you are looking into. Our Lord Jesus is the living Translator and Interpreter of all the Holy Words of both Testaments. Take care not to read the Bible like other books by mere men, and lay aside any personal perceptions, preconceived ideology or particular points of view that would obscure or override the clear sense of the Scriptures. God does not lie, and He keeps every promise—whether it is for good or ill. The Scriptures contain more than an accurate history of ancient kingdoms. They are a powerful moral teacher because God has shepherded these writings since He directed men to write down those things they heard from Him and sometimes saw with their own eyes. The Lord was instrumental in ensuring that each word was exact, as are the thoughts expressed. Therefore, you can trust this whole body of work. *"All Scripture is given by inspiration of God, and is profitable for doctrine, for reproof, for correction, for instruction in righteousness, that the man of God may be complete, thoroughly equipped for every good work."*[1]

One of the Old Testament gifts to all believers is the timeless and universal moral Law of God to both warn and protect us throughout our lives. This Law is the spotlight revealing the character of God and His will for mankind. This standard He has given us to use to govern our lives and deepen our relationship with Him. The Lord has told us in the Scriptures how men are to love the Lord of Life and also love each other. We are to live in the pursuit of holiness for the body, the mind and the will.

The Lord also gave specific religious codes and civil governmental codes to govern the theocracy under which the people of God lived in the Kingdom of Israel. We also see the gift of generations of our Father's dealing with His people to understand and apply the wisdom gained—both negative and positive. The Old Testament is a record of God's complicated provisions for Jesus to come at the right time and the right place and to be born of the right lineage, so that Jesus is the permanent king from the tribe of Judah promised to David so long ago. Jesus is, of course, the promised Priest of God,[2] the final permanent Intercessor appointed by God.

Jesus quoted the Old Testament passages that were written about Him[3] to show that He is the "Anointed One," the point of both testaments. Through the Spirit's work in the mind and heart of the apostles, including Paul, they heard Jesus. Their writings testify that the promised New Covenant[4] is realized in Jesus Christ, the Messiah. The sum of all things is gathered in Christ Jesus, and He is the final fulfillment of the offices of prophet, priest and king combined. There is no new revelation that is of God because the Holy Scriptures are fixed, full, complete with everything that

---

1. 2 Timothy 3:16
2. See Hebrews 4:14-16 and 1 Samuel 2:35
3. Just a small sample: Matthew 12:18-22—Isaiah 42:1-4 and 49:3; Matthew 13:14-16—Isaiah 6:9-10
4. See Jeremiah 31:31-34 and Ezekiel 36:26-27

He has chosen to reveal to us. The Scriptures sweep us through time, telling their own story, and your thinking, emotions, imagination and suggestions as to the meaning of these scriptures has been limited by God Himself.

We need to understand the very words used to convey the principles of God. The grammar that is being used is important. The verbs used can change the depth of meaning and open up a greater grasp of the content. *"God inspired"* means that all words are particular words used in a particular way to convey the mind of God and His thoughts exactly in both testaments. Therefore, readers are not to add anything to this body of work nor subtract anything from this body of work.[5] Our Bible is a specific history of God's work and a completed prophecy of both the past and the coming future.

---

5. See Revelation 22:18-19

HOW TO USE AND TEACH YOUR STUDENTS TO USE A CONCORDANCE

Begin with reading the book of John through a few times to understand who John was and what his message was. John reveals Jesus, the Son, sent to us through the love and mercy of God our Father. Take notes as you read and ask questions. It is very important to understand the context, as well as the content of what you are reading.

Follow the thinking of the writer. Who is the author talking about? Who is he talking to? Why are these verses John wrote so very important? What was going on in the political and religious arenas of the day? What does the verse say as it is read in the context of the chapter and of the entire book of John? How does John add to our knowledge of the Father and His beloved Son? What does the author mean by his words?

How many of the words used and the thoughts expressed apply personally today to you? What is God's message to you? Think about Christ's Messages: what do they tell us about Jesus or His suffering or His purpose? What does Jesus say about His second coming? What do we learn about the Father and the Holy Spirit? Are there commands to obey, sins to be confessed, apologies to be made and practices to be changed?

List the principles Jesus upholds including the Ten Commandments. Find the answers to your questions and put them into your notebook, including the name of the book, the chapter and the specific verse or verses.

If, for example, you have read the first verses of John, you have a puzzle to solve. *"In the Beginning was the Word, and the Word was with God, and the Word was God. The same was in the beginning with God. All things were made by him; and without him was not anything made that was made. In him was life; and the live was the light of men. And the light shined in darkness; and the darkness comprehended it not."*

Now, skip to verse 14: *"And the Word was made flesh, and dwelt among us, (and we beheld his glory, the glory as of the only begotten of the Father,) full of grace and truth."*

Purchase and dedicate the time necessary to learn to use a Bible concordance so that you can find the meanings of biblical words. I have found *Strong's Concordance*[6] to be easy to use, but there are many good concordances that use Strong's same numbering system.

Once you have your copy, turn to the large first section, which is an alphabetical listing of the words used in the Scriptures. To find the word *word*, for example, look under the W section. Next, look for the book of John, which is abbreviated as *Jn*. Look through the listings, and find the particular word used in John 1:1-5 and 14. The number found to the right of the word you are searching for in John 1:1-5 and 14 is *G3056*. This is the New Testament portion, primarily written in Greek.

---

6. *Strong's Exhaustive Concordance of the Bible* by James Strong, S.T.D., LL. D. (Peabody, Massachusetts, Hendrickson Publishers: 2007)

Now, go to the back of the concordance to the section called "The Greek Dictionary," which contains the explanations of words used in the entire New Testament. The white letters GRK are placed upon a small black background and are seen on the right-hand side of all these pages. As an example, see page 1599. The first information mentioned is the fact that 3056 is formed from *Logos* G3004, which is a primary verb meaning "to lay forth, to relate in words usually of a systematic or set discourse." Other meanings are listed after this. The Greek "Word" is 3056, which means, "Something said (the thought), reasoning (mental faculty) motive. When used specifically with the article *the*, it means, "The divine Expression" (i.e. the Christ).

To summarize, the words used here identify Jesus Christ as "The Divine Expression" of God. Jesus Christ is the exact representation of the Lord God in human flesh. Therefore, He is both fully divine and fully human.

Jesus Himself made some amazing statements, *"I am the way, the truth and the life: no man comes to the Father, but by me."*[7] Jesus said to Philip, *"Have I been with you so long, and yet you have not known Me, Philip? He who has seen Me has seen the Father: so how can you say, Show us the Father?* "*Do you not believe that I Am in the Father and the Father in Me? The words that I speak to you I do not speak on My own authority: but the Father who dwells in Me does the works. Believe Me that I am in the Father and the Father in Me, or else believe Me for the sake of the works themselves."*[8] Look at John 1:17-18 (NKJV): *"For the law was given through Moses, but grace and truth came through Jesus Christ. No one has seen God at any time. The only begotten Son, who is in the bosom of the Father, He [Jesus, the Christ] has declared Him [God the Father]."* Jesus came to reveal the Father and the universal Truth unto men and to sacrifice Himself to save mankind.

When Jesus was talking to the woman at the well, He told her that neither on this mountain upon which her people worshiped, nor the Jewish worship site in Jerusalem would be where men worshiped God. *"But an hour is coming, and now is, when the true worshipers will worship the Father in spirit and truth; for such people the Father seeks to be His worshipers. God is spirit, and those who worship Him must worship in spirit and truth."* The woman said to Him, I know that Messiah is coming (He who is called Christ); when that One comes, He will declare all things to us." Jesus said to her, *"I who speak to you am He."*[9] Jesus told His disciples in John 13:19 and 14:29, that He had revealed things to them before they had happened so that they might believe.

Our Lord Jesus is very plain-spoken, He cannot lie, and He does not make mistakes. He has the exact character as the Father. He says exactly what He means, and He has made it very clear that He means what He has said. Remember, the Father allowed Jesus Christ to die, taking the debt of sin we owed upon Himself, therefore making it possible to justify true believers by and through Jesus' blood and righteousness, thereby making us acceptable to God.

God has a vested interest in us, and we, His children, are accepted in the beloved Son.[10] Remember

---

7. John 14:5 and 9-11
8. John 14:9-11, NKJV
9. John 4:23-26, NASB
10. See Ephesians 1

that this is God's book, and He interprets His Scriptures using the Scriptures themselves. He knows very well that the temptation to slide some personal view in among the Scriptures comes from the corrupt nature of man. The Scriptures are also His means of enlightening the heart and mind of men through the indwelling Spirit of Christ, which leads to the conversion of the soul. The Scriptures are the Truth, and the Lord sends the Spirit of Christ to indwell the souls he is converting[11] that they might see the Truth and know the Living Truth. Remember that this is necessary because we all have a sin nature that cannot know God nor can men be in the presence of God because He is holy and perfect in all His ways.

---

11. See John 8:12-59 and John 14

AN OVERVIEW OF THE FIVE SECTIONS OF THIS STUDY

SECTION ONE: THE NATURAL MAN

The natural man is used here to make the student aware of where we stand in relation to the quality of our core being. The only source of objective truth is found in the God-inspired ancient Scriptures we call the Bible, which have been passed down through generations for thousands of years. We cover how the Law functions in relation to mankind.

SECTION TWO: SPIRIT-FILLED MAN

In this section, we study God's biblical work of grace and how His grace functions to fulfill His objectives to save the people He loves. We show how this grace of God working through the indwelling Jesus Christ, works in us to perform His will. We see the opening of the mind\heart of man to hear the truths of God. The Father brings rebirth, with godly repentance being worked into our hearts. We discuss the principle of the justification of man through faith in Jesus Christ alone. The Lord is clear in His intentions: we are to reflect the character of Christ in all of His fulness.

SECTION THREE: PRIDE A PATTERN OF THINKING

This section takes the sinful attitude of pride, which is at the center of our thinking, and shows how far it is from the heart\mind filled with love for God and love for men. There is almost no sin that we commit that is not in some way connected to our pride, for most wrong thinking springs from this sinful core of pride in self.

SECTION FOUR: ISRAEL AS AN EXAMPLE

This is the largest section, and it is broken into three parts. Part 1 concerns the Northern Kingdom, Part 2 the Southern Kingdom, and Part 3 the Gentiles in the Assyrian and Babylonian kingdoms. We also see God's assessment of all of these kingdoms. We begin with a brief view of the history of Israel to give you a framework in which to put the rest of the section. Here is a more detailed description of the lives of the Jewish people. Many of the people in the Old Testament were filled with pride. Being stubborn and rebellious, they refused to follow God. We would expect this to be true of the sin-nature described in the Scripture as man's true nature. The exception is found in those prophets or judges called by God for specific purposes, as well as in a remnant of the people who had set their hearts to follow God.

The first kingdom was formed by God from the family of Abraham. The Hebrew people were the descendants of the twelve sons who were born to Abraham's grandson Jacob. [1] We discuss Solomon and watch his grandson Rehoboam as he alienated most of the twelve tribes. Jeroboam took ten of

---

1. See Genesis 24 through 35

the tribes as the base of the Northern Kingdom and established his own priesthood and worship sites. The two tribes of Judah and Benjamin, as well as the loyal priests of Levi formed the Southern Kingdom. These examples are given to help us understand the results which follow from sinful thinking. We cover the false religious leaders of both testaments who lied about God and bent His Word any way they wanted, or ignored the precepts of God and inserted their own perceptions or traditions.

This section includes examples taken from the leaders and peoples of the northern and southern kingdoms of Israel and from the Assyrian and Babylonian empires of the Gentile or non-Jewish peoples, to see how pride impacts all individuals and all countries. Pride has been a universal trait of men within all cultures throughout time.

NOTES ON SPECIFIC LESSONS

PART I: THE NATURAL MAN

CHAPTER 1

MAN'S THINKING

It is important for children to know that sin breaks the commandments of God. In discussing sin, it is a good idea to look up the Ten Commandments [1] and spend a while discussing them. The admonition to honor parents is particularly relevant because these days few are expected to obey their parents as God intended. This is serious because any failure to honor parents is sin because God has commanded that children young or old obey their parents. Children, however, are the center of their own world and will try their hand at manipulation to maintain this position, even against the will of the parent.

Parents daily confront this truth of the innate selfishness and sin nature in the determined will of their offspring. A child is told to pick up his room; instead, he shoves everything under the bed. Has he obeyed his parent? The natural tendency of the sin-nature is to do only what pleases self. Children who are not taught to respect the Lord and their parents became impatient, demanding and often have no regard for others. Having no regard for the will of God or their own good, [2] children must be taught to obey, to have self-control. This is very important.

The Word of God gives children insight into the qualities of evil within men and within self that students will recognize. If they are taught the truth of the Scriptures, they can develop sound judgment based on the wisdom of God. We are obliged, as Christian parents, to exhibit and teach the qualities found in godly love—such as kindness, gentleness, self-control, truthfulness and courtesy—and help our children develop these qualities.

We are not born into this world as innocents; we all have a natural bias toward the breaking of God's eternal Law. No one bound by the sin nature has the discernment and knowledge necessary to submit self to the will of the heavenly Father. Our sin nature is terminally self-absorbed, with absolute trust in our perceptions. We cannot see ourselves as being as self-absorbed as we actually are because sin deceives the one committing the sin. We justify our choices, even if our own conscience protests. We are self-deceived.

The truth is we camouflage the desires of our heart/mind in order to pursue them. Such willful self-absorption clearly exists in the nature of parent and child; we both actively display this same bias. This sin nature separates us from God and corrupts man so that he cannot know the Lord, love Him or keep His laws. The Lord says to man: "the thought of your heart is only evil continually." [3] If we consider this truth seriously, it humbles our heart and helps us see that our

---

1. Exodus 20

2. Jeremiah 10:23: *"0 Lord, I know that the way of man is not in himself; it is not in man who walks to direct his steps."*

3. Genesis 6:5: *"And Jehovah saw that the wickedness of man was great in the earth, and every imagination of the thoughts of his heart was only evil continually."*

dark thoughts and deeds sent Jesus to the cross, to shed His blood, to atone for our bone-deep sin nature.

Those of us who are redeemed once had no regard for the Lord, but He graciously extended mercy by opening our heart/minds to know Him. He changed the intent of our heart/mind to have regard for Him and His truth and to obey His will. When we are given new life through Jesus Christ, we pray and teach our children the wisdom of God. This is no guarantee that they will submit their hearts/minds to the Lord. Our Lord must also open their hearts/minds to see the truth of the sin nature which blinds us and separates all of us from the Lord. The Lord is full of mercy and will graciously grant new life to those who seek Him with their whole heart for worship and submission.

CHAPTER 2

MAN AS A FREE AGENT

As a preparation for this chapter, read Romans 1:15-32, which describes the general downward moral spiral taken by natural man without serious devotion to God. Read Romans 2:1-13, where Paul discusses the hypocrisy of a man who judges others, and Romans 3:9-32, where he explains that among men, none do good, no one is righteous, none understand and none seek God. We also learn that God is not a respecter of persons but deals with all men by the same standard of truth. So, it matters not if we are Jewish people under the Law of God or Gentiles under the laws invented by men. Both will be judged by God.

Men fail to keep the Law because of their natural propensity for sin and rebellion against God. *"For all have sinned, and come short of the glory of God"* (Romans 3:23). God has declared that His righteousness is displayed through our faith being placed in Jesus Christ for salvation. This is so contrary to the expectations of men, who place faith in their ability to do the things which they have determined will gain salvation. Jesus is the only true Keeper of God's Law, the only sacrificial Sin-Bearer whose shed blood made possible the forgiveness of our sins. Only Jesus is designated by God to be both just and the Justifier of all who trust/obey Him by faith. So, no man can boast in self. [4]

---

4. See Ephesians 2:4-9, Romans 9:13, 2 Corinthians 5:21, Galatians 2:21, 3:21 and 5:5, Philippians 3:9 and Hebrews 11:7

CHAPTER 3

GOD'S ASSESSMENT OF MAN'S THINKING

Unregenerate men are unaware of the fact that God has declared mankind to be evil from his youth. Listen to this from Genesis 6:5, NKJV: *"Then the Lord saw that every intent of the thoughts of his heart was only evil continually."* In Genesis 8:21, the Lord is making a promise to us and giving us this truth: *"I will never again curse the ground on account of man,"* although, He said, *"the intent of man's heart is evil from his youth."*

Young people do not evaluate their behavior or attitudes, and we want to open their understanding of self. The Ten Commandments are the excellent standard that covers our natural propensity for sin. We must use every opportunity that presents itself to us to allow our children to see the comparison between God's Word and our wretched self. This requires the consistently used standard of the Commandments to illustrate the right from the wrong. After some time has passed, the children will recognize sin and understand that sin begins within self. They will begin to have an idea that we all are responsible for our attitudes, behavior and speech.

Often, we can observe our sins being reflected in the attitudes, actions and speech of our children. Start to use the Commandments for your own behavior also. Why? Because our young people can see our sin, and our failures need to be acknowledged. Here are some important things to remember: Even older children need to have definite penalties for misbehavior.[5] Be cautious if you are dealing with multiple children because they will try to pass the ownership of sin to another. Stay alert because when we are tired and overloaded, we tend to have less patience and will pass judgment before we have heard all the information.

Least you think God is too harsh in His judgments, read Leviticus 26:1-46, which was written before the people went into the Promised Land.

---

5. See Proverbs 29:15 and 17

CHAPTER 4

THE LAW (PART 1)

In preparation for teaching this lesson, read all the context of the related references so that you can help broaden the understanding of your student. You may want to expand this lesson by make your own questions from the references. You could also read Matthew 22:37-39 and Mark 12:30-31. Please share all of the information you gather with the students. See what great things the Lord has done for us by sending the Law. Without this Law, man would only do what is right in his own eyes. We know what corrupt men do when power comes to them, and there are no restraints upon their cruelty. Out of the Lord's bountiful goodness, He left the imprint of His commandments in our conscience. It is also interesting to delve into the laws from the Babylonian civilization and compare them to the Ten Commandments.

You will find references to the Decalogue, the moral law, throughout Genesis, before the Law was officially given at Sinai. For instance, in Genesis 4, we read that Cain slew Abel. Although the Decalogue had not yet been given at Mt. Sinai, [6] Cain's murder of Abel was still declared as sin. Without God's law we would not know what He requires of us nor what constitutes evil. The Decalogue defines evil, for in our spiritual darkness, we would be only guessing as each man made his own definitions of good and evil, according to his perceptions of truth.

There are six laws which feature human relations found in the Ten Commandments. The sins of men are stated clearly and invite our heart/mind to see the opposite of the stated evil, thereby also defining for us the good. The Ten Commandments cover the main streams of evil which flow from men. We need this information to begin to understand the qualities of evil. With our natural bias toward sin, we are unable to discern, with any degree of accuracy, even our own sin, and it is certain we cannot see the sinful motivations of another. The Lord has shown us great kindness, for without an objective observer to present to us the truth of His Law, which reveals our real natures, we would be eternally lost.

THE LAW (PART 2)

How do you have a consistency of obedience to the Word of God? King David said this to the Lord, *"Your commandment is exceedingly broad."* [7] Think of an iceberg and imagine you see the top. The hidden bottom layer is about five times the area and weight of the top layer. This is a good

---

6. See Exodus 20
7. Psalm 119:96

picture of the Law. We see the Ten Commandments and generally understand them, but we are ignorant of the depth of their application … unless and until Jesus expands our understanding by showing that our thoughts, motives and behavior are covered by the same law. Jesus was consistently elevating the Law of God as His standard before the people.

Jesus explained what happened to God's Law under the Jewish Leaders: *"Why also do you violate the commandment of God for the sake of your tradition [handed down by the elders] (depriving it of force authority and making it of no effect)."*[8] This same truth is revealed by God in Isaiah 29:13, *"Uselessly do they worship me, for they teach as doctrines the commandments of men."*[9] The Jewish leaders had, over time, inserted their perceptions of truth and righteousness around these sacred texts, and the result was that the Holy Word was obscured. When an eclipse takes place, you can watch it happening through devices which drastically reduce the scale and the full glory of the sun. This is what men did and still do to God's Word.

Approach the Law with respect for the Lawgiver and with humility. These Laws were written to identify sin clearly for us, curb our sin natures and teach us of the glory of the Living God and those things that please Him. Christians can understand that the Lord's person and character are, to a degree, revealed by the Ten Commandments. This moral Law is still in effect today, and it is to be our standard of conduct and thought. It will be the standard God uses for the final judgment of all mankind.

The next question is: "How do you keep it?" You cannot! Therefore, it was necessary for someone pure and full of holiness to be substituted for us. And who among human beings is pure and holy enough to take our sin upon himself. None, of course! Sometime before the world was made, Jesus offered to do just that for His children. He would offer His blood and righteousness for each one condemned by their own sin. He became a sacrificial Lamb, to endure the wrath of God against our sin. This obedience to the will of the Father by the Son paved the way for those destined by their sin to Hell to be called into a new kingdom. Only those who come to God for mercy, after hearing the truth, will find it in His Son Jesus.

---

8. Matthew 15:3, 6, 9. AMP
9. AMP

CHAPTER 5

SPIRITUAL DARKNESS

All of the lessons require the study of the footnotes and the indicated scriptures, as well as the discussions, so that you and your student may have a clear understanding of what happened to mankind when sin entered the heart. Adam and Eve were the first representatives of man and, as such, their choices would impact the history of all mankind. Explain to the students how God has made a way for man to be reconciled to God. This study will enable you to enrich the student's understanding. You may wish to expand this lesson to include the Genesis account and make your own questions. Share the information given with the students.

Read the account of the Fall of man in Genesis chapters 1 through 3. God has given to us this truth, that He created Adam and Eve and pronounced them pleasing in His sight, and they heard what God had said. Adam was the appointed leader, but he chose to defer to Eve's wishes rather that trust and obey God. Eve allowed herself to be persuaded to disregard God's clear word, choosing, instead, to put her trust in Satan's implication that God was withholding information that they needed to become like God.

Satan's sly insistence that Eve would not suffer death because of her choice to disobey the living Lord was a slick lie. He successfully manipulated her by using deception. 1 Timothy 2:14 says this of Eve: *"And Adam was not deceived [cheated, deluded], but the woman being deceived [cheated, deluded] was in the transgression [violation, breaking, transgression]."*[10]

As the representatives of mankind, Adam and Eve's violation of God's word brought the promised punishment of death and separation from God down upon all generations. After this, human beings were spiritually dead, unable to love God or man as God had intended. We now have death attached to us like a malignant shadow, to limit our life. Remember that man is unaware that he lives in spiritual darkness, and this condition is permanent, unless God sends His Holy Spirit into man, to open his mind, so that man can grasp the truth of his bondage to sin and seek salvation through Jesus Christ.

In Romans 5 and 1 Corinthians 15, Paul explained this truth:

Therefore, even as through one man (Adam), sin entered into the world, and death by sin, so death passed on all men inasmuch as all sinned ... .   Romans 5:12

For if, when we were enemies, we were reconciled to God through the death of His Son, much more, being reconciled, we shall be saved by His life.   Romans 5:10

---

10. Strong's G538

For since death is through man, the resurrection of the dead also is through a Man. For as in Adam all die, even so in Christ will be made alive. But each in his own order: Christ the first-fruit, and afterward they who are Christ's at His coming then is the end, when He delivers the kingdom to God, even the Father; when He makes to cease all rule and all authority and power. And so it is written, The first man Adam was made a living soul; the last Adam was made a life-giving Spirit. ... The first man was out of the earth, earthy; the second Man was the Lord from Heaven ... . And according as we bore the image of the earthly man, we shall also bear the image of the heavenly Man.

1 Corinthians 15:21-22, 45, 47 and 49, KJV

Notice that in Adam all die because all sin, but in Christ, His people are given new spiritual life by His Spirit. Jesus is called the Lord from Heaven. We shall bear His imprint upon our character, to joyfully do His will. *"... but the free gift shall not be also like the offense, for if by the offense of the one many died, much more the Grace of God, and the gift in grace; which is of the one Man, Jesus Christ, abound to many"* (Romans 5:15, KJV).

God loved human kind to such a degree that He sent His Son to atone for our spiritual blindness, our innate hostility toward God and our inability to keep His Law. Jesus chose, before the earth was made, to atone for His children's trespasses. His life's blood paid the penalty due our sin, in order that God might justly forgive our sin and produce in us the imprint of His dear Son.

CHAPTER 6

THE FLESH AND THE SPIRIT

We want our teens to understand the precepts of God, for they are wisdom. David said that God's precepts gave him wisdom, so that he understood more than his teachers and more than the aged of his kingdom.[11]

We have remaining sin within us that can interfere with Christian growth for too long a period. As followers of Christ, we can no longer afford to be urged into sin by our own thoughts. We are to learn to control our mind, for it can be the birthplace of more sin. *"(For the weapons of our warfare are not carnal, but mighty through God to the pulling down of strong holds;) casting down imaginations, and every high thing that exalteth itself against the knowledge of God, and bringing into captivity every thought to the obedience of Christ."*[12] What does self-control of the mind and spirit look like? Consider what needs to be controlled—anger, malice, carnal desires, evil intentions, evil reasoning and covetousness. The dictionary gives these words to describe covetous thinking: "To wish for excessively and culpably (for what you do not have or for that which belongs to another), avaricious, greedy, crave, envy." The Scriptures have a lot to say to those who lack self-control:

He who is slow to anger is better than the mighty,
And he who rules his spirit than he who takes a city.   Proverbs 16:32, NKJV

Whoever has no rule over his own spirit
Is like a city broken down, without walls.   Proverbs 25:28, NKJV

He who leans on, trust in, and is confident of his own mind and heart is a {self-confident} fool..."
          Proverbs 28:26

He who trusts in his own heart is a fool,
But whoever walks wisely will be delivered.   Proverbs 17:20, NKJV

Be renewed in the spirit of your mind.   Ephesians 4:23, NKJV

I beseech you therefore, brethren, by the mercies of God, that you present your bodies a living sacrifice, holy, acceptable to God, which is your reasonable service. And do not be conformed to this world, but

11. See Psalm 119:99-100
12. 2 Corinthians 10:4-5

be transformed by the renewing of your mind, that you may prove what is that good and acceptable and perfect will of God.   Romans 12:1-2, NKJV

There may be some restraints that we have acquired because of family, our traditions or cultural influences. Our spirits are generally not in open conflict with self (the sin-nature) before we become Christians. Therefore, we are surprised to find ourselves in a battle with our own spirit when the Holy Spirit indwells us. Paul, in Romans 7, describes the situation that existed with him. He genuinely delighted in the law of God but found a battle raging within when he wanted to obey the Lord and do what was right before Him. He found that his sin nature was reveling in all manner of covetous. He was aware that there was nothing good in self and this knowledge comes to us by the Spirit's work in our heart. Paul seemed to be shocked to find this depth of sin within. The Holy Spirit convicted him, using the Law that this sin was worthy of death. The Spirit uses the Law and the Scriptures in the same way to convict us, to correct us and to transform our minds.

In Romans 8, Paul revealed that those who are indwelt by the Spirit of Christ Jesus are not under condemnation because Jesus has paid the penalty for our law breaking. This frees us to continue fighting self because the Spirit of Christ enables us to bring our spirit under His control and work on eradicating the sins one by one. Let your children know that this is a lifetime battle, so don't be fooled when quiet comes.

NOTES ON SPECIFIC LESSONS

PART II: THE SPIRIT-FILLED MAN

CHAPTER 7

CONVERSION

The next two chapters will be discussions of Romans 7 and 8. Help the student to understand that the new law of the Spirit is unlike the old Law. The new law has the built-in provision of power through the indwelling Spirit of Christ and kinship through adoption as a son. When men decided to divide the Testament into chapters, some divisions, like this one, seem arbitrary because Paul's discussion of the internal war that exist and the pathway of victory over remaining sin in the believer continue from Romans 7 through chapter 8.

CONCERNING ROMANS 7:7-25:

Paul starts the chapter making the point that the Law has jurisdiction over individuals as long they live. He is explaining the necessity of the Law to point out sin within all individuals. When the natural man is ignorant of the Law, he does not brand himself as a sinner. But he must understand that the Law is holy, spiritual and good, operating like a nail gun and nailing us to the barn. We are given no cover for our sin but are exposed, and sin multiplies as we are compelled to delve into our hearts. Knowledge of the Law points out sin and produces condemnation under a just death sentence. Sin is revealed in its true form: our soul is corrupt, just as if it were a malignant cancer. But there is hope in Jesus. He kept the Law perfectly, as the Substitute for us. He also paid the sentence of death piled up against us because of our trespasses.

We have fruit trees in our yard, and it takes perfect conditions and about six months to produce a lemon. The external conditions required are continuous sunshine, periodic rain, warm nights and a high temperature during the day. We can also experience white fly infestations, which produce a horrible black, sooty, moldy fungus that covers the entire tree, limiting the sunlight that reaches the plant, and the result is that the whole plant declines. In the winter, we must cover the trees and put a heat producing light under the tarp near them to raise the temperature slightly. Some winters, this is not enough, and later in the spring we must prune off the branches that have frozen and split. If there are too many lemons on the tree, they will be small, but if you reduce the number of lemons growing on each branch, the lemons grow much larger.

Our heavenly Father supervises our condition and our fruit production, just like we watch over our fruit trees. He brings changing circumstances, to condition us for spiritual growth. He is working in us to produce all the fruit of the Spirit. This fruit [13] is the opposite of the sin we had produced.[14]

---

13. Galatians 5:22 *"But the fruit of the Spirit is love, joy, peace, patience, kindness, goodness, faithfulness, gentleness, self-control ... ."* (NASB)

14. Galatians 5:19-21 *"Now the deeds of the flesh are evident, which are: immorality, impurity, sensuality, idolatry, sorcery, enmities, strife, jealousy, outbursts of anger, disputes, dissensions, factions, envying, drunkenness, carousing, and things like these, of which I forewarned you, that those who practice such things will not inherit the kingdom of God."* (NASB)

This means we have to trust our Lord, listen to His Word, believe it and follow His directions for our lives. We are in a steady state of flux under His hand, as we are moved to let go of those sins that impede our growth. The Lord continually goes deeper, revealing yet more thoughts, attitudes and responses that are contrary to the love He is teaching us. In this journey, we are seldom at ease. We are pressed on all sides, with seasons of warfare within and without, and the truth is that we could not bring to ourselves one virtue. But God is the purposed and faithful Gardener. In Christ, we have died, and sin is no longer our Master. We are shielded forever from the Law's condemnation and death. We are given new life, to produce fruit for our heavenly Father. The Spirit is working in us to produce the virtues of our Lord Jesus.

CHAPTER 8

THE LAW OF THE SPIRIT IN CHRIST

ON ROMANS 8:1-17

There is therefore now no condemnation to them which are in Christ Jesus, who walk not after the flesh, but after the Spirit. For the law of the Spirit of life in Christ Jesus has made me free from the law of sin and death that the righteousness of the law might be fulfilled in us, who walk not after the flesh, but after the Spirit. For they that are after the flesh do mind the things of the flesh; but they that are after the Spirit the things of the Spirit.   Romans 8:1-5

Here Paul discusses the understanding he gained through the Spirit about the work that the Spirit was doing in him and the work done through the good Law in giving sin its malignancy. Paul had become aware of the war that existed between his mind (that loved the Lord) and the old sinful ways of thinking and behaving that clung to him. The Spirit gave Paul insight into the inner workings of God within redeemed men.

The biblical language is not always easy to understand because it speaks in phases that may not be familiar, but once you get the concepts, the phrases become clearer. For instance, in chapter 8 of Romans, there are two basic laws discussed. One of them, in verse 7, is the *"Law of God"* (basically the Ten Commandments or moral law), and the other is *"the law of the Spirit of Life in Christ Jesus"* in verse 2. See again what verses 2 and 3 are saying, *"For the law of the Spirit of life in Christ Jesus has made me free from <u>the law of sin and death</u>. For what the law could not do, in that it was weak through the flesh, God sending his own Son in the likeness of sinful flesh and for sin, condemned sin in the flesh."* What then, does the moral law, *"the law of sin and death,"* have to do with the discussion of natural sin-bound man? If a law had been given which was able to impart spiritual life to the natural man, dead in his trespasses and separated from God, then righteousness would have been based on that law. [15] However, the Law could never give life, only condemnation for failure to keep it, [16] hence the phrase, *"the law of sin and death"* in verse 2. After all, the Law was given because of the transgressions of men. Even though the Law is both good and spiritual, [17] it has no way to control what is in your mind, or what you choose to do. Remember, our thinking and our choices are the products of our sin nature. All men are under just condemnation for our failure to keep the moral law. The moral law is like a Roman arch: if one stone is removed, the arch collapses. If one law is broken, the whole is corrupted.

---

15. See Galatians 3:21-22
16. See Galatians 3:19 (MKJV)
17. See Romans 7:12 and 14 (NASB)

James, disciple of Jesus, said this: *"for whoever shall keep the whole Law and yet offend in one point, he is guilty of all"* (James 2:10).

> *But when the fullness of the time was come, God sent forth his Son, made of a woman, made under the law, to redeem them that were under the law, that we might receive the adoption of sons. And because you are sons, God has sent forth the Spirit of his Son into your hearts, crying, Abba, Father. Wherefore you are no more a servant, but a son; and if a son, then an heir of God through Christ.*
>
> Galatians 4:5-7 [18]

God's purpose is to build our heart\mind, our character, to conform to the character of His Son, [19] and teach us to love the Lord with our whole being and practice godly love by placing great value on our family, our church family, our neighbors and even our enemies. *"Owe no one anything, except to love one another; for he who loves another has fulfilled the law. For: Do not commit adultery; Do not kill; Do not steal; Do not bear false witness, Do not lust; [20] and if there is any other commandment, it is summed up is this word, 'You shall love your neighbor as yourself.' Love works no ill to his neighbor: therefore love is the fulfilling of the law"* (Romans 13:8-10, MKJV).

Now, through the love of Jesus Christ, because of His atoning sacrifice and perfectly-lived sinless life, believers have been redeemed from under the righteous condemnation of the Law and filled with God's Spirit. Therefore, we have been adopted as sons, to love our Father and to love one another. Christ is our Refuge, our Peace and in Him we will overcome. God has become our Father. Such mercy is beyond expression!

Jesus always obeyed the Father. As He lived upon this earth, He was a strong man of exceptional character, like none other. He did not lie in any way, but always told the absolute truth. He had no need for pride, for He had laid aside His privileges as Lord and King. He was good, full of integrity and complete within Himself. He did not lust after material gain or fame, work to build a worldly empire or engage in self-indulgent behavior. Instead, He longed to save men. This mission was on His mind, and He set His face like flint [21] to fulfill the Fathers plan of redemption.

We must be always on our guard, for, if not, we can allow sin to gain a staging area, a source of corruption, within us. Each time you mentally or physically engage sin, your will grows weaker. Set yourself to regard temptation as a red flag. Then, remove yourself physically or mentally and go immediately to the Lord, praying for strength and spiritual awareness of the cost of sin to you and to the name of our Lord. Don't follow temptation into sin. Don't be arrogant and think you can do this alone. *"Therefore let him who thinks he stands take heed lest he fall. No temptation has overtaken you except such as is common to man; but God is faithful, who will not allow you to be tempted beyond what you*

---

18. See also Romans 8:18 and 39
19. See Romans 8:29
20. Do not lust after or covet.
21. See Isaiah 50:7

are able, but with the temptation will also make the way of escape, that you may be able to bear it."[22] *"Resist the devil and he will flee from you."*[23]

Being born again and having the gift of faith is just the beginning of our walk. God has prepared the Bible to provide His wisdom to direct us into His thinking in the mighty display of His perfect truths. The Lord gives us knowledge of Himself through the Spirit who indwells us. The Spirit uses the Scriptures, giving us understanding of our Lord's amazing grace and mercy and our obligations as His children.

Jesus used the Word of God as His weapon and protection when tempted in the wilderness. We grow stronger spiritually as we use all the means that God has prepared for us. He commands us not to forsake gathering together in His name. We need to bond ourselves to each other to worship God in the Spirit, to pray in earnest continually and to encourage each other. Taking the Lord's Supper regularly with a grateful heart and love for the Lord, remembering His sacrifice, is also important. We are to seriously study the Word of God. Set your mind and spirit to obey His moral Law, for this promotes holiness and keeps you safe under the Spirit's care. Keep watch over each other, for we can all forget that we are in a battle.

22. 1 Corinthians 10:12-13, NKJV
23. James 4:7, NKJV

CHAPTER 9

THE SPIRIT OF CHRIST DWELLING WITHIN US

In John 14, Jesus was discussing the fact that He would soon leave and was giving His disciples knowledge of His relationship with the Father. Thomas wanted to know the way to follow Jesus. Jesus said to him, *"I am the way, the truth, and the life. No one comes to the Father except through Me."*[24] When Philip wanted to see the Father, Jesus said this: *"He who has seen Me has seen the Father."*[25] *"Do you not believe that I am in the Father, and the Father in Me? The words that I speak to you I do not speak on My own authority; but the Father who dwells in Me does the works."*[26] He also said, *"He who has My commandments and keeps them, it is he who loves Me."*[27] *"And I will pray the Father, and he shall give you another Comforter, that he may abide with you for ever; even the Spirit of truth ... ."*[28] Jesus repeated twice more the truth that if we love Him we will keep His commandments. Later, He said, *"If you abide in Me, and My words abide in you, you will ask what you desire, and it shall be done for you. By this My Father is glorified, that you bear much fruit; so you will be My disciples. As the Father loved Me, I also have loved you; abide in My love."*[29]

This "fruit" is first the fruit that the Holy Spirit works into your heart and mind, to motivate and encourage you, as He continues changing you to be like Christ in character and intentions. Here is the list of the Spirit's work in us: love, joy, peace, patience, kindness, goodness, faithfulness, gentleness, self-control.[30] This internal reworking by the Spirit is necessary to do those things Jesus asked us to do. For instance, we are to love our neighbor and our enemies, to love and encourage other believers here and in the rest of the world, to see the wide range of needs all around us and personally help in whatever way we can. We are also to pray without ceasing.

Serving others in the local body of believers means that through the work of the indwelling Spirit you will really love the people you meet with every Lord's Day. We are unable, within ourselves, to create this fruit, and this is what Jesus has determined for us, so that we will be holy and blameless before Him. I have seen men seek to lead before they actually have this fruit for all to see. Later, they fall away because they do not have this foundation within them. Some succumb to depression or create a ministry that hides serious spiritual and moral corruption.

---

24. Verse 16, NKJV
25. Verse 9, NKJV
26. Verse 10, NKJV
27. Verse 21, NKJV
28. Verse 16, NKJV
29. John 15:7-9, NKJV
30. See Galatians 5:13-25

This extraordinary love from the Father and from the Son are a great comfort. The gift of the Spirit[31] is amazing, and something to remember is that the Spirit's job is to reveal the person of Christ to us, His continuing love for us, His concern, His very words, His power to settle us down and still our hearts, giving us peace as the Lord Jesus promised. Jesus told the disciples that the *"Helper, the Holy Spirit, ... will teach you all things and bring to your remembrance all that I said to you."[32] "He who has My commandments and keeps them is the one who loves Me; and he who loves Me will be loved by My Father and I will love him and will manifest Myself to him."[33]* We must study the Scriptures and ask Jesus our Lord to put His words into our mind/heart, so that the Spirit can use them to comfort us, guide us and gives us the wisdom of Christ that comes from the Father. We find in Jesus the power to continually boycott these sins that so easily trick us. This is how we can overcome the remaining sin continually, but we will have a running battle that never stops until we go to with our Lord and Savior.

We are never alone, and in faith we can run to the Lord Jesus and find help in our difficult times. However, it is wise to seek the Lord Jesus very often, to learn how to love Him and to let Him guide you through the Scriptures. The supernatural work of the Spirit of Christ opens your mind and directs your understanding as you read the Word, study the Word and hear the Word.

Something that happens sometimes to Christians is strange but predictable. We focus on the gifts and begin to see the gifts and not the Lord Jesus. Every gift comes to us because we are *in* Christ Jesus.[34] We cannot separate Christ from the gifts because He is the Gift. Without Him, there is no hope for us. I have seen more than one man brought to disgrace because He pursued the gifts and leadership before the changes in character and faith had emerged. We must all be brought into a mature faith and character. We go to the Lord Jesus to direct our steps, to give us courage to face our fears, to give us strength to resist evil and obey the truth, and to give us love for the unlovable.

---

31. See John 14:16-24 and Galatians 3:13-14
32. John 14:26
33. John 14:21
34. See Ephesians 1:1-17

CHAPTER 10

OPENED AND RENEWED MINDS

Read and discuss all of the information given with the student. This is a very full lesson, and you may wish to expand it into two lessons. Have the student memorize Proverbs 16:1 and 3.

Help the student understand God's amazing grace extended unto us through His Son Jesus Christ. Our Lord Jesus has done for us an astounding thing: He stepped out of time into our world to sacrifice Himself for those who were estranged from Him and alien in mind\heart. As Gentiles, the great promises given to Israel were not ours to receive. We had no merit to recommend us, and we were not seeking God that we might worship Him. Jesus came so that we who were not walking with the Lord could be cleansed of our sin, forgiven and reconciled to God, having our consciences purged through His blood. *"He shall receive the blessing from the LORD, and righteousness from the God of his salvation"* (Psalm 24:5). Our Lord Jesus lifted us into the New Covenant by His sacrifice. [35] He begins transforming our hearts\minds so that we become new creatures, no longer believing the darkness, but living in the light and knowing the truth. We adopt the Lord's world-view, as presented in the Scriptures and we adopt His agenda to *"love the Lord your God with all our heart, and with all your soul, and with all your mind .... And love your neighbor"* (Matthew 22:37-39).

Through Christ, we begin to love our heavenly Father and set our heart\mind to learn how to love others, instead of always relating everything to ourselves. Every believer understands the things of God at a different rate and to a different degree, as the Lord decides. But as we put our whole heart into the study of the Lord, with careful consideration upon His Word, and practice obedience into His ways, we will all be changed through the internal work of the Holy Spirit. "He restores my soul: he leads me in the paths of righteousness for His name's sake" (Psalm 23:3). In the long run, all believers will become a reflection of the Son of God. *"Being confident of this very thing, that He which has begun a good work in you will perform it until the day of Jesus Christ"* (Philippians 1:6).

---

35. See Hebrews 8:1-13 and 10:1-24

CHAPTER 11

NEEDED ARMOR

Jesus is the final Prophet sent from God, and He used the Old Testament frequently in His teachings. He came to establish the New Covenant promised by God in the Old Testament. Why? Because the people under the Old Covenant had failed to follow God, except for a small remnant. God told Jeremiah this, *"Behold, the days are coming, says the LORD, when I will make a new covenant with the house of Israel and with the house of Judah—not according to the covenant that I made with their fathers in the day that I took them by the hand to lead them out of the land of Egypt, My covenant which they broke, though I was a husband to them, says the LORD. But this is the covenant that I will make with the house of Israel after those days, says the LORD: I will put My law in their minds, and write it on their hearts; and I will be their God and they shall be my people."[36]* When Jesus came to preach to His people the New Covenant, they did not receive Him as the promised Messiah sent by God to remove the sins of Israel.

"He [the Lord God] has delivered us from the power of darkness and conveyed us into the kingdom of the Son of His love, in whom we have redemption through His blood, the forgiveness of sins. He is the image of the invisible God, firstborn over all creation."[37] It is when we believe the Scriptures are fact and that Jesus is our hope and redemption that we know we have been transferred out of this dark world and put into another Kingdom. This God-given faith in Christ Jesus is a gift.[38] The first part of this spiritual transaction is that the Holy Spirit gives us an understanding of the Word of God as He leads us to our Savior, and, at some point, our eyes are opened and we believe in Jesus Christ our Redeemer and our Lord. The helmet of salvation comes to us because of the gift of faith we now experience in believing the truth of God and the veracity of Christ. Under the direction of Jesus, our Lord, the Spirit opens our minds[39] to understand God's truth and, if believed, it functions to protect our minds. God changes what we think and how we think by using the wide field of truth given in the Scriptures. Without the helmet of salvation, we are defenseless, like Adam and Eve, and would be open to all the lies and manipulations of Satan as he rules this dark world.

The promised Messiah is Jesus, the Anointed One, perfectly pure in mind, heart, body and soul. Therefore, He is the only perfect man who could qualify to take the burden of His people's sin natures. Christ's sacrifice of His life and blood atoned for all of His people's sins. Christ's righteousness is eternal, never wavering, never diminished, and He has supplied this righteousness to His people as a gracious gift.[40] Christ is our righteousness.[41] This breastplate of the righteousness of Christ protects us from the open assaults of Satan and this

---

36. Jeremiah 31:31-33, NKJV
37. Colossians 1:13-15, NKJV
38. See Ephesians 2:8
39. See Acts 16:14-15
40. See Romans 15:15-17
41. Hebrews 9:8-9: *"A scepter of righteousness is the scepter of Your Kingdom. You have loved righteousness ... ,"* NKJV

dark world, primarily as a defensive weapon. But this is not the only purpose for Christ's righteousness. His righteousness covers us and makes us acceptable to the Father.

The Sword of the Spirit is the Word of God. This is both our offensive and defensive weapon. In order to use this Word, it must be embedded within our thinking and become a part of us. We develop understanding of the truths found within God's Word in order to live according to His will. Our prayers join with this Word through the indwelling Spirit to become much more effective, as the Lord Jesus teaches us how to pray and love others.

Believers cannot stand against the wiles of Satan without the full armor of God and the words of life abiding within. The words are not magic; they are piercing Truth. We will find ourselves in spiritual warfare at the strangest times. Sometimes it is through temptation, sometimes because of sin and sometimes when alone or afraid or unsure of what to do about a situation. The Spirit will not throw verses at your mind and hope they stick. He uses the verses that you have memorized or those that you know from Bible study, preaching, Sunday school and seriously reading His Holy Word. Every word has meaning, and we are to drop our thinking and pick up God's thinking, found within the Holy Scriptures.

Believers cannot be passive in this arena, lazy, or have a cavalier attitude. Why? Because you will be spiritually crippled and open to Satan's seductions.

For though we walk in the flesh, we do not war according to the flesh, for the weapons of our warfare are not carnal but <u>mighty in God</u> for pulling down strongholds, casting down arguments and every high thing that exalts itself against the knowledge of God, bringing <u>every thought</u> into <u>captivity</u> to the obedience of Christ.   2 Corinthians 10:3-5, NKJV

CHAPTER 12

JUSTIFICATION BY FAITH

Take your time. There is no rush. We want the student to really understand the Christian faith. Please read Romans 3, 4 and 5 so that you can help them understand the importance of this principle of Justification by Faith. We hang the principles of God in both Testaments upon this cable of Justification by Faith in God alone that runs through them. These chapters in Romans show how the intentions of the Father, presented in Genesis, as He gives insight and promises to Abraham, are fulfilled in the New Testament with the sacrifice and resurrection of our Lord Jesus. This will help give the student the means to think differently about the intentions of the Father on behalf of all believers over the expanse of time.

I must give you a word of caution here: there will be a running battle with the old sinful patterns of thinking and behavior, which go against the indwelling Spirit's guidance. Believers cannot always keep the Law perfectly because we still struggle to overcome the imprint of sin in the way we think and the things we do. We are not always careful to follow the leading of the Spirit given in His holy Word. We do not always stay alert to avoid our heart being deceived by the misdirections of Satan or self. These failures are called "grieving" the Spirit, [42] and we are admonished not to cause the indwelling Spirit to be in heaviness of sorrow because of this remaining sin. Even in these failures, the Spirit continually causes us to recognize our sins and brings us again to repent, and he never abandons us, but continues to work in our hearts. As we yearn to be holy, renewal continues in our mind, and we learn. Dependence upon our Lord, as we trust His character and believe His Word, is how we live.

All believers are justified by their faith being placed in Jesus alone as the Perfect Sacrifice appointed by God who did <u>atone</u> [43] for our sin. *"For if, when we were enemies, we were reconciled to God by the death of His Son, much more, being reconciled, we shall be saved by His life. And not only so, but we also joy in God through our Lord Jesus Christ, by whom we have now received the atonement"* (Romans 5:10-11).

We need to see the truth of the Law and the just condemnation of the Law, to know the darkness of our sin. We see that Justification by Faith in Christ Jesus is far superior to man's false belief in the keeping of ritual or some law or deeds to provide justification. *"Therefore by the deeds of the law there shall no flesh be justified in his sight: for by the law is the knowledge of sin"* (Romans 3:20). The Scriptures say clearly that no person shall be justified by law-keeping, but this truth does not negate the Law. We see that the new law of the Spirit working through the indwelling Jesus Christ has given us the

---

42. Ephesians 4:30"*And grieve not the Holy Spirit of God whereby you are sealed unto the day of redemption.*" The word *grieve*, according to Strong's Concordance, means "to distress; to be sad: cause grief, be in heaviness, sorrowful, be made sorry."

43. *Atonement*, Exchange, that is, restoration to divine favor: reconciliation. See Romans 5:10-11

motivation and power to walk, generally, keeping the commandments. We now walk, mindful of the things of God that are given value by the Word. This <u>justification by faith</u> exalts the abundant grace of God in giving us the gift of faith and of the righteousness of Christ because of His willing and sufficient sacrifice. To know that such mercy is applied to us lifts up our hearts to our Father in praise and thankfulness. The imputation of Christ's righteousness for belief in God's character and trustworthiness has relevance throughout all time.

Paul is explaining what happened to men through the Fall and what Jesus has done that nullified the death sentence upon men who come to Him.

The gift is not like that which came through the one who sinned; for on the one hand the judgment arose from one transgression resulted in condemnation [Adam's], but on the other hand the <u>free gift</u> arose from many transgression [sinful heart\minds] resulting in <u>justification</u>. [44] For if by the transgression of the one [Adam], death reigned through the one, much more those who receive the abundance of grace and the gift of righteousness will reign in life through the One, Jesus Christ. So then through one transgression [Adam's] there resulted condemnation to all men, even so through one act of righteousness [Jesus'] there resulted justification of life to all believers. For as through the one man's [Adam's] disobedience many were made sinners, even so through the obedience of the One [Jesus] the many will be made righteous ... , so that, as sin reigned in death, even so grace would reign through righteousness to eternal life through Jesus Christ our Lord. Romans 5:16-21 (NASB)

For we through the Spirit wait for the hope of righteousness by faith. For in Jesus Christ neither circumcision availeth anything, nor uncircumcision; but <u>faith</u> [45] which works <u>by</u> [46] <u>love</u>. Galatians 5:5-6

Faith works by love through the power of the indwelling Jesus Christ, as we are motivated and changed by His love for us. The better we understand the qualities of this love within His heart, the more our hearts\minds are moved to love our Lord and Savior in return.

---

44. *Justification*, to render (shown as or regarded as) just or innocent:-be righteous, free, justified.
45. *Faith*, persuasion, that is, credence; moral conviction (of religious truth, or the truthfulness of God, or a religious teacher), especially reliance upon Christ for salvation; abstractly constancy in such profession; by extension the system of religious (Gospel) truth itself: assurance, belief, believe, fidelity. *Strong's*
46. *By*, a primary preposition denoting the channel of an act; through (in very wide applications).

NOTES ON SPECIFIC LESSONS

PART III: THE POWER OF PRIDE

PRIDE, A PATTERN OF THINKING

What do natural men think? How do they make decisions and guide their own lives? There are so many examples available from the Scriptures that I decided to take pride as one pattern of thinking so that we could concentrate on the particular traits common in pride. As you go through this section with your student, refer to the list after each lesson and discuss which ones mentioned apply to the men we are studying from various cultures.

CHAPTER 14

THE LOVE OF THE WORLD

"Love not the world or the things that are in the world. If anyone loves the world, the love of the Father is not in him."[47] This is considered by many to be a radical belief because men always love the things of the world. Men cannot conceive of life without or apart from the world and the things in it. Jesus taught believers that the world is actually passing away, and this is not our future. Our Lord Jesus will create a new world unspoiled in anyway by the sins of men.[48]

Love could be described as "an intense desire for someone or something." When this determined will and emotional response is focused upon the things of the world and not upon the living Lord, there lies the problem. God is not in all our thoughts.[49] He created us out of deep love, and we did not care, but, instead, preferred to decide all things for ourselves.[50] That men knew God but would not glorify Him as God nor were thankful is a strange and twisted response. However, it is understandable because men, by the deliberate suppression of this truth, had lost the knowledge of God and become futile in their thoughts and dark in their hearts. Men would not love God, but would love everything else.

I saw a movie that gave the viewer a sense of the emotional agony and hopelessness of an assortment of friends and family in a small town. They were to die in a horrific collision between earth and another heavenly body. I bring this up because we are all in the grip of a wide range of ongoing circumstances, without power or protection, and without God there is no peace or hope in anything else.

We are at home in this world, but Jesus has taught, through the Scriptures, that the world cultures are, in fact, ruled by Satan. Satan took Jesus up on the highest mountain and showed Him all the kingdoms of the world and their glory. Satan told Jesus that he would give Him all of it if He would worship Satan. Jesus did not dispute Satan's claim to rule the world kingdoms, but added that men should only worship the Lord and serve Him only.[51]

Paul wrote that the Gentiles, who are not part of the Jewish peoples, were, therefore, not entitled to *"the covenants of promise, having no hope and without God in the world."*[52] This is an accurate account of the plight of the Gentiles of the whole earth. But we, the Gentiles, were never victims but, rather, active participants in the evil led by Satan in continuous rebellion against God. Satan desires to continue reveling in his power over all men. When you are taken out from under Satan's rule, by becoming part of the Kingdom of

---

47. 1 John 2:15-17, VERSION?
48. See 2 Peter 3:12-14
49. See Psalm 10:4
50. See Romans 1:18-21
51. See Matthew 4:8-11
52. Ephesians 2:12, NKJV

God and His Christ, a continuous assault begins. Satan cannot force you anymore to obey his desires, but now he seduces you into making deadly compromises, to destroy your witness to the power and provisions of the Lord Jesus.[53] He wants to make you a liar and hypocrite because it smears the Church and, more, it devalues the Kingdom of God before unbelieving men.

What are the implications of this? We are not to have close relationships with unbelievers, for they function as the idols did in the Old Testament, to turn our hearts away from God and His Kingdom's obligation of love for one another. No close partnership with unbelievers, such as marriage or business or close friendships, are to be entered into. We can know that the Lord will make it possible to live under old conditions that were in place before we became believers. It may take a while to untangle ourselves, but it must be done in a way that glorifies our Lord, and while you are in a state of flux, be on your guard. There is one exception to this, and that is believers are not to seek divorce if the other person wishes to stay married and sin is not an issue.[54] Remember Paul's admonition to the Church to turn the unrepentant believer over to Satan for the destruction of the body that his soul might be saved.[55]

Another implication to consider is this: *"The natural man does not receive the things of the Spirit of God, for they are foolishness to him: nor can he know them, because they are spiritually discerned."*[56] This, in effect, means that it is impossible for the nonbeliever to understand or believe the things of God. We, therefore, cannot any longer try to maintain close friendships with the world, not because we do not love the unregenerate and long for reconciliation for them with the Father through the Son. But we must remember that they are part of Satan's system and will be led to the worst conclusions possible about Christ's Kingdom because it holds no value to the world system but, rather, is a constant irritant.

---

53. See 2 Corinthians 6:14-18
54. See 1 Corinthians 7:9-17
55. See 1 Corinthians 5:1-13
56. 1 Corinthians 2:14

CHAPTER 15

A SELF-RIGHTEOUSNESS AND CRITICAL SPIRIT

This is a long lesson, and you may want to divide it into two or more mini-lessons. Be sure to study the references so that you can enrich the lessons for the students and correct any misunderstandings they may have.

Notes on Specific Lessons

PART IV: ISRAEL AS AN EXAMPLE

CHAPTER 16

OLD TESTAMENT ISRAEL

The history of Israel began thousands of years ago, when the Lord singled out one man that He had chosen to become the progenitor and patriarch of His new nation. Roughly some four hundred plus years passed, and then the Lord spoke through Moses at Mount Horeb and gave statues and laws for the people to form a new nation under God.[57] Here Moses again addressed the people and reviewed their experiences and the obligations as a nation under God.

Moses said something interesting in Deuteronomy 7. *"For you are a holy people to the LORD your God; the LORD your God has chosen you to be a people for Himself, a special treasure above all the peoples on the face of the earth. The LORD did not set His love on you nor choose you because were more in number than any other people, for you were the least of all peoples; but because the LORD loves you, and because He would keep the oath which He swore to your fathers, the LORD has brought you out with a mighty hand, and redeemed you from the house of bondage, from the hand of Pharaoh king of Egypt. Therefore, know that the LORD your God, the faithful God who keeps covenant and mercy for a thousand generations with those who love Him and keep His commandments, and He repays those who hate Him to their face, to destroy them."*[58]

Israel went into the Promised Land and prospered … until the people allowed themselves forgetfulness and chose not to keep the covenant that God had made for them. The rest of the years were spent with various judges raised up by God to deliver His people again and again. The next phase was introduced by the request for a king rather than direct rule by God. God graciously granted the request, and Israel had a long line of kings. Both the kings and the people became so corrupt that the destruction promised by the Lord came upon them. The Northern Kingdom was destroyed by the Assyrians, and Judah, to the south, some years later was carried away into Babylon. After this kingdom was destroyed, there was a diminished state of Israel that arose until the time when Messiah should come.

Shortly after the assent of Christ to His Father, Jerusalem and the surrounding areas were leveled to the ground by the Romans. After this, there was no large separate state for Israel but, instead, the people were scattered over the known world, just as God had said would happen. Why did the people choose this route against the Lord? We are given many reasons in the New Testament, but primarily it was their hearts and minds choosing to disregard the Lord their Savior and count the graces given to them as nothing. Israel's long-time allotted-for rebellion foretold in prophecy entered into the final, awful harvest. Even with this history, ancient Israel has not been completely

---

57. See Deuteronomy Chapters 4-7
58. Deuteronomy 7:6-9, NKJV

destroyed, but has been promised by the Lord a short time to glorify Him after the time of the Gentiles is complete.[59]

Jesus Christ is the reason that the qualities necessary for real civilization were first brought to the mind of men. Individual men's minds were changed by the extraordinary truths of God through the power of the indwelling Spirit of Christ. I think that we Gentiles benefited greatly from the power of good to push back evil, but the darkness of sin is once again seducing the Gentiles of the world. Remember the words that God spoke to Abraham, that when *"the iniquity of the Amorites"* was *"full,"* He would bring His people out of bondage.[60] Does this phrase used in the Pentateuch directed against the Amorites also apply to the similar phrase used in Romans? Does it, in fact, mean that the Gentiles have a time allotted to them for rebellion against God, and that the same warning against the Amorites evil being *"full"* is for all the Gentiles of the world? Today, our world celebrates evil and calls evil good. We are becoming as spiritually blind as Israel, following the same pattern set by Israel and are probably facing the same awful harvest because we have relegated the living Lord to the status of myth.

59. Romans 11:25: *"... until the fullness of the Gentiles has come"* (NKJV).
60. See Genesis 15:16

CHAPTER **17**

THE KINGDOM SPLITS

If Solomon's gift of wisdom was not enough to keep him on the path of righteousness, how are we, who are not nearly so wise as he, to keep on the path of righteousness? Jesus reproduces a likeness of His wholeness within men who are born again. Through His indwelling Spirit of grace, He causes us to travel the path of righteousness. The first consideration we should have is to learn from Christ words in both Testaments how we are to live, love others and worship our God. The Scriptures are the exact words inspired by the Holy Spirit of Christ. His admonitions about our responsibilities to our Savior and Redeemer are somewhat similar in both Testaments. The moral law still informs our mind and hearts of what constitutes sin and what the Lord desires within our lives, to reflect Him to those around us. Our minds must be renewed for us to think like our redeemer.[61] As our mind is renewed, our hearts yearn to be like Jesus, to love the Father and love others with such grace as we have been given. Godly love values and promotes gentleness, patience and humility, thinks no evil, cannot produce evil, endures with grace, wholly believes and rejoices in the truth, and this love cannot fail.[62] The narrow way is the pathway of God's love and requires God-generated, God-powered and motivated love to walk therein.

Solomon saw much truth, but his heart was heavy and his mind weary with the knowledge gained. He seemed to know that the goal of man was to fear God and keep His commandments, but he knew nothing about the love of God. He must have read or heard the psalms of his father, David. King David poured out his heart in the Psalms and repeatedly mentioned the love of God toward him. Unfortunately, Solomon did not learn the lessons that could be taken from his father's life with God. Sin and great pride had imprisoned this man, who was so gifted by God, and it tuned away his God-given potential for good toward God and His own people. Solomon no longer seem to love or respect or reverence the living God who had interacted twice with him. Solomon did not value the Word of God as did his father, David. His heart\mind had lost light, and his soul became insensitive to the things of God. I believe that Solomon wrote this about himself: *"Better is a poor and a wise child than an old and foolish king, who will no more be admonished."*[63]

I have no way of knowing what the eternal outcome was for Solomon. Perhaps he did repent. He wrote this: *"Let us hear the conclusion of the whole matter, Fear God, and keep His commandments: for this is the whole duty of man."*[64]

---

61. See Ephesians 4:20-25, Colossians 310-16 and Romans 12:1-2
62. See 1 Corinthians 13 and Matthew 7:13-14
63. Ecclesiastes 4:13
64. Ecclesiastes 12:13

Jesus said, *"All that the Father gives Me will come to Me, and the one who comes to Me I will by no means cast out."*[65] Call out to Jesus and ask Him to take your life as His and bring light to your mind and His love to your heart. The Lord builds us anew at salvation, changing the will and emotions and the heart\mind to meet His purpose in bringing the knowledge of the love of Christ Jesus to us and through us, to a spiritually-darkened world.

65. John 6:37, NKJV

CHAPTER 18

JEROBOAM AND REHOBOAM AS EXAMPLES

Study the references so that you can enrich the students understanding of Jesus Christ and the fact that His thinking and actions were so very different than those of ordinary leaders who are filled with pride. Jesus' words and actions show that He had a nature vastly different from natural man. Jesus kept even more than the "Law of Kings" and was not at all like the early kings of Israel. Jesus Christ did not pursue the power or pleasures of this world, nor did He rebel against the law. His heart\mind was intent upon the expressed will of His loving Father. Jesus did not collect wives, wealth or material goods like the kings we are studing. Jesus purposefully dedicated every resource at His disposal to accomplish the purpose for which He had been sent. Jesus' prayers and thoughts, His conversations, even His ability to walk, all of His time, and all of the things He did were for and under the direction of His holy Father. No king, president or leader has ever been so pure in his devotion to God or in his love of the people.

Jesus is the final King promised to David. Through the Scriptures, we see in Jesus those qualities of character which provide for integrity, justice and truth in His Kingdom, as the purposes of His Father are complete. Jesus makes no compromises with the truth. He does not show favoritism to persons of power, wealth or achievement, nor the poor or criminal. Instead, His judgment of men is pure, coming out of a mind\heart set to obey the will of His heavenly Father in bringing sinful men to salvation.

We are to strive to be like Jesus in yielding ourselves to our Father's will. Our Lord Jesus was nothing like Solomon, Rehoboam or Jeroboam. He held His position in relation to His Father as precious, but out of His love for the Father, Jesus held it lightly in His hand, always joyfully entering into the will of the Father. Jesus did not covet the power or position of His Father, but continually looked out for the interests of His Father and of His beloved children in everything He did. Jesus humbled Himself, to do the work of His Father, and He did this for us, knowing what we were. How much more do we need humility today?

Paul taught the Philippians that they, as followers of Christ, were to have a certain attitude toward their fellow Christians, the same attitude that Jesus had. *"Have this attitude in yourselves which was also in Christ Jesus, who, although He existed in the form of God, did not regard equality with God a thing to be grasped, but emptied Himself, taking the form of a bond-servant, and being made in the likeness of men. Being found in appearance as a man, He humbled Himself by becoming obedient to the point of death, even death on a cross"* (Philippians 2:5-8, NASB). *"Therefore if there is any encouragement in Christ, if there is any consolation of love, if there is any fellowship of the Spirit, if any affection and compassion, make my joy complete by being of the same mind, maintaining the same love, united in spirit, intent on one purpose. Do nothing from selfishness or empty conceit, but with humility of mind regard one another as more important than yourselves; do not merely look out for your own personal interest, but also for the interest of others"* (Philippians 2:1-4, NASB)

We are to have this same kind of love and regard for one another as Christ has for His Father and for His children. We are to think carefully how to work out this loving regard in obedience. *"For this reason also, God highly exalted Him, and bestowed on Him the name which is above every name, so that at the name of Jesus EVERY KNEE WILL BOW, of those who are in heaven and on earth and under the earth, and that every tongue will confess that Jesus Christ is Lord, to the glory of God the Father"* (Philippians 2:9-11, NASB, Emphasis added).

CHAPTER 19

JEROBOAM TOOK OVER THE PRIESTHOOD

Study and discuss with the student the priesthood of Jesus Christ and the depth of the sin of Jeroboam. You may expand this lesson by reading Hebrews chapters 8 and 9, to gain a clearer view of what Christ has done and make your own questions. Read the references given in the lessons to have a more in-depth understanding of the material and share the information with the students.

God had set in motion a long-term plan to bridge at least a thousand years. He instituted the priest-led sacrificial system. Their animal sacrifices were to function as a covering over the sin of His people until our Lord was ready to present His final and permanent Priest. *"For if the first covenant of law and sacrifice had been faultless, there would have been no occasion sought for a* second" (Hebrews 8:7). For natural man to be used as priests to teach and be intercessors for men and to employ animal sacrifices to cover the sin of men was but a short-term fix for man's continual sin. Our Father, knowing the fault with the first covenant, promised a new covenant with Israel. *"And I will put my spirit within you, and cause you to walk in my statutes, and you shall keep my judgments, and do them"* (Ezekiel 36:27).

MEMORIZE

Aaron and his descendants, all of them of the tribe of Levi, were to be the only anointed priests and were given the responsibilities and duties surrounding the Altar of Incense and were also the only priests allowed into the Holy of Holies. A priest had two huge responsibilities: the first was to present the things of God to the people, primarily teaching the people the words and thoughts as well as the requirements of God. The second required the priests to intercede for the people and represent the people before God, with the proscribed sacrifices for sin. Jesus Christ is the final Great High Priest, [66] being by nature holy and undefiled, the Permanent Intercessor and Teacher appointed by God, continually making intercession for the people of God. Jesus Christ, as the eternal High Priest, gave His own blood as the final and perfect atoning sacrifice before His Father, [67] removing sin forever, thereby reconciling men to God. Covering us with His blood, He cleans the corrupting stain of sin from our souls, for He is both our Priest and our Sacrifice.

But we see Jesus, who was made a little lower than the angels for the suffering of death, crowned with glory and honor; that he by the grace of God should taste death for every man, for it became him, for whom are all things, and by whom are all things, in bringing many sons unto glory, to make the captain

66. Hebrews 4:14-16 *"Seeing then that we have a great high priest, that is passed into the heavens, Jesus the Son of God, let us hold fast our profession. For we have not an high priest which cannot be touched with the feeling of our infirmities; but was in all points tempted like as we are, yet without sin. Let us therefore come boldly unto the throne of grace that we may obtain mercy, and find grace to help in time of need."*

67. Hebrews 9:7-15 *"Neither by the blood of goats and calves, but by his own blood He entered in once into the holy place having obtained eternal redemption (for us)."*

of their salvation perfect through sufferings. For both he that sanctified and they who are <u>sanctified</u> [68] *are all of one: for which cause he is not ashamed to call them brethren ... . Wherefore in all things it behoved Him to be made like unto his brethren, that He might be a merciful and faithful high priest in things pertaining to God, to make reconciliation for the sins of the people.* Hebrews 2:9-11 and 17

---

68. *Sanctified*, to make holy that is, to purify or consecrate ceremonially for use (refers to Christ's work in setting us apart for use in the Kingdom of God)

CHAPTER 20

THE PEOPLE OF THE NORTHERN KINGDOM AS EXAMPLES

Study and discuss the information in the references found in the lesson with the students. Give them an overview of what was happening and why the people could not evaluate their own sin or change their evil intentions for good. When you have finished discussing the Amos chapters, then bring to the student's mind the contrast between these people and Jesus Christ.

"Jesus went through the grain fields on the Sabbath day. And His disciples were hungry and began to take and eat the heads of grain. The Pharisees saw this and said 'Your disciples do what is not lawful on the Sabbath day' " (Matthew 12:1-2). They had just judged the disciples as evil for eating grain on the Sabbath, and Jesus as evil for allowing them to profane the Sabbath. Jesus reminded them of the incident recorded in the Scriptures where King David and his men were hungry and entered the House of God. The priest allowed them to eat the showbread [69] which was set aside for the priests. Jesus brought to their attention the fact that the priests also worked in the Temple on the Sabbath and, thus, profaned the Sabbath, but were held blameless. Jesus confronted them with this truth, *"One greater than the Temple is in this place"* (Matthew 12:6). These Pharisees seemed to pass over the phrase, and Jesus then made this comment, *"If you had understood this verse, 'I desire mercy and not sacrifice,' you would not have condemned those who are not guilty"* (Matthew 12:7). The Pharisees saw that the disciples were hungry and ignored their needs but then jumped on their failure to keep the Sabbath. In other words, Jesus was saying that mercy is far better than keeping rules in a godless manner and forgetting mercy.

Jesus went even further, *"For the Son of Man is Lord even of the Sabbath"* (Matthew 12:8). [70] Jesus was quoting a verse from the Old Testament, making the clear assertion that He was Lord of the Sabbath and, therefore, He was the living God in human form, the "Son of Man." As He rested from His labors, the Lord created the Sabbath, giving men a day of rest from their labors, a day to be spent in worship. Jesus, as Lord of the Sabbath, declared the disciples innocent of wrongdoing.

The Pharisees were like the men in Amos, depending on circumcision, sacrifices and participation on the feast days to gather enough "good deeds" to make them acceptable before God. This was done in spite of God's teaching that none shall be justified [71] by law keeping for even their righteousness was *"as filthy rags"* (Isaiah 64:6). [72] The Pharisees could have listened to Jesus' rebuke and,

---

69. *Shewbread*, hallowed bread, see 1 Samuel 21:1-6. (God did not punish David or his men for eating this bread).

70. Matthew 12:7-8 (God did not hold them guilty for eating the grain on the Sabbath)

71. Galatians 2:16 "Knowing that a man is not justified by the deeds [works] of the law, but by the faith of Jesus Christ, even we have believed in Jesus Christ, that we might be justified by the faith of Christ, and not by the deeds [works] of the law: for by the works of the law shall no flesh be justified." See also Romans 3:20

72. Isaiah 64:6 *"But we are all as an unclean (thing), and all our righteousnesses (are) as filthy rags; and we all do fade as a leaf; and our iniquities, like the wind, have taken us away."*

in sorrow, asked for mercy, but they would not even consider His point. They were like the people in Amos, *"Who hated him who rebukes in the gate and they despise him who speaks uprightly"* (Amos 5:19). This kind of response to the truths of God is natural to the sin-bound man, whose mind is hostile to God. Here is what Jesus said: *"Woe to you, scribes and Pharisees, hypocrites! For you pay tithes of mint and dill and cumin, and you have left undone the weightier matters of the Law, judgment, mercy, and faith. You ought to have done these and not leave the others undone"* (Matthew 23:23).

Jesus Christ desires that we honor the Father out of thankful and redeemed hearts, remembering always mercy, as He does. Real love glorifies the Lord with worship and obedience. Godly love regards others as more valuable than our selves and, therefore, will not use, hurt or deceive others. Jesus made it clear that He deals with our hearts, as we yield to His will, understanding that justice accompanies sacrifice, and mercy accompanies the letter of the Law. We are not to be like the people under Amos, nor the Pharisees nor the kings who built a wall separating the truth of God from the deeds done and added corruption to His Law.

We have the Spirit of the Lord indwelling us. *"For whosoever is born of God overcomes the world: and this is the victory that overcomes the world, (even) our faith"* (1 John 5:4). Our faith is not dependent upon our will, mind or emotions. It is a gift from God to each of His children. [73] It is a permanent and active link to our Savior. He is continually forming a bond of trusting belief. We depend upon Jesus Christ, and He lives within us, actively loving us and teaching us to overcome the world, walk in integrity and keep justice. He even teaches us many things from our failures. The children of God have this promise, *"You are of God, little children, and have overcome them [the false spirits \ false prophets speaking forth a vision of their own]: because greater is he that is in you, than he that is in the world"* (1 John 4:1-4). [74] The Spirit of Jesus Christ warns our spirit when something is wrong in the literature, speech and lifestyle of the false prophets and teachers, as well as our own lives. We see many deceptions described within the Scriptures as we study the Word of God.

The Word of God holds the absolute truth before our hearts\minds, and if we heed this truth, the indwelling Spirit will guide us around the false teachers found operating among the believers in the Church of our Lord. Satan's best shot is to work through a person who appears as an *"angel of light,"* (2 Corinthians 11:14) [75] one who disregards, devalues, dilutes or <u>casts aspersions</u> [76] upon both the truth of God and the person of our Lord.

---

73. Ephesians 2:8-10 *"For by grace are you saved through faith; and that not of yourselves: (it is) the gift of God: not of works, lest an man should boast, For we are his workmanship, created in Christ Jesus unto good works ... ."*

74. See also Deuteronomy 13:1-18, 18:9-22, Matthew 7:15, 24:11 and 24, Galatians 2:4, 2 Peter 2:1 and Acts 13:6

75. 2 Corinthians 11:13-15 and 26 *"For such are false apostles, deceitful workers, transforming themselves into the apostles of Christ. And no marvel; for Satan himself is transformed into an angel of light ... . His ministers also be transformed as the ministers of righteousness; whose end shall be according to their works."*

76. Cast aspersions (asperse or asperge = to sprinkle), to make false or spiteful statements or damaging imputations within the neighborhood or community

CHAPTER 21

PRIDE AND WEALTH (AMOS 8, 787 BC)

Every commandment which I command you today you must be careful to observe, that you may live and multiply, and go in and possess the land of which the Lord swore to you fathers. And you shall remember that the Lord your God let you all the way these forty years in the wilderness, to humble you and test you to know what was in your heart, whether you would keep His commandments or not. So He humbled you, allowing you to hunger, and fed you with manna which you did not know nor did your fathers know, that He might make you know that man shall not live by bread alone; but man lives by every word that proceeds from the mouth of the Lord. Deuteronomy 8:1-3, NKJV

Why did the Lord need to humble the Israelites? After all, they had been treated harshly in Egypt and then had wandered in the desert wilderness for forty years. But we know that they looked Moses in the eye and refused to go into the Promised Land, even after witnessing ten horrendous judgments against Egypt. Plus, they traveled under a cloud by day and had light that dispelled the darkness at night, their clothes did not rot, nor did their feet swell, and God fed them manna every morning. What then?

The answer is that they were full of pride, and pride always refuses to acknowledge any other's will but its own. The generation of slaves that came out of Egypt had gradually died in the wilderness before this time because they had disobeyed the Lord's clear command to go into the Promised Land. It appears that those slaves who had suffered were full of pride. God knew what was in their hearts, but the rescued slaves did not. They were unthankful and ungrateful for God's supernatural care and their own deliverance. The former slaves would not trust the Lord and learn the truth that man does not live by bread alone but by every word of God.

Beware, for a practice of not keeping the Lords commandments could mean that your choice has been made to put God out of your sight and soon out of your life. Trials are one of the Lord's ways to humble us to hear Him. Difficulties in our lives test us as to what is in our hearts and reveal wrong attitudes, unconfessed sins, anxiety, lack of trust and wrong thinking. We still have remnants of old thinking, even as our minds are being renewed. We still have remnants of the old pride in self, traditions, talents, opportunity's given and much more. Pride is like the contents of Pandora's Box, and we do not understand the depth of our remaining sin. Everyone carries a load of pride—rich or poor alike.

Amos was dealing with a lethal combination of pride and wealth in the upper class of Israel. The prophecy of the Lord foretold in Deuteronomy 8 was exactly what happened to the hearts and minds of the people when they gathered wealth unto themselves. Apparently, wealth promoted certain characteristics,[77] such as keeping the poor from obtaining justice and leveling taxes upon the poor, which took food from their mouths. The wealthy hate those who rebuke them and those who speak the truth. They afflict the just and take bribes. As a result, the people of Israel were oppressed within. The nation would not repent or receive correction, even after the Lord sent many trials to humble them, that they might hear the Lord and save their nation from destruction. Pride will not bend or yield, and it is an unreasonable response, but it is a visible trait of the sin nature.

---

77. See Amos 3, 4 and 5

CHAPTER 22

PARALLELS

But know this, that in the last days perilous times will come. For men shall be lovers of themselves, lovers of money, boasters, proud, blasphemers, disobedient, unthankful, unholy, unloving, unforgiving, slanderers, without self-control, brutal, and despisers of good, traitor, headstrong, haughty, lovers of pleasure rather than lovers of God, having a form of godliness but denying its power, And from such people turn away!

2 Timothy 3:1-5, NKJV

In this letter to Timothy, Paul named two of the magicians of Pharaoh and said that *"They resisted the truth: men of corrupt minds, disapproved concerning the faith; but they will progress no further, for their folly will be manifest to all, as theirs also was."*[78] Their *"folly"* was to cling to their false god, even as Moses, as God's representative, did miracles far beyond their attempts to duplicate. It had to be evident to all those present that Pharaoh's magicians were false, but they did not relent, and it is possible that these men could have repented when the truth was so obvious and Moses was clearly sent by God, who had been shown to rule the natural world.

In Chapter 4, Paul mentioned that *"For the time is coming when they will not endure sound doctrine, but according to their own desires, because they have itching ears, they will heap up for themselves teachers; and they will turn their ears away from the truth, and be turned aside to fables."*[79] This is what we encounter in the Old Testament as we study Israel through the prophets and kings. They were men of corrupt minds who resisted the truth and found for themselves other men who would tell them what they wanted to hear or false prophets to tell them what seemed true in their own minds.

Jeremiah, spoke with the Lord. *"Then I said, 'Ah LORD God! Behold, the prophets say to them, you shall not see the sword, nor shall you have famine, but I will give you assured peace in this place.' And the LORD said to me, 'The prophets prophesy lies in My name. I have not sent them, commanded them, nor spoken to them; they prophesy to you a false vision, divination, a worthless thing, and the deceit of their heart. Therefore thus say the LORD concerning the prophets who prophesy in My name, whom I did not send, and who say, 'Sword and famine shall not be in this land,' by Sword and famine those prophets shall be consumed."*[80]

It seems that religious and political prophets abound and have loyal followers with allegiances to some philosophy or to particular leaders. Our culture is naive about the nature of evil within men. The future is unknowable because the time of the Gentiles has been upon us for two thousand years now, and our evil

---

78, 2 Timothy 3:8, NKJV
79. 2 Timothy 4:3-4, NKJV
80. Jeremiah 4:3-4, NKJV

is not yet *"full,"* but it will be. When? I have no idea. What is clear is that in this nation our people have put the Word of God behind their backs, choosing instead to follow their own desires. We have come full circle and are about to repeat the horrors and miscalculations of terminal selfishness carried out in so many others places.

NOTES ON SPECIFIC LESSONS

PART V: THE SOUTHERN KINGDOM AS AN EXAMPLE

CHAPTER 23

THE FRAMEWORK FOR THE BEHAVIOR OF MEN

The Lord revealed to His people the universal underlying pattern of mankind's drive to satisfy his desires, no matter what culture he was born into. In Exodus, we read of the Ten Commandments, and truly they apply across all time and are easy to understand. We are to seek the Lord only to the exclusion of all other supports that men devise and cling to. We are not to be casual, flippant or callous about the things belonging to God—including His name. God's name is who He is, and the names used to describe His character traits give us insight and more knowledge into the Lord's majesty. The Lord guards His reputation, and those who deliberately slander His name will be judged accordingly and their guilt openly revealed to all. Believers are to give one day a week to worship God and study from the Scriptures, so that they learn to trust, love, follow and fear the Lord. Why? Because He holds their very next breath in His hands, and His heart is set to present them blameless before all.

We are to hold our parents as dear to us, especially in view of our own sins and shortcomings. The fact that this is actually a commandment, one that demands this loving care as a test of our faith, is an arresting thought. Are we preparing our hearts to seek and obey our Lord? To love those in your house who are not worthy is, in fact, exactly how Jesus loved us, even while our own sins were in full view.

In ancient Israel, the death penalty applied to anyone who deliberately struck a man so that he died or who exhibited premeditation in killing another man or struck his father or mother or even cursed his father or mother. If a man kidnapped another person or had immediate control over him, then he was to be put to death.[81]

It is easy to see that human desires create the motivation for adultery, as well as all the other sexually-motivated sins. These desires have little in common with love, which values another over self. I hate to see what is happening in the Church because so many have chosen the world's way of decision making, which involves feelings or false perceptions of truth rather than God's clear mandate for marriage and the family. Again, each partner's innate selfishness provides the motivation to satisfy desires, regardless of the scriptural view of the sacredness of marriage. This culture is playing with fire and has no understanding of where it leads.

Over time, women become incidental and easily interchangeable. This pattern also applies to men. Some women already think of men as being interchangeable and incidental. In such a society, children have no intrinsic value either because the heart of our people has become stone cold. The

81. See Exodus 21:12-17

integrity of a nation is formed within the families of believers. Children are taught not to steal nor engage in any form of a lie. "Do not covet" is a strong teaching of the people of God. To the contrary, to absolutely covet is a very visible trait of our culture, perhaps because it is and has been a mantra of popular advertising since the 1950s.

The blessings and curses found in Deuteronomy[82] are very instructive. They are a lesson in God's seriousness concerning the direction taken by Israel in the Old Testament. But the same direction is being taken by our culture to disavow the Lord, and the results of our rebellion will be awful indeed.

82. See Deuteronomy 28

CHAPTER 24

A TALE OF TWO SISTERS (EZEKIEL 23)

Perhaps you could find current material that illustrates this truth of the downward spiral taken by our country. We once had a commonly-held belief in the Ten Commandments as moral truth in the eighteenth and nineteenth centuries. But in the span of time from 1950 to now, we have developed a general consensus for amorality. Breaking the Commandments is the norm for our society. Even the church has bowed under the assault of immorality that has rushed through the doors into the hearts of the men professing Christ. The natural result of today's churched men under bondage to sin is wholesale disregard for the words and ways of our Lord, just as the men of Jerusalem turned away while still calling themselves people of God. These same specific areas of gross idolatry, trust in the power of ungodly men and joint ventures with unbelieving men laden with sin still trap men like mice made immobile by sticky paper.

Christians, therefore, must be tied to the truth of Jesus and not to the culture they live in or men who are considered successful. It breaks my heart to see the distress of adults and children tossed back and forth by the dictates of this amoral society, in a seemingly-permanent state of flux, having abandoned the fixed moral and spiritual truth of the Lord.

CHAPTER 25

IN BONDAGE IN BABLYON

This is a long lesson and should be taught in three or four sections, as you decide would be best for those you are teaching. The narrative is compelling because there is no place for us to hide; we are caught in the strong spiritual light of the universal truth of the timelessness of God's Word. This land we consider to be ours was given to us to provide protection for those under religious persecution and unbelievable stress in the Old World. Yet, we see people within the church today who resist the truth in the same way and follow other men (false prophets) who manipulate and squeeze the perfect truth into a form that pleases their listeners.

For the time will come when they will not endure sound doctrine, but according to their own desires, because they have itching ears, they will heap up for themselves teachers; 4 and they will turn their ears away from the truth, and be turned aside to fables.   2 Timothy 4:3-4

2 Peter 1:16-2:22 describe the false teachers and those "professing Jesus Christ" who follow these false teachings. Basically, they're refusing the truth and are, therefore, open to all kinds of fruit from the imaginations of their false teachers. They will buy whatever they are told and be forever removed from the knowledge and grace found in the Gospel of Jesus Christ.

CHAPTER 26

"THEY WOULD NOT HEAR"

Study the references and the discussion so that you can aid the student's understanding of the Hebrews selection. Stress what happens to the heart\mind if we do not yield to the Lord.

"But to the one who does not work, but believes [trusts-obeys] in Him who justifies the ungodly, his faith is credited as righteousness" (Romans 4:5, NASB), just as *"Abraham believed God, and it was credited to Him as righteousness"* (Romans 4:3, NASB). How did this work? Abraham was made promises by God. One promise was that Abraham would be the father of many nations. The scriptures concerning Abraham in the New Testament describe Abraham's thinking process: *"Without becoming weak in faith He contemplated His own body, now as good as dead since he was about a hundred years old, and the deadness of Sarah's womb; yet, with respect to the promise of God, he did not waver in unbelief but grew strong in faith, giving glory to God, and being fully assured that what God had promised, He was able also to perform, Therefore IT WAS ALSO CREDITED TO HIM AS RIGHTEOUSNESS"* (Romans 4:19-22, Emphasis added). *"Now not for his sake only was it written that it was credited to him, but for our sake also, to whom it will be credited, as those who believe in Him who raised Jesus our Lord from the dead, He who was delivered over because of our transgressions, and was raised because of our justification"* (Romans 4:23-25).

Today we live in this same faith in God, not having received complete salvation because we are still earth bound, but we are persuaded of the fulfillment of the promises of God and embrace them and confess that our allegiance has changed. We are a citizen of the family of God. We submit our wills by obeying the Word given in the Testaments, for they are life-giving words. If you hear the Word but have no faith, call out to the Lord for mercy. Listen to this man's cry to Jesus: *"Jesus said... if you can believe, all things are possible to him that believes. And straightway the father of the child cried out, and said with tears, Lord I believe;* [83] *help thou mine unbelief"* (Mark 9:24).

---

83. *Believe*—to have faith (in, upon, with respect to, a person, here by implication, it means to entrust one's spiritual well-being to Christ: commit to, trust, put in trust with (trust to the degree of active obedience to the Word of Christ

CHAPTER 27

FALSE SHEPHERDS VS. TRUE SHEPHERDS

This may be a good place to give the student a lesson on how to use *Strong's Concordance,* known officially as *The Exhaustive Concordance of the Bible,* or one that is keyed to *Strong's* numbers. I have prepared pages for you, the parent\teacher, on the use of the *Strong's Concordance,* primarily as an example that you can use to guide the student's efforts to use this source for information. I use the 1 Timothy 4:1-3 quote in this lesson as the example. Guide the students through this selection until they understand how to tackle the verse. The students need to be able to search the meaning of words for themselves.

Now the Spirit speaks expressly, that in the latter times some shall depart from the faith, giving heed to seducing spirits, and doctrines of devils; speaking lies in hypocrisy; having their conscience seared with a hot iron; Forbidding to marry, and commanding to abstain from meats, which God has created to be received with thanksgiving of them which believe and know the truth.   1 Timothy 4:1-3

There would be people at a later time who would depart from the faith in Christ. They would pretend to be true believers, but would actually seduce believers by teaching false doctrines fostered by demons. These teachers have sinned to such a degree that their own moral conscience was no longer sensitive to the things of God. Gathering people to themselves, they start ministries for there own use. They are arrogant and proud, with only feigned respect for the words of our Lord. The false teachers invariably twist and pervert the Gospel, by adding to or subtracting text, putting emphasis upon, casting doubt upon or ignoring certain doctrines. Using private interpretations, which shade or devalue or lie, in effect they nullify the truth. There are many books available that give clear descriptions of the various false teachings that existed yesterday and that still exist today.

Notes on Specific Lessons

PART VI: THE GENTILE KINGDOMS AS EXAMPLES

CHAPTER 28

THE CRUEL ASSYRIANS

The Assyrians were famous for their extreme cruelty and had become a clear menace to all the nations in that part of the world. God gathered this kingdom together to take away the kingdom of northern Israel, also called "Samaria," because the evil of the Israelites was full. Shalmaneser, the King of Assyria, came against Hoshea, the King of Samaria (which was northern Israel). Shalmaneser prevailed and Hoshea became the vassal of Shalmaneser and paid him tribute taxes. Hoshea had sent messengers to Egypt, calling upon them to help him against the Assyrians, and when the Assyrians uncovered his plot, they put him in jail. Then the Assyrian King, Shalmaneser, went throughout the land, and his armies terrorized the people of Samaria, engaging in wholesale murder and rape, ripping open pregnant women and dashing their unborn children to pieces. Everyone who was left became a slave to serve the interest of Assyria.

In the ninth year of Hoshea, Shalmaneser removed the remnant of the people of the Northern Kingdom to other places. This series of events happened in 722 B.C. He put the Israelites in Halah, Habor, the area of the River Gozon and the cities of the Medes.[84] In the place of the Israelites, the Assyrians brought in people from other places, such as Babylon, Cuthah, Ava, Hamath and Sepharvaim, and placed them in all the cities of the Northern Kingdom.[85] This was exactly what God had said would happen to those descendants of Abraham brought out of Egypt.[86] He had waited generations, while showing mercy and grace to the people. During those years, out of mercy, He sent prophets continually to warn the people, again and again, of the consequences of choosing other gods and other ways of living. Now, finally, the Lord was holding the people accountable for practicing their ungodly ways of thinking and their horrible deeds that included burning their own children as sacrifices in occult practices. They had become a violent and oppressive people who naturally followed this path because of their deliberate unbelief.

In the fourteenth year of Hezekiah, King of Judah, the Assyrians came again (in 701 B.C.), this time to take the Southern Kingdom of Israel. Sennacherib was the next king of Assyria, and he came up against all the walled cities of Judah and took them. Hezekiah sent a message to the king of Assyria saying, "I have offended you and will pay your tribute." Then Hezekiah sent him all the silver and gold he could gather. The Assyrian king sent two of His trusted captains with a large army, and they placed themselves in front of Jerusalem as a clear threat to the city. These spokesmen for

---

84. See 2 Kings 1-6
85. See 2 Kings 17:23-24
86. See Deuteronomy 28:1-14 for the promised blessings for obedience to God and 15-68 for the curses for the deliberate and continued choice for evil as opposed to God's mercy for obedience. See Leviticus 18 through 20 to see how the people were to live, honoring God, their kindred, and the stranger. See Leviticus 26 for the results of deliberate noncompliance.

Assyria then tried to separate the people of Israel from their rulers by turning them against each other. They tried to convince the rulers and people that it was impossible to escape this war alive because their armies had destroyed all of the surrounding kingdoms and their gods. They also tried to convince the hearers that the Egyptians could not rescue them from the mighty King Sennacherib. They said that God Himself had told Sennacherib to go against this land and to destroy it and assured the hearers that they could not depend upon their God for deliverance, for no god had been able to deliver their people or kingdoms from the hand of Sennacherib.

When the Assyrians sent a threatening letter to Hezekiah, he took it into the temple and prayed to God to help him stand against Sennacherib and his Assyria hordes. Soon a message came from the Lord through the prophet Isaiah. The message was that God had heard Hezekiah's prayer. What happened next was nothing short of astounding. The next morning 185,000 Assyrian troops lay dead. Later, Sennacherib himself was killed by his own sons in the temple of their god. Jerusalem had been delivered yet again by the mercy of the Lord.

A very interesting thing happened sometime after Hezekiah had recovered from an illness. The king of Babylon sent him letters and presents. Out of pride, Hezekiah foolishly showed the Babylonian envoys everything of value in his kingdom, all of his treasures. They were even able to see the defenses inside the walls of the city. Then God sent the prophet Isaiah to tell Hezekiah that Babylon[87] would be back and would take everything of value. Even some of his sons would be made eunuchs in the palace of the king of Babylon.[88] For some reason, Hezekiah didn't seem to care much about the plight of his descendants. He was only interested in the fact that the promised destruction would not come in his lifetime. Isaiah foretold these events in his prophecies of the Babylonian invasion and the deportation of the citizens of the kingdom of Judah. About a hundred and fifty years later, it happened just as Isaiah had prophesied. Isaiah spoke of these awful events in graphic language,[89] but he also gave the people hope, assuring them that God is powerful and full of mercy, and He does not lie. The Lord was at work bringing all that He had said to pass.

There are many lessons to be learned from the encounters between two continually adversarial positions. The Lord is always confronting His people about the deep, wide and generational battle between the evil one (who opposes God) and His people. Satan rules in the kingdom of men and spends his time interposing between God and His purposes. If Israel could be destroyed spiritually or physically, then Satan believed he could stop the advance of God's Kingdom, as revealed in the promised Messiah. Satan knew the Old Testament Scriptures and moved over the chess board of the world, working to achieve mastery over all men and nations.

All the kingdoms involved here were visibly corrupted. The rulers of these kingdoms wanted control of all resources and all peoples, and there is no pity or mercy in men who are saturated with pride and become drunk with power. The Assyrians were not good people, and yet God used them

---

87. See Isaiah 39:6-7
88. See 2 Kings 18 through 20
89. See Isaiah 40 through 66. The prophet even named the king, Cyrus, who would eventually allow the people of Judah to go back home.

to destroy or remove the people who had called themselves by God's name but were saturated with evil. Their rebellion was against God.

History shows us the true nature of man. No form of government can ever stop the natural proclivities of man with his sin nature. His drive for power is not logical, for what is the point of having everything when God has destroyed every civilization by raising up another kingdom to oppose them or through physical changes such as earthquakes, floods or droughts. Pride is an opened gate into every man and nation, shaping them to follow their desires.

Numbers records a truth that all men need to remember: *"The LORD is longsuffering, and of great mercy, forgiving iniquity and transgression, and by no means clearing the guilty ..."* (Numbers 14:18). The Lord will not clear the guilt men accumulate for their sins, nor clear the sin deliberately done. Instead, He holds all men accountable for their sin and the results of those choices. All men—past, present and future—will be judged according to God's moral law.[90] This is the reason we need the Lord Jesus to remove all sin and guilt. He will do this when the Spirit has opened our mind to see that we carry our weight in sin and, therefore, have real guilt. No one has forced self to produce this body of sin with its accompanying guilt.

This new awareness is accomplished as we read and absorb the Scriptures as the Truth. Through the Holy Spirit's charter to reprove all men,[91] it is revealed to us through the Scriptures how and why we incur sin and guilt. The Holy Spirit must also reveal what righteous actually is, for we know sin well, but we are devoid of righteousness.[92] The fact is that only Jesus has this righteousness and purity of character[93] that reflects His divinity. Therefore, only Jesus the Christ—the Anointed One, the Messiah—could be the Sin-bearer for the people of God. And Jesus, by His resurrection, has already judged Satan, the prince of the world.[94] I wonder if the people of Israel who were taken to the cities of the Medes by the Assyrians became part of the great army God called to destroy Babylon?

90. See Romans 1:18-32
91. See John 16:7-11
92. See Romans 6:20-21
93. See Jeremiah 23:4-6
94. See John 16:1-11

CHAPTER 29

THE BABYLONIANS

Babylon had a birth that is recorded in Genesis 11:4. Later, this whole area became the land of the Chaldeans after much conquest spread out over long years. The Chaldeans were the bastions of all types of occult practices. Abraham was called by God to leave the land of Ur of the Chaldeans and go into a land chosen by Him. God gave Abraham many explicit promises, for He was to be the progenitor of a new peoples,[95] a nation formed to be an example and messenger of the grace and the government of the Holy God. Much later, the Babylonian Empire formed and then absorbed the Assyrian kingdom through war. The city of Babylon grew to be the principal city of commerce, religion, government and also of the armed forces. Nebuchadrezzar ruled over this vast kingdom, intending to capture or coerce other kingdoms. Babylon was considered to be the most beautiful and powerful kingdom upon the earth, and the Babylonians were acknowledged and feared throughout the known world.

God used Nebuchadrezzar to crush all the various nations, from Egypt to Babylon, including Judah. I believe that the Lord had waited until the evil in all these nations had reached full capacity, just as He had done with the Amorites.[96] The Lord said of Nebuchadrezzar: *"You are my battle axe and weapons of war: for with you I will break in pieces the nations."*[97] Matthew Henry said, "God serves His own wise and righteous purposes by the impudence and iniquities of men and snares sinners in the work of their own Hands."

The Lord said something unexpected about Judah through Jeremiah the prophet: *"Whom I have sent away from this place for their own good."*[98] Jeremiah had been raised up to preach the words of God against Jerusalem and her people for about twenty-three years. They had been warned multiple times and were told of the awful things that would happen to the city, as well as the whole of Judah, if they failed to obey. The people knew exactly what had happened to their cousins in the Northern Kingdom of Samaria.

The first time Babylon came against Jerusalem was after Jehoiakim was made king of Judah by Egyptian forces. Babylon chased after the Egyptians and took everything they had fought to have jurisdiction over. The Egyptians did not come again to Judah, but the Babylonians came to Judah and made the people vassals and demanded a high tax every year. King Jehoiakim sent tribute for three years and then revolted. This act brought the Babylonian army to the land of Judah again.

---

95. See Genesis 11:27-12:9, 15:1-19, 17:1-18:15, 21:1-7 and 22:1-19
96. Genesis 15:16: "But in the fourth generation they shall return here, for the iniquity of the Amorites is not yet complete."
97. Jeremiah 51:20
98. Jeremiah 24:5

In 605 B.C., Babylon began the first deportation of the people of Judah. The Book of Daniel records this bit of history: *"In the third year of the reign of Jehoiakim king of Judah came Nebuchadnezzar king of Babylon unto Jerusalem, and besieged it. And the LORD gave Jehoiakim king of Judah into his hand, with part of the vessels of the house of God."*[99] Jehoiakim had killed God's prophet Urijah, who spoke against Jerusalem in the same way that Jeremiah had.[100] Nebuchadnezzar carried the sacred vessels away from the Temple of God into his land and put them into the treasure house of his god. The king told the master of his eunuchs that he should bring certain children to Babylon and train them to be used in his service. This included Daniel and his three friends.[101]

Jehoiakim died and His son Jehoiachin reigned in his stead. Then Babylon came again and laid siege against Jerusalem in 597 B.C. Now in the eighth year of his reign, Jehoiachin went out of the gate in surrender with his family and officials. They were all exiled to Babylon. The captain of the guard gathered the king's treasures and more of the treasures of the Temple that was in Jerusalem. Jehoiakim's brother, Mattaniah, the twenty-one-year-old uncle of Jehoiachin, was named as the new King, and his name was changed to Zedekiah. He served nine years as king and then rebelled. This was a most serious breach, as he lied and refused to abide by the contract with the King of Babylon. That contract had been made in God's name, so this meant a far harsher punishment. The Lord was angry with the king of Judah.[102]

Now we can fast forward to the third Babylonian invasion. In 585 B.C., King Nebuchadnezzar's army came again, this time because of rebellion by Zedekiah. Jeremiah brought a message from God to Zedekiah: *"... If you surely surrender to the king of Babylon's princes, then your soul shall live; this city shall not be burned with fire, and you and your house shall live. But if you do not surrender to the king of Babylon's princes, then this city shall be given into the hand of the Chaldeans, they shall burn it with fire, and you shall not escape from their hand. ... Please, obey the voice of the Lord which I speak to you. ... Now behold, all the women who are left in the king of Judah's house shall be surrendered to the king of Babylon's princes ... . So they shall surrender all your wives and children to the Chaldeans ... and you shall cause this city to be burned with fire."*[103]

Zedekiah was so filled with pride that no one existed in his world but himself. He cared not for his wives or children; he cared not for the whole city of Jerusalem with all of the desperate people in it. Out of God's mercy, Jerusalem did not have to be burned, nor did the people who were left have to be deported. God sent Jeremiah to tell Zedekiah that he would be the cause of his wife and children being given to the Chaldeans and the direct cause of the burning of Jerusalem. But Zedekiah had a heart of granite, as well as a mean streak of cruelty. Therefore, he was deceived and thought escape possible from the King of Babylon and the words of the living God. Remember that pride will not allow the person bound by it to judge or assess his situation accurately. Nebuchadnezzar's army had already been outside of Jerusalem for two years, enforcing the siege. When the walls of

99. Daniel 1:1-2
100. See Jeremiah 51:20
101. See Daniel 1:1-6
102. See 2 Chronicles 6:11-14 and 36:22-23
103. Jeremiah 38:17-23 , NKJV

Jerusalem began to fall, the Babylonian king sent his army after Zedekiah, his nobles and some of the soldiers who had deserted the people and sneaked out of Jerusalem, escaping into the night. Nebuchadnezzar's army was able to capture them all and return to the Babylonian King's encampment in Hamath.

According to the information contained in the book of Daniel, King Nebuchadnezzar had an explosive temper.[104] Daniel had been transferred from Jerusalem to Babylon roughly sixty-six years before this, in the first wave of deportations from Judah. Now all of the sons of King Zedekiah of Judah were killed in front of their father, and all the nobles that were with him were also killed. The Babylonian king blinded Zedekiah himself, bound him in bronze fetters and sent him to Babylon. Listen to this message from the Lord against the king: *"He [Zedekiah] did not humble himself before Jeremiah the prophet, who spoke from the mouth of the Lord. And he also rebelled against King Nebuchadnezzar, who had made him swear an oath by God; but he stiffened his neck and hardened his heart against turning to the Lord God of Israel."*[105] This was the God of Daniel, Jeremiah and Isaiah, and King Zedekiah's rebellion against Nebuchadnezzar meant that he had committed perjury against God, as well as breaking God's covenant.

Ezekiel has an interesting backstory that I had not discovered before: *"And he [Nebuchadnezzar] took the king's offspring, made a covenant with him, and put him under oath. He also took away the mighty of the land, that the kingdom might be brought low and not lift itself up, but that by keeping his covenant it might stand. But he [the king of Judah] rebelled against him [Nebuchadnezzar] by sending his ambassadors to Egypt."*[106] He was seeking help from the Egyptians just as Hosea, King of Samaria, had done years earlier when surrounded by the Assyrians. *"'As I live,' says the Lord God, 'surely in the place where the king dwells who made him king, whose oath he despised and whose covenant he broke—with him in the midst of Babylon he shall die."*[107] Nebuchadnezzar had great respect for the God of Israel and Judah because of the personal humiliation he had suffered through his inordinate pride.[108] This proud, gentile king knew that God ruled over the kingdoms of men, but Nebuchadnezzar never turned to God in humility for his own salvation. He allowed his will to become his trust, a personal law.

About a month later, the Chaldeans came again and burned all the houses. The captain of the guard, servant to the Babylonian king, finished breaking down the walls of Jerusalem. He pillaged the Temple of God again, breaking to pieces anything of value to send to his King. Our Lord called Jeremiah to send a letter to the people who survived the journey to Babylon. They were to: *"Build houses, live in them; plant gardens and eat the fruit."* [109] *"take wives for your sons and give your daughters to husbands, so that they may bear sons and daughters—that you may be increased there, and not diminished."*[110] *"Seek the peace of the city where I have caused you to be carried away captive, and pray to the Lord*

---

104. See also 2 Kings 23 through 25
105. 2 Chronicles 36:12-13 , NKJV
106. Ezekiel 17:13-15 , NKJV
107. Ezekiel 17:16 , NKJV
108. See Daniel 4:20-35
109. Jeremiah 29:28 , NKJV
110. Jeremiah 29:6 , NKJV

for it; for in its peace you will have peace."[111] The Lord also warned them: "*Do not let your prophets and your diviners who are in your midst deceive you, nor listen to your dreams which you cause to be dreamed. For they prophesy falsely to you in My name; I have not sent them, says the Lord. For thus says the Lord: After seventy years are completed at Babylon, I will visit you and perform My good word toward you, and cause you to return to this place. For I know the thoughts that I think toward you, says the Lord, thoughts of peace and not of evil, to give you a future and a hope. Then you will call upon Me and go and pray to Me, and I will listen to you. And you will seek Me and find Me, when you search for Me with all your heart.*"[112]

Powerful words from God came to Jeremiah, Isaiah, Daniel and Ezekiel against Babylon: "*Because you were glad, because you rejoiced, you destroyers of my people,*"[113] "*for she [Babylon] has sinned against the Lord,*"[114] "*call together the archers against Babylon. All you who bend the bow, encamp against it all around; let none of them escape. Repay her according to all she has done, do to her; for she has been proud against the Lord, against the Holy One of Israel.*"[115] "*Behold, a people shall come from the north, and a great nation and many kings shall be raised up from the ends of the earth, they shall hold the bow and the lance; they are cruel and shall not show mercy.*"[116] "*For it is the vengeance of the Lord,*"[117] "*vengeance for His Temple.*"[118] "*Your end has come, the measure of your covetousness.*"[119] The Lord called down upon Babylon the armies of the Persians and the Medes, and they took Babylon in 539 B.C.

God sent His prophets to the kingdoms of Samaria, Judah and Babylon, as well as to men who came to their defense during the dangerous times of speaking on God's behalf. The Lord protected Jeremiah in two ways: Nebuchadnezzar told the captain of the guard to look after Jeremiah and do what he said. This was an amazing demonstration of God's power over men and kingdoms.[120] The Lord sent a message to Baruch, a man who helped Jeremiah, that both would be safe. The lone Ethiopian who believed God received a message from Him through Jeremiah: "*'But I will deliver you in that day,' says the Lord, 'and you shall not be given into the hand of the men of whom you are afraid. For I will surely deliver you, and you shall not fall by the sword; but your life shall be as a prize to you, because you have put your trust in Me,' says the Lord.*"[121]

God also called Jeremiah to issue warnings to His people in Babylon, to flee the destruction that would come upon that kingdom for the pride of her people in contending with Him. "*Flee from the midst of Babylon, and everyone save his life! Do not be cut off in her iniquity for this is the time of the Lord's vengeance ... .*"[122] Unfortunately, many did not heed this warning.

---

111. Jeremiah 29:7, NKJV
112. Jeremiah 29:8-13, NKJV
113. Jeremiah 50:11, NKJV
114. Jeremiah 50:14, NKJV
115. Jeremiah 50:29, NKJV
116. Jeremiah 50:41-42, NKJV
117. Jeremiah 50;15, NKJV
118. Jeremiah 51:11, NKJV
119. Jeremiah 51:13, NKJV
120. See Jeremiah 38:7-13 and 39:11-14. In verses 16-18, He gave assuranaces to the Ethiopian. See also 40:1-6
121. Jeremiah 39:17-18, NKJV
122. Jeremiah 51:6

Darius the Persian ruled Babylon first and then Cyrus, the King of the Medes, ruled. This King Cyrus was named by Isaiah the prophet more than one hundred and fifty years before he came to power. In the first year of his reign, King Cyrus signed a proclamation to let the people of Judah go. God had promised to let them return to their homeland after the seventy years were accomplished.[123]

123. In 1879, a cylinder was found in the ruins of ancient Babylon which was from Cyrus himself. This so-called Cyrus Cylinder was a record of how the exiled nations were ordered home. See Ezra 1:2-4 and 6:2-5. This information was taken from Derek W. H. Thomas' book, Strength for the Weary. (Orlando FL, Reformation Trust Publishing, 2018).

NOTES ON SPECIFIC LESSONS
PART VI: THINKING DIFFERENTLY

CHAPTER 30

HOW ARE WE TO THINK?

This is a long lesson because I wanted the students to see that the Bible has a history that reveals much about the Lord's thinking. The New Testament is also filled with this different way of thinking found within the Godhead. The Holy Spirit is sent to indwell the people who believe God, in order to reveal this different way of thinking and give believers a foundation in Jesus.

There is no randomness in Jesus' plans for each of His children. Nothing touches us except those things ordained by Jesus Christ. He makes no arbitrary decisions; therefore, whatever affects you was sent deliberately to increase your faith or enlarge you heart to actively love others or reveal sin or hypocrisy. Suffering of various kinds usually make us more aware of the suffering of others. Trials often reveal the depth of hidden sin and the shallowness of our faith. God disciplines His children, not as a punishment, but to bring us into His will.[124] This is necessary because it is too easy for us to lose touch with what is true and forget the Lord. We forget that His judgment against sin includes sins that we allow after we have been grafted into His Kingdom.

His will has been clearly revealed: we are to be like Christ in our character and in our love for others. The Lord insists that believers are to be righteous, holy and loving in all our thoughts and deeds, and He will make it so.[125] We are saved to honor our Lord, by growing in holiness, which is seen in the fruits of the Spirit[126] and in our conformity to the character and moral excellence of our Lord.[127] We are not to let sin reign in our body,[128] and we are to actively abhor all evil and cling to that which is good.

A clean conscience is the only way to have peace within yourself and follow the Lord Jesus in truth. No one can pursue holiness unless his conscience is routinely swept clean by the Holy Spirit, using the Scriptures to identify and convict the reader of sin. The reading of the Word just for information without application is a subtle trap because knowledge without conviction can build pride. Do not trust yourself, but depend upon the living Word, as the Holy Spirit enlightens your heart and mind with the truth. God actually knows what we think and do in the dark. David managed to sear his own conscience and commit murder because of His open desires and a self-indulgent pride. God humbled David and brought the sword of rebellion into his house.

Warn the students that if, while calling themselves a "Christian," they are continually engaged in fulfilling the worldly desires of the heart and mind, then they are balanced upon an unraveling

---

124. Proverbs 15:3, 17-20. *"Great is the Lord, and highly to be praised, His greatness is unsearchable...."*
125. See Philippians 1:6 and Isaiah 26:3
126. See Galatians 5:16-24
127. See Romans 12:1-2 and 9-20
128. 1 John 2:15-17

tightrope. We must not ignore or dismiss the Scriptures or nothing preached will move heart or mind. Are the students dismissing the prompting of the Holy Spirit and the warning of righteous leaders in the church? Are their parents concerned about their spiritual condition? Are the students hiding the truth of their real thoughts and opinions? If this is a pattern, then the student is, at the very least, a hypocrite and may have experienced a false conversion.

Men are dealing with the God of infinite knowledge and limitless understanding. He is pure everlasting love, and His hatred of sin is perfect. He created everything seen and unseen, including time, but the Lord lives outside of all constraints of time. He is present at all times and in all places. He is immutable, therefore, changeless in all of His determinations. We are finite and cannot even begin to measure or quantify Him, and our minds cannot grasp infinite life, love, mercy or grace.

Our Father has determined that only by faith and through faith, which He gives as a gift to His children,[129] can He be known by mankind. This faith is brought to us by the indwelling Spirit of Christ, which leads to active belief, and this faith leads to reconciliation with our Father through and because of the deliberate sacrifice of the Lord Jesus, our great High Priest. If we are in Christ, we are not now under God's wrath, because Jesus bought our debts of sin with His own blood. His sacrifice reveals to us His deep personal love, which brings us peace with God and peace within our own hearts and minds. The test of our love for our Lord is this: do you keep His commandments?[130]

---

129. See Ephesians 2:1-10
130. The test of Love (see 1 John 1:9, 2:1-6 and 15-16)

CHAPTER 31

THE REPENTANCE OF KING DAVID
(SOME CONCLUSIONS ABOUT DAVID'S REPENTANCE)

Because of the clarity found in God's Word, I have come to a few inescapable conclusions about suppositions that are found in our culture. One idea I hear repeated is this: "All men are basically good." It sounds plausible, but here is another traditional urban legend that is not possible. The Lord has given us wisdom in His Truth to search out for a reason. All human beings are involved in producing the ills of civilizations. This truth concerns all men, as their behavior is visible in the span of history and in all modern cultures. Mankind is not basically good, but, rather, desperately wicked.[131] No matter the time, place, people or circumstances involved in the creation of any culture or subculture, sooner or later it becomes saturated with evil and, consequently, oppression is used to stifle opposition. Lies, covetousness, immorality of all kinds, murder (by hand, mind or law), oppression of all degrees and confusion are common among men.

All cultures exhibit elitism, which fosters the inclusion of special interest provisions of laws affecting the wealthy or powerful, and, therefore, justice fails. The whole tenet of the Scriptures concerning the communities of God's people is that the visible and invisible justice for all is to be a hallmark.[132] The Lord told Moses that the Law was not to favor the rich or the poor, but all were to be under the exact same prescriptions.[133]

The Atonement tax instituted in Exodus 30:15 was for all God's people to make atonement for themselves. It would be used to pay for the service of the "Tent of Meeting," which would eventually become the Temple in Jerusalem. The Lord indicated that, *The rich shall not give more, and the poor shall not give less*" (Exodus 30:15). Later, in Leviticus 19:15 (NKJV), we see this: *"You shall do no injustice in judgment. You shall not be partial to the poor, nor honor the person of the mighty. In righteousness you shall judge your neighbor."* All through Exodus and Leviticus, see warnings to the people about their future treatment of the poor among their own kin and the poor people of the nation: *"You shall love your neighbor as yourself: I am the LORD!"*[134] From the Old Testament covenants to the New Covenant sealed by the blood of Jesus Christ, love from the heart of spiritually newborn and repentant men of God were to produce the visible hallmark of fair justice for all.

---

131. *"The heart is deceitful above all things, and desperately wicked: who can know it? I, the LORD, search the heart, I try the reins, even to give every man according to his ways, and according to the fruit of his doings."* (Jeremiah 17:9-10)

132. *Hallmark*, "any conspicuous indication of the character or quality of something.

133. See Exodus 23:3 and 6, 30:15 and Leviticus 19:15 and 17

134. Leviticus 19:18, NKJV (OT: See also Proverbs 24:23 and 28:21, and NT: see James 2:1-4 and 9, Romans 2:11, Ephesians 6:9 and Colossians 3:25

Remember: it was said of King David that he rendered justice for all the people.[135] The Lord sent the prophet Samuel to anoint David to be the second King of Israel. *"And the Lord said, 'Arise, anoint him in the midst of his brothers; and the Spirit from the Lord came upon David from that day forward.' "*[136] This is what made the difference between an ordinary man and a man of God. God sealed David to be His forever. This is why David could be brought to repent of his many sins during his lifetime. The Holy Spirit was within David and did not let his sin go underground to be hidden from himself, as men routinely do.

David valued his Lord above all and poured out his hurting soul as the sons of his family departed from David in rebellion. The Lord had told David this was to be because he had despised the Lord and taken the Lord's name as a vain thing. David asked the Lord not to take His Holy Spirit from Him, and He never did. Neither will the Lord take His Spirit from those sealed through His Spirit, as they are also His forever.

135. 2 Samuel 8:15

136. 1 Samuel 16:12-13

CHAPTER 32

OUR NEED FOR REPENTANCE

To enrich the understanding of the student, give them the information discussed. Perhaps assign the scripture selections to the class and have a discussion of each one. Notice that our Lord chose Jesus to be the Creator of all, visible and invisible. If you wish, you can make this material into two separate lessons.

CHAPTER 33

SAVED BY GRACE

To enrich the understanding of the student in the grace of our Lord, read through Romans chapters 5 through 8 for yourself, as a review for this last lesson. Check the references and the verses given to have an overview of the wonders our Lord has accomplished through His abundant grace, a grace seen in all He has done for men, men who despised Him and had contempt for all His ways.

And the Word was made flesh, and dwelt among us, (and we beheld his glory, the glory as of the only begotten of the Father), full of grace and truth ... . For the law was given by Moses, (but) grace and truth came by Jesus Christ. John 1:14 and 17

Such grace was granted to us through the willing self-sacrifice, abundant mercy and pity that flowed from the heart of our Lord Jesus. This grace encompasses the divine work by the Spirit of Christ upon the heart of man. *"But we believe that through the grace of the Lord Jesus Christ we shall be saved, even as they"* (Acts 15:11). Paul was writing to reveal to the Jewish believers in Jerusalem the miracles and wonders God had wrought among the Gentiles through him. These God-motivated, God-given powers illustrated that the Gentiles were being saved, just as the Jews had been saved by the work of Christ in their hearts.

The Law and prophets both testify to the righteousness of God. In the New Testament, we see the righteousness of God demonstrated through Christ Jesus, faith being placed in the righteous Christ because of His atoning sacrifice by all who believe, whether Jew or Gentile. [137]

Being justified freely by His grace through the redemption that is in Christ Jesus: whom God has set forth (to be) a <u>propitiation</u> [138] through faith in his blood, to declare his righteousness for the remission of sins that are past ... . Therefore being justified by faith, we have peace with God through our Lord Jesus Christ: by whom also we have access by faith into this grace wherein we stand. Romans 5:1-2

For if through the offence of one (Adam) many be dead (because of the curse of sin), how much more the grace of God, and the gift by grace which is by one man, Jesus Christ, has abounded unto many. For if by one man's (Adam's) offence death reined by one; much more they which receive abundance of grace and the gift of righteousness shall reign in life by one, Jesus Christ. Romans 5:15 and 17

137. See Romans 3:19-23
138. Propitiation: Expiatory (the act or place of making an atonement), that is, (concretely) an atoning victim, or (specifically) the lid of the Ark (in the Temple): mercy seat.

Remember that the Law reveals sin against God and each other. The Law is a spotlight shone upon all our external and internal sin, and we are exposed to the light. *"Moreover the law entered, that the offence might abound"* (Romans 5:20). We were justly condemned, but now, by the grace of God given us through faith deposited in Jesus Christ, we are to count ourselves dead to pervading sin [139] and, through Jesus, alive to God.

Those who have been born again do have this promise: *"(There is) therefore now no condemnation to them which are in Christ Jesus, who walk not after the flesh, but after the Spirit. For the law of the Spirit of Life in Christ Jesus has made me free from the law of sin and death"* (Romans 8:1). Through grace we are motivated and empowered to walk after the Spirit, practicing the good instead of following the carnal nature. We glorify the Lord by honoring His eternal Son: *"Being then made free from sin, you became the servant of righteousness, that is, a servant to God"* (Romans 6:18). We are to serve the Lord Jesus Christ and, through Him, the eternal Father.

Grace focuses your heart upon the exceeding greatness of the Father the Son and the Spirit. We are now tethered to Jesus through faith, as if we were with Him through His death and resurrection. This is the picture the words of Romans 6 form: our old man is crucified with Christ so that we can reckon ourselves dead to sin. We have an iron-clad promise that our attachment to the sin nature has been severed. [140] Therefore sin is no longer our Master. *"Therefore if any man be in Christ he is a new creature: old things are passed away; behold all things are become new"* (2 Corinthians 5:17). *"For in Christ Jesus neither circumcision availeth anything, nor uncircumcision, but a new creature"* (Galatians 6:15). *"Sin shall not have dominion over you, for you are not under law, but under grace"* (Romans 6:14). [141]

This grace moves our hearts to study and learn from the Scriptures how to walk in the Spirit so that we will not fulfill the lusts of the flesh. Remember: those old ways of thinking, speaking and behaving must change to reflect the character of our Savior and Father. We cannot do this by ourselves; it is through Christ alone that we overcome our old habits and remaining sin. Through Jesus Christ, our nature has been changed. Therefore, we desire to please the Lord, and we do not wish to grieve [142] His indwelling Spirit. Through faith in Jesus, we have access to this grace, *"being justified by faith, we have peace with God through our Lord Jesus Christ"* (Romans 5:1).

During His time on the earth, Jesus showed forth the heart of God, the culmination of the grace of God on behalf of those who believe. Jesus Christ was gracious, slow to anger, circumspect in all of His speech, gentle to the humble, patient with His disciples and kind to the lost children of men.

In one of King David's prayers to the Lord, he said this: *"I will run the way of your commandments, when you shall enlarge [143] my heart [144]"* (Psalm 119:32). I realize that this is a figure of speech, but the grace of God in salvation does enlarge our hearts through the Lord Jesus. The grace of God, through the Lord Jesus, has done much for us. Through Him, we have been given a greater capacity to love God and our neighbor, as well as our enemies.

---

139. Romans 6:11 (read the entire argument in verses 1-13)

140. See Romans 6:18

141. Read Romans 6:1-16 to have a clearer understanding of the work of grace

142. Ephesians 4:30: "And grieve not the Holy Spirit of god, whereby you are sealed unto the day of redemption."

143. *Enlarge*: to broaden (literally or figuratively) (intransitively or transitively): be an en-(make) large (-ing), make room, make (open) wide

144. Heart: also used (figuratively) very widely for the feelings, the will and even the intellect; likewise for the centre of anything: care for, comfortably, consent, considered, courageous, friend, friendly, broken (heart), hard (heart), merry (heart).

JESUS AS PROPHET, PRIEST AND KING

All the lessons presented were done so for this reason, to demonstrate to the reader that Jesus is the point of the Old and the New Testaments. Use the last student section as a review, just to remind your student/s of the amazing love and wisdom of our Almighty God. Jesus came to redeem lost men throughout the centuries who believed the Scriptures and, therefore, trusted and obeyed Him. His companions are and will be a vast new family, grateful for His righteousness that covers us. His sacrificial love rescued us from eternal darkness, and Jesus takes us into everlasting life.